STRATEGIC CUSTOMER MANAGEMENT

STRATEGIC CUSTOMER MANAGEMENT

Strategizing the Sales Organization

Nigel F. Piercy and Nikala Lane

OXFORD
UNIVERSITY PRESS

OXFORD

UNIVERSITY PRESS

Great Clarendon Street, Oxford OX2 6DP

Oxford University Press is a department of the University of Oxford.
It furthers the University's objective of excellence in research, scholarship,
and education by publishing worldwide in

Oxford New York

Auckland Cape Town Dar es Salaam Hong Kong Karachi
Kuala Lumpur Madrid Melbourne Mexico City Nairobi
New Delhi Shanghai Taipei Toronto

With offices in

Argentina Austria Brazil Chile Czech Republic France Greece
Guatemala Hungary Italy Japan Poland Portugal Singapore
South Korea Switzerland Thailand Turkey Ukraine Vietnam

Oxford is a registered trade mark of Oxford University Press
in the UK and in certain other countries

Published in the United States
by Oxford University Press Inc., New York

© Nigel F. Piercy & Nikala Lane, 2009

The moral rights of the authors have been asserted
Database right Oxford University Press (maker)

First published 2009

British Library Cataloguing in Publication Data
Data available

Library of Congress Cataloging in Publication Data
Data available

Typeset by SPI Publisher Services, Pondicherry, India
Printed in Great Britain
on acid-free paper by
the MPG Books Group,
Bodmin and King's Lynn

ISBN 978–0–19–954450–9

Acknowledgements

Many people have played a part in shaping this book. Certainly, our research partnership with Professor David W. Cravens, Emeritus Professor at Texas Christian University, has been incredibly important in guiding and correcting our thinking in these areas. Our friend Professor Malcolm McDonald remains our model for pragmatism. The managers who have participated in our Sales and Strategic Customer Management network at Warwick Business School have shared with us many important practical lessons relevant to the subject of this book, and have helped to motivate us to write it. Our interactions with the members of the Sales Special Interest Group at the American Marketing Association have also been important, and we have been grateful for the chance to learn from the insights of people like Greg Marshall, Rollins College; Bill Cron, Texas Christian University; Eli Jones, University of Houston; and the many other dedicated sales educators in that group. The work of figures like Professor Christian Homburg, University of Mannheim, and Professor Ove Jensen, University of Koblenz, and our discussions with them have also been instrumental in deciding the direction for this book.

We also thank Professor Howard Thomas, Dean of Warwick Business School, for providing us with the space and leeway to work in this area, even though it is profoundly unfashionable for a leading business school like Warwick—though that may be about to change. Our colleagues have been very tolerant. Finally, we thank Sheila Frost, Department Secretary in the Marketing and Strategic Management Group at Warwick Business School, for her assistance in producing and delivering this book.

Naturally, the limitations of this book and any errors contained remain the responsibility of the authors (or actually the sole responsibility of the second author, who gets blamed for everything, but she is used to it . . .)

Preface

This is not a book about academic research. It is concerned with the realities that executives are confronting in aligning their sales and account management structures and processes with the radical changes in the demands that customers make and the relationships they require with their suppliers. Those realities are driving what can only be described as a revolution, a radical transformation in buyer–seller relationships.

What we have tried to produce is a manifesto for strategic change in the role and management of sales and account management activities at the front of the organization. The key ideas underpinning our approach are strategic customer management (making the customer portfolio a key driver of business strategy) and the strategic sales organization (one which is capable of implementing a new type of role).

Nonetheless, while it is not a book about research, our thinking has been shaped by the research we have been doing in this field over a number of years. It is a special pleasure to do academic business school research in an area which actually matters to people in the real world of business. That pleasure derives from people being interested in what we do and looking for the practical implications that they can use to improve performance. Our work in the area of strategic sales management and strategic relationships with major customers definitely falls into this category. Our challenge now is to make that knowledge more available and operationally relevant to executives.

The sales and account management functions in companies constitute a massive area of economic activity and a huge cost to business. Yet aside from traditional textbooks about sales management techniques, and enthusiastic (though often banal and naïve) prescriptions of the apparently newly discovered merits of 'key account management' as the answer to all major customer problems, business schools have largely ignored the 'front-end' of companies where they meet their customers. While every business school in the world does 'marketing' in its teaching and research, very few have any real critical mass in the sales and account management fields. Research-based business schools responsible for new knowledge creation are especially guilty in this respect. This is foolish. We hope that this book will play a small part in redressing the balance.

But while giving greater recognition to the contribution of sales and account management effectiveness to superior business performance is good, it is not really the whole point of this book. The point is that we are in the early stages of an amazing and profound organizational transformation in how relationships with customers are managed. We have called this transformation the move to strategic customer management, in which the management of the customer portfolio and the design of relationship strategies for major customers are recognized as key issues driving business strategy and performance. Strategic customer management is the shift from sales as a tactical activity concerned only with implementing business and marketing strategy to a strategic process that aligns corporate resources with customer needs and confronts the hard decisions about investment in customers and the risks in dependence.

We have said this book is not a set of research findings. Naturally, if anyone wants to see that material it is freely available elsewhere. (It is listed on our website www.wbs.ac.uk.) This book focuses on the broader implications of our research for managers.

Our target reader is the chief executive, the general manager, the marketing director, the sales manager, the account director, as well as specialists in organizational design—in fact, any executives from any specialization who want to put a handle on how companies are re-shaping their 'front-ends' to improve how they perform in the customer marketplace.

Contents

List of Figures and Table

Figures

Table

About the Authors

Professor Nigel F. Piercy, BA, MA, PhD, DLitt, is one of the best-known business school academics in marketing and strategy in the UK. He is Professor of Marketing and Strategy at Warwick Business School. He was previously Professor of Strategic Marketing at Cranfield School of Management, where he was head of the marketing group. Earlier he held the Sir Julian Hodge Chair in Marketing and Strategy at Cardiff University. In addition, he has been a visiting professor at Texas Christian University; the University of California, Berkeley; Columbia Graduate School of Business, New York; the Fuqua School of Business, Duke University; the Athens Laboratory of Business Administration; and the Vienna University of Business and Economics. He has managerial experience in retailing, and was in business planning with Nycomed Amersham plc (now part of GE Healthcare). He has consulted with companies and worked with executives throughout the world.

His research interests are in strategic marketing, most recently emphasizing the sales/marketing interface and the impact of strategic customers on buyer–seller relationships. Nigel has published 20 books and written around 300 articles and papers appearing in the management literature throughout the world. Recent books include *Marketing Strategy & Competitive Positioning*, 4th edn. (with Graham Hooley and Brigitte Nicoulaud, Hemel Hempstead: FT/Prentice-Hall, 2008) and *Strategic Marketing*, 9th edn. (with David W. Cravens, Burr Ridge, Illinois: McGraw-Hill/Irwin, 2009). His best-selling book for managers is *Market-Led Strategic Change: Transforming the Process of Going to Market*, 4th edn. (Oxford: Butterworth-Heinemann/Elsevier, 2009). Among other awards and prizes, he was the UK Marketing Author of the Year for three years. He has published academic papers in the *Journal of Marketing*, the *Journal of the Academy of Marketing Science*, the *Journal of World Business*, and the *Journal of Business Research*, and has written on management and marketing issues in *The Sunday Times* and *The Independent* newspapers.

Dr. Nikala Lane, BSc, PhD, is Associate Professor in Marketing and Strategy at Warwick Business School. She attended Cardiff University, though mainly on the cold, wet days. She was previously Senior Research Associate at Cardiff Business School and Visiting Fellow at Cranfield School of Management, where she participated in the work of the sales consortium. She is Co-Director of the Sales and Account Management Research Unit, and Co-Chair of the Sales and Strategic Customer Management practitioner network, both at Warwick Business School.

She has research interests emphasizing the impact of gender on career paths and on management effectiveness, and she is co-author of several influential papers concerned with the impact of the female sales manager on sales organization effectiveness. Her interests extend to the development of effective management control strategy in the sales area and the factors driving higher levels of salesperson effectiveness. Currently she is working on projects related to the choice of sales careers by business graduates and the strategic sales capabilities underpinning business strategy implementation. She has published papers in such journals as the *Journal of Management Studies*, the *British Journal of Management*, the *Journal of Personal Selling & Sales Management*, the *Journal of the Academy of Marketing Science*, and the *Journal of Strategic Marketing*.

Dr. Lane is also dedicated to empirical studies and participant evaluation of retail locations throughout the world, mainly focused on fashion and jewellery, which has caused many of her credit cards to go into serious melt-down. She denies being a classic brand victim and claims that reducing expenditure on clothes and jewellery is just a sign of meanness and weak character, which is to be despised.

What the Experts Say About *Strategic Customer Management*

As a team, Professor Nigel Piercy and Dr Nikala Lane represent the highest global standards in research, teaching and practice. This book is outstanding because it represents a breakthrough in strategic marketing and sales. When was the last really groundbreaking new thinking in marketing? Yes, it was a very long time ago!!. We have all waited with anticipation for their work to hit the market and I for one will use their ideas as soon as possible in my work with some of the world's biggest and best companies.

(Professor Malcolm McDonald, Emeritus Professor of Marketing, Cranfield School of Management, Cranfield University, UK)

I am impressed with this book. The radical transformation underway toward strategic sales organizations is not recognized in many firms and this cutting edge contribution promises to play a pivotal role in guiding the change process in organizations. As thought leaders Nigel Piercy and Nikala Lane provide impressive action guidelines concerning the key role of *strategic customer management* in gaining competitive advantage and superior business performance. Designing and managing the *strategic sales organization* is at the center of this change process.

(Professor David W. Cravens, Emeritus Professor of Marketing, M. J. Neely School of Business, Texas Christian University, USA)

Nigel Piercy and Nikala Lane have written the *defenitive* book about the new world order of sales and marketing. This is an incredibly insightful and important work that provides the specific approaches necessary to compete successfully in this changed environment. Piercy and Lane have captured the essence of managerial and organizational actions needed to successfully develop and implement integrated customer management strategies in the 21st century. They have correctly articulated and exemplified the need for alignment of people, processes, systems, and strategies in order to shift the whole organizational focus to one of customer management. No thoughtful sales or marketing manager should be without a copy.

(Professor Grey W. Marshall, Ph.D., Charles Harwood Professor of Marketing and Strategy and Vice President for Strategic Marketing, Crummer Graduate School of Business, Rollins College, Winter Park, Florida, USA)

Any sales or marketing manager who reads this book and does not find ideas to improve their business should seek a new career! Professors Piercy and Lane have developed a long-overdue and radically different view of managing sales organizations. Informed by their extensive consulting and research activities, rich with colourful examples, and incorporating practical tools to aid implementation, their work should be required reading for managers everywhere.

(Professor James Mac Hulbert, R. C. Kopf Professor Emeritus, Columbia Business School, and Visiting Professor, Guanghua School of Management, Peking University)

Part I

Making the Case

1

Introduction: Is Sales the New Marketing?

There is nothing short of a revolution taking place at the front-end of our manufacturing and services organizations.[1] It has been a long time coming, but it is fundamentally changing the way we deal with customers and how we manage customer processes in our businesses. That front-end may be called sales, account management, business development, the commercial department, or it may masquerade under other names yet to be invented. The front-end is where our company meets its customers, relationships are formed, and deals are done, or where relationships fail and business is lost.

The front-end of our companies is moving into an era of strategic customer management. The sales organization is becoming a strategic imperative rather than a tactical tool. For many companies, the strategic management of customers and customer relationships has become a higher priority than conventional marketing activities, which is why we are already seeing major organizations transferring resources from marketing to strategic sales and account management initiatives, to achieve better alignment and to achieve the goals of business strategy.[2]

---

[1] Yes, we are aware that every management book in the world refers to an imminent 'revolution', but we think this time it is actually true.

[2] Webster, Frederick E., Alan J. Malter, and S. Ganesan, 'The Decline and Dispersal of Marketing Competence', *MIT Sloan Management Review*, Vol. 46 No. 4 2005, pp. 35–43.

Hence, the question (which is profoundly irritating to many marketing executives, and probably worthwhile for this achievement alone): is sales the new marketing?[3]

Marketing has always taken a somewhat snooty view of sales as a quite separate entity in the organization concerned with tactics and the execution of their marketing strategies. Marketing gurus generally concurred. According to Theodore Levitt: 'Selling focuses on the needs of the seller; marketing on the needs of the buyer'[4] (where by implication buyer needs are a higher priority than seller needs). The conventional subordination of sales (tactical and down-market) to marketing (strategic and clever) was elaborated by statements like Peter Drucker's that 'the aim of marketing is to make selling superfluous'.[5] However, let us get real here. Levitt was writing almost 50 years ago, and Drucker more than 30 years ago. Their views may have dated somewhat. The world has changed. Part of that change impacts the relationship between marketing and sales in companies, and what it means for effective relationships with customers.

The End of the Marketing Dream

There are more and more signs that marketing, as an organizational function, is coming to the end of its useful life. The signs that matter are not just the breaking-up of marketing departments, the growing absence of marketing from top management teams, the reducing expenditures on conventional marketing, the shortening job tenure for chief marketing executives, and the like—all of which have been documented. It is not even that marketing is no longer the company powerhouse it once thought itself to be, or that frequently other people

---

[3] Actually, some people say the more important question is 'Is marketing the new sales?', but this is no place for that kind of sloppy, post-modern thinking.

[4] Levitt, Theodore, 'Marketing Myopia', *Harvard Business Review*, July–August 1960, pp. 45–56.

[5] Drucker, Peter F., *Management: Tasks, Responsibilities, Practices*, New York: Harper and Row, 1973.

in the company no longer listen to marketing about the things that matter—which has also been documented.

The problem is more that conventional marketing has simply run out of ideas in the areas that matter most to companies: developing value-creating opportunities in new market segments and niches; creating radical innovation in product and service offerings; using customer value as the basis for price positioning; coping with a disruptive new communications landscape where the rules are fundamentally different from those in the past; protecting and enhancing corporate reputation as a competitive resource; building cross-boundary collaborations for innovation and partnership; and managing effective relationships with major customers—some of which may have considerable power and dominant market positions.

Instead, in too many places, marketing has clung to fixed and unchanging definitions of markets and segments, incremental innovation in tired brands, mechanical pricing formulae, conventional communications (sometimes crudely re-shaped for online delivery), unimaginative public relations efforts, and the management of customers as though they had no power. Marketing has not run out of technical expertise so much as it has run out of ideas. Most particularly, marketing no longer looks to have the big ideas that can drive innovative and effective business strategy.[6]

It is almost as if marketing is so concerned about marketing communications—'marcoms'—brochureware and design that they have forgotten why and how people buy products.[7]

A New Type of New Sales Organization

While traditional marketing has buried its head in the tactics of advertising and promotion, the world has moved on. The ability of a company to manage its relationship with its markets is probably

[6] If you want more in this vein, perhaps with which to challenge your marketing people, then you can find more details in: Piercy, Nigel F., *Market-Led Strategic Change: Transforming the Process of Going to Market*, 4th ed., Oxford: Butterworth-Heinemann, 2009, Chapter 3.
[7] Parmar, Arundhati, 'Flight Path', *Marketing News*, 15 June 2005, pp. 9–10.

a higher priority now than it has ever been. The problem is that traditional marketing was never designed for complex, consultative, and collaborative, technology-based relationships where, for example, the 'product' is being created jointly by the buyer and the seller as it is being 'sold'. In fact, in many markets this is likely to be one of the core capabilities for survival and performance. Marketing is not addressing these capabilities. Sales is going to have to, before it is too late.

The urgency of addressing these capabilities is underlined by escalating customer power and buyer concentration in market after market. The complex demands of powerful customers alone mean that the field salesforce can no longer passively accept and execute plans produced by corporate marketing. (Actually, the best sales organizations probably never did.) The reality is that 'As power shifted from the seller to the buyer, it also shifted from headquarters to the field'.[8]

In fact, there have been several suggestions that the revolution in the relationships between marketing and sales has already arrived, even if marketing executives (and many educators) have yet to notice. There is growing evidence of the expanding influence of sales over strategic decisions. For example, research finds that the sales department has more influence than the marketing department on many so-called marketing decisions,[9] and that 'primary marketing coordinators increasingly reside in sales rather than the marketing organization',[10] while sales plays a growing role in formulating as well as executing marketing strategies.[11] Similarly, the sales organization often has a decisive influence on the direction of new product innovation through

[8] Shapiro, Benson P., *Creating the Customer-Centric Team: Coordinating Sales and Marketing*, Harvard Business School Note 9-999-006, Boston, MA: Harvard Business School, 2002.

[9] Krohmer, H., Christian Homburg, and John P. Workman, 'Should Marketing Be Cross-Functional? Conceptual Development and International Empirical Evidence', *Journal of Business Research*, Vol. 35 2002, pp. 451–65.

[10] Homburg, Christian, John P. Workman, and Ove Jensen, 'Fundamental Changes in Marketing Organization: The Movement Toward a Customer-Focused Organizational Structure', *Journal of the Academy of Marketing Science*, Vol. 28 No. 4 2000, pp. 459–78.

[11] Cross, J., S. W. Hartley, W. Rudelius, and M. J. Vassey, 'Sales Force Activities and Marketing Strategies in Industrial Firms: Relationships and Implications', *Journal of Personal Selling & Sales Management*, Vol. 21 No. 3 2001, pp. 199–206.

the intelligence they collect and interpret,[12] and on assessing and accessing key market segments.[13]

There is growing consensus that traditional approaches to marketing and sales are doomed to fail, and in particular that 'the shaping of the selling function has become a strategic corporate issue', requiring clarity about the new sales role, new structures, and new management approaches.[14] But in addition to positioning sales as a boardroom issue, we should recognize that the new processes and structures required to enhance and sustain value delivery to customers through the reinvented sales organization are likely to demand evaluation and appraisal that extends far beyond the domain traditionally associated with selling activities.[15]

The conclusion to which we are drawn is that increasingly the ability of companies to achieve competitive superiority and enhanced business performance through the way they manage customer relationships is a core capability, but one which has been largely ignored by conventional sales and marketing thinking.

Let us not forget that it is traditional thinking that has got us in the position where in many companies profits depend on the most dissatisfied customers—unhappy because we encouraged them to make bad purchases (so they have to pay penalties, buy add-ons, or replace the product prematurely, which is why these products are very profitable in the short term)—is it surprising they hate us?[16]

The future requires a sales organization that behaves differently, does different things in different ways, and delivers value to the business in new ways. It will involve a strategic responsibility for the

---

[12] Lambert, D. M., H. Marmorstein, and A. Sharma, 'Industrial Salespeople as a Source of Market Information', *Industrial Marketing Management*, Vol. 17 May 1990, pp. 111–18.

[13] Maier, J. and J. Saunders, 'The Implementation Process of Segmentation in Sales Management', *Journal of Personal Selling & Sales Management*, Vol. 10 February 1990, pp. 39–48.

[14] Shapiro, Benson P., Adrian J. Slywotskyl, and Stepehn X. Doyle, *Stratgeic Sales Management: A Boardroom Issue*, Harvard Business School Note 9-595-018, Boston, MA: Harvard Business School, 1998.

[15] Ogbuchi, Alphonso O. and Varinder M. Sharma, 'Redefining Industrial Salesforce Roles in a Changing Environment', *Journal of Marketing Theory and Practice*, Vol. 7 No. 1 1999, pp. 64–71.

[16] McGovern, Gail and Youngme Moon, 'Companies and the Customers That Hate Them', *Harvard Business Review*, June 2007, pp. 78–84.

management of the links between a company and its market, and for confronting the important choices and decisions that exist. The core responsibility of the strategic sales organization will be strategic customer management—placing the management of the customer portfolio and its implied investment decisions at the centre of business strategy. This book attempts to map out what we know so far about how it is possible to achieve this reinvention of the front-end of a company.

It is now a decade since Neil Rackham concluded: 'Sales functions everywhere are in the early stages of radical and profound changes comparable to those that began to transform manufacturing 20 years ago.'[17] Think about it. Total quality deployment was a big idea in operations management. It has run its course. Business process re-engineering was a big idea in internal systems. It has run its course. The marketing concept was a big idea. It has run its course. The lean supply chain was a big idea. It has run its course. Strategic customer management is a big idea. The time for this idea is now. It is the customer's turn at last.

The Priority for Strategic Customer Management

There are some really powerful and compelling reasons why the big idea of the strategic sales organization capable of implementing strategic customer management is emerging. They identify the forces driving and re-shaping the sales organization, the escalating demands from major customers for something new and better from their suppliers, and the impact of strategic sales capabilities on business performance.

Forces Driving the Sales Organization

For some time sales organizations in companies have been under powerful company and customer forces that have re-shaped the salesforce

---

[17] Rackham, Neil and John DeVincentis, *Rethinking the Sales Force: Redefining Selling to Create and Capture Customer Value*, New York: McGraw-Hill, 1999, p. 3.

Fig. 1.1 Forces driving the sales organization

role and operation.[18] The major forces acting to re-shape the sales function in organizations are summarized in Figure 1.1. The implementation of new types of marketing strategy, driven by customer relationships and value, requires the realignment of sales processes with the strategy—many sales organizations have inherited structures and processes that were set up to do a quite different, largely transactional, job.

At the same time, multi-channelling and the growth in Internet-based direct channels are substituting for many traditional sales activities, so direct channels compete with the traditional salesperson. Moreover, in most places management wants more for less—the days of throwing money at marketplace problems have gone for most of us, and the issue is enhanced productivity. Higher productivity in sales is very attractive to management if we can achieve both top-line and bottom-line effects at the same time—sell more, cheaper, and profit rises as well as volume. In fact, evidence from the United States suggests that many senior managers are dissatisfied with the productivity of their sales organizations, and many see salesforce cost poorly aligned with their strategic goals.[19]

---

[18] For example, see: Jones, Eli, Stephen P. Brown, Andris A. Zoltners, and Barton A. Weitz, 'The Changing Environment of Selling and Sales Management', *Journal of Personal Selling & Sales Management*, Vol. 25 No. 2 2005, pp. 105–11.

[19] *Strategic Sales Compensation Survey*, New York: Deloitte Touche Development LLC, 2005.

For example, when Mark Hurd became CEO of Hewlett-Packard and began that company's remarkable performance improvement, he found that there were 11 layers between him and a customer, which he thought a touch excessive. H-P was slower to respond to customers than its competitors, and yet of the 17,000 people working in corporate sales, only 10,000 directly sold to customers—the rest were support staff or managers. Hurd's overhaul of H-P's vast corporate salesforce involved closing a large sales group that sold a broad portfolio of products and reallocating salespeople to product-specific groups, so they could master the products they sell; cutting hundreds of under-performing salespeople; removing three levels of sales management; and paring back internal meetings so salespeople can spend more time with customers. H-P's salesforce now spends more time in front of customers, responds faster to their needs, and is winning more corporate sales deals.[20]

But then, to cost saving issues, you have to add the simple truth that business-to-business customers want much more from their suppliers as well.

What Customers Want

One of the most dramatic changes in business-to-business marketing in the twenty-first century has been the breathtaking escalation in the demands for enhanced service, new types of relationships, and greater added-value by business-to-business customers of all kinds. The H. R. Chally consultancy's *World Class Sales Excellence Research Report*[21] investigates the views of corporate purchasers and their expectations for the relationship with the salesperson from a supplier, and mandates that the seller will:

1. *Be personally accountable for our desired results*—the sales contact with the supplier is expected to be committed to the customer and accountable for achievement.

---

[20] This illustration is based on: Tam, Pui-Wing, 'System Reboot—Hurd's Big Challenge at H-P', *Wall Street Journal*, 3 April 2006, p. A.1.
[21] H. R. Chally, *The Chally World Class Sales Excellence Research Report*, Dayton, OH: The H. R. Chally Group, 2006.

2. *Understand our business*—to be able to add value, the supplier must understand the customer's competencies, strategies, challenges, and organizational culture.

3. *Be on our side*—the salesperson must be the customer's advocate in his or her own organization, and operate through the policies and politics to focus on the customer's needs.

4. *Design the right applications*—the salesperson is expected to think beyond technical features and functions to the implementation of the product or service in the customer's environment, thinking beyond the transaction to the customer's end state.

5. *Be easily accessible*—customers expect salespeople to be constantly connected and within reach.

6. *Solve our problems*—customers no longer buy products or services, they buy solutions to their business problems, and expect salespeople to diagnose, prescribe, and resolve their issues, not just sell them products.

7. *Be creative in responding to our needs*—buyers expect salespeople to be innovators, who bring them new ideas to solve problems, so creativity is a major source of added value.

These qualities characterize how world class salesforces are distinguished in the eyes of their customers. They describe a customer environment which is radically different from the transactional selling approaches of the past, and which poses substantially different management challenges in managing business-to-business customer relationships. The sales and service organizations which meet these customer demands and expectations and develop sustainable and attractive customer relationships are likely to look very different to those of the past, and to work very differently.

Most changes in company sales organizations to respond to this profound change in what customers want have barely got past the most trivial and superficial adjustments. This will not hack it. More is required.

Why Strategic Sales Capabilities Matter More than Ever Before

For many companies, the growing significance of strategic sales capabilities is underlined by issues like these. These are the reasons why strategic customer management has to be on the boardroom agenda, if it is not already there.

The Real Importance of Customer Relationships

In a lot of companies channels development has included the establishment of direct channels, such as those based around Internet websites. Even in consumer marketing, by 2007, 10 per cent of all retail spending took place on the Internet,[22] and this figure is much higher for many business-to-business sellers. At the same time, there is a growing trend in major companies towards the outsourcing to third parties of routine sales operations[23]—while in the United States Proctor & Gamble has a 200-person team wholly dedicated to Wal-Mart (the single customer that constitutes 20% of P&G's business), it is relatively easy for P&G to outsource routine sales visits to stores to a third-party sales organization. Similarly, global corporate expenditure on customer relationship management (CRM) technology is measured each year in billions of dollars, and individual spends by companies can be in tens of millions of dollars. CRM explicitly aims to automate many of the functions traditionally associated with the salesforce.

But the question people are now asking is whether a company's most important business-to-business customer relationships can really be managed securely and to full advantage through a website, a third-party seller, or a call centre? Consider, for example, that Home Depot in the United States has asked a number of suppliers, including Black & Decker, to pull back from their more extreme Internet strategies, or risk losing the Home Depot business.[24] CRM, for example, in spite of all its promises, is really no more than a way of managing customer transactions, not impacting strategically on relationships with major customers. Answering this question is really important to understanding the strategic role of sales, rather than considering only the routine activities involved in taking and processing orders.

For instance, Dell Computers is an Internet-based company—the majority of sales and service provisions are on the Web. Nonetheless, Dell maintains both account executives in the field and internal salespeople in branches, because their view is that the technology exists

---

[22] Rigby, Elizabeth, 'Shopping gets Tougher for Online Supermarkets', *Financial Times*, Monday 9 April, 2007, p. 19.

[23] Anderson, Erin and Bob Trinkle, *Outsourcing the Sales Function: The Real Costs of Field Sales*, Mason, OH: Thomson, 2005.

[24] Friedman, Lawrence G., *Go To Market Strategy*, Woburn, MA: Butterworth-Heinemann Business Books, 2002.

to free salespeople to sell and develop customer relationships, not to process orders (which the technology generally does better and cheaper). Indeed, part of Dell's fightback against the decline of its direct model in delivering sales growth is developing multiple, global sales channels. There is a substantial business and competitive risk in underestimating the role of the salesforce in defending and sustaining a competitive position.

Writing in *Harvard Business Review*, Thomas Stewart summarizes the new and emerging role for the sales organization in these situations in the following terms:

> ... Selling is changing fast and in such a way that sales teams have become strategic resources. When corporations strive to become customer focused, salespeople move to the foreground; engineers recede. As companies go to market with increasingly complex bundles of products and services, their representatives cease to be mere order takers (most orders are placed online, anyway) and become relationship managers.[25]

Understanding and enhancing the ways in which sales resources add value and protect customer relationships is becoming of strategic importance in markets being driven towards commoditization (see below). To the extent that a marketing strategy depends upon strong and sustained customer relationships, there is an implicit reliance on strategic sales capabilities. Moreover, to the extent that a salesforce has built and sustains strong customer relationships by creating value for customers, then this provides a strategic resource for the company, which should impact on its strategic choices.

Customer Sophistication and Complexity

In addition, the growing sophistication and aggressiveness of purchasers in business-to-business markets has escalated the strategic importance of effectively managing buyer–seller relationships.[26] The urgent challenge to sellers is to implement effective marketing

[25] Stewart, Thomas A., 'The Top Line', *Harvard Business Review*, July–August 2006, p. 10.
[26] For example, see: Jones, Eli, Stephen P. Brown, Andris A. Zoltners, and Barton A. Weitz, 'The Changing Environment of Selling and Sales Management', *Journal of Personal Selling & Sales Management*, Vol. 25 No. 2 2005, pp. 105–11.

strategies in a dramatically changed world of sophisticated buyers.[27] This change is underlined by the shift in the traditional role played by purchasing functions in customer organizations. Increasingly, purchasing has become a strategic function directly linked to the customer's strategic plans, with a major level of responsibility for profitability, cost control, and enhanced shareholder value.[28]

Professional purchasing managers use complex sourcing metrics to select the 'right' suppliers, and to dictate the terms on how they will be supplied, so more than ever before supplier profitability is determined at the point of sale, where the sales organization meets the customer.[29] Correspondingly, the sales task has become much more complex and the stakes much higher.

Sellers in business-to-business markets face much more complex decisions about their marketing and sales investments in customer relationships than in the past. Historically, seller profits were generally in line with account size, because prices tended to be cost-based, sales costs were relatively low, and the size of accounts did not vary dramatically. However, consolidation by merger and acquisition and attrition has changed this situation in many markets. In industrial markets, sales situations are increasingly characterized by fewer, larger, and more complex purchasing organizations, and in consumer markets there has been a massive shift in power to retailers.[30]

Unsurprisingly, very large customers are powerful and demand customized sales and account management, and are challenging for the supplier in terms of profitability. Other customers also demand special treatment, but it is likely to be different. Small- and medium-sized accounts require yet more different approaches, mainly because of the cost of serving them. The strategic challenge is to match sales efforts

---

[27] For example, see: Shapiro, Benson P., Adrian J. Slywotsky, and Stephen X. Doyle, *Strategic Sales Management: A Boardroom Issue*, Note 9-595-018, Cambridge, MA: Harvard Business School, 1998.

[28] Janda, S. and S. Seshandri, 'The Influence of Purchasing Strategies on Performance', *Journal of Business and Industrial Marketing*, Vol. 16 No. 4 2001, pp. 294–306.

[29] De Boer, L., E. Labro, and O. Morlacci, 'A Review of Methods Supporting Supplier Selection', *European Journal of Purchasing and Supply Management*, Vol. 7 No. 2 2001, pp. 75–89. Talluri, S. and R. Narasimhan, 'A Methodology for Strategic Sourcing', *European Journal of Operational Research*, Vol. 154 No. 1 2004, pp. 236–50.

[30] Shapiro, Benson P., Adrian J. Slywotsky, and Stephen X. Doyle, *Strategic Sales Management: A Boardroom Issue*, Note 9-595-018, Cambridge, MA: Harvard Business School, 1998.

and approaches to different parts of a complex portfolio of customers, to balance revenue and profitability with business risk. These choices impact substantially on corporate performance.

In many sectors, traditional sales models may be obsolete as a result of growing customer sophistication. For example, in the pharmaceuticals business, high sales pressure placed on doctors to prescribe new drugs has resulted in formal training courses in medical schools to teach future doctors how to resist sales pitches.[31] This is just symptomatic of the search by the pharmaceutical industry for new and better ways to get to market. Companies like Pfizer, Wyeth, Novartis, and GlaxoSmithKlein recognize that the era of 'hard sell' is over in their sector and are working to develop new sales models.

Our logic is that such fundamental changes in the requirements of business customers mandate a strategic response from sellers that is more robust than simple acquiescence to demands for lower prices and higher service levels. The challenge is to reposition sales as a core part of a company's competitiveness, where the sales organization is closely integrated into a company's business strategy.[32]

These market trends have elevated the importance of the effective deployment of sales capabilities to a strategic issue. Many traditional approaches to marketing and sales simply ignore the implications of customer sophistication, complexity, and scale. Continuing to do so is a route to potentially devastating losses in profits and business performance, because customers are well aware of what the new realities mean, even if sellers are not.

Commoditization

One impact of the revolution which has taken place in operations management and supply chain design has been to reduce product and service differentiation in many sectors. Competing products are frequently built on near-identical modularized platforms, and supply chains are designed for maximum speed and lowest cost. Benchmarking systems encourage suppliers to achieve similar performance against each other on the same metrics. It is unsurprising that the result

---

[31] Weintraub, Arlene, 'Just Say No to Drug Reps', *Business Week*, 4 February 2008, p. 69.
[32] Stephens, H., CEO, The H. R. Chally Group, Presentation at the American Marketing Association summer Educators' Conference, August 2003.

is growth in product similarity rather than differentiation. Products as diverse as mid-market cars, personal computers, and financial services are close to impossible to distinguish one from the other, once the brands and badges are removed. So, where now is the competitive differentiation that gives an advantage against the rest?

Moreover, at the same time, customer organizations have increasingly pursued aggressive commoditization strategies with their suppliers—from their perspective, if all competitive offerings can be made essentially similar, then differentiation can only be achieved through price, because that is how commodities are sold. This is a preferred situation for the purchaser, but not usually for the seller. The chief purchasing officer's modern armoury includes RFPs (Request for Proposal or an invitation to suppliers to bid for business on a specific product or service); Internet auctions; purchasing consultants; and buying consortiums. These mechanisms all seek to reduce purchasing to a comparison of prices and technical product specifications. The challenge to sellers is to constantly expand the scope and value of the offering to the customer, and the impact of the offering on the customer's business performance. Achieving differentiation with strategic customers requires new types of buyer–seller relationships that assist customers in implementing their own strategies. This underlines the priority for a strategic sales role in developing and implementing business and marketing strategy.

In fact, for many of us, one outcome of modularization and benchmarking in operations, and lean design in supply chains, is that the sales/customer interface is the *only* place where competitive differentiation can actually be achieved. For example, research by the US consultancy H. R. Chally suggests that salesperson effectiveness accounts for as much as 40 per cent of business-to-business customer choice of supplier, simply because technology has made the products themselves increasingly substitutable.[33]

Strategic sales capabilities may be a vital component of competitive advantage or even the only source of competitive differentiation that is left. For example, SKP is the world's largest maker of industrial bearings—a business highly susceptible to commoditization. SKF's fight to overcome commoditization threats relies on the company's

[33] Stephens, H. (2003), op cit.

5,000 sales engineers developing close relationships with customers and liasing with technical experts deep inside their own business. The goal for sales is to align customer needs with complex technical solutions, often involving customized products. The sales engineer stands between the company and commoditization.[34]

Corporate Expenditure

Notwithstanding the impact of the Internet, CRM, and all the other things that were supposed to reduce the cost of sales, it is worth remembering that corporate expenditure on sales operations exceeds that on higher profile advertising and sales promotion activities. Only rough estimates exist, but 2000 levels of UK expenditure on personal selling by British companies were estimated at £20 billion, compared to £13 billion on advertising and £14 billion on sales promotion.[35] Sales activities are frequently among the most expensive in the marketing budget. US survey data suggest that in 2006 the average salary for salespeople was approximately $150,000, while high performers averaged more than $160,000. Survey participants expected sales incomes to continue to increase.[36] Research in the United States also finds that while in some sectors companies spend as little as 1 per cent of sales revenue on their salesforce (e.g. banking, hotels), the average company spends 10 per cent of sales on its salesforce, and some spend as much as 22 per cent (e.g. printing and publishing).[37] In fact, it is not uncommon for sustained salesforce costs to be as high as 50 per cent of sales in some companies.[38]

It is also commonly the case that the sales function employs more people and consequently in many companies is a much larger function than marketing. Interestingly, estimates in both the UK and the United States suggest that sales employment is expected to increase up to

---

[34] Marsh, Peter, 'Back on a Roll in the Business of Bearings', *Financial Times*, 7 February 2007, p. 10.

[35] Doyle, Peter, *Marketing Management and Strategy*, 3rd ed., London: Prentice-Hall, 2002.

[36] Kornik, Joseph, 'What's It All Worth?', *Sales and Marketing Management*, May 2007, pp. 27–39.

[37] *Dartnell's 30th Sales Force Compensation Survey: 1998–1999*, Chicago: Dartnell Corporation, 1999.

[38] Zoltners, Andris A., Prabhakant Sinha, and Sally E. Lorimer, *Sales Force Design for Strategic Advantage*, New York: Palgrave Macmillan, 2004.

2010. The 'death of the salesman' forecast as a result of the expansion in Internet marketing and other direct channels appears to have been somewhat exaggerated—indeed, the 'dearth of the salesperson' may be more apt, as companies compete for scarce talent.

Strategic sales capabilities focus on important customer relationships in ways which the technology cannot do, and this is mandated by the complexity, sophistication, and scale of major customers. These capabilities may be the last line of defence against commoditization. And, apart from anything else, they cost you a fortune and there is no sign this will change. Just on their own, the expenditure levels and the growth in employment in sales demands that we should be asking more searching questions about the full utilization of these resources to add value to the company. But perhaps the larger issue is evolving and developing these capabilities because they can change a company's competitive position for the better or for the worse. But the organization that will effectively deploy strategic sales capabilities will look a lot different to the traditional sales department.

The Evolution of New Organizational Processes and Forms

Organizations do not stand still. They evolve and change as the outside world changes, as demands on the company re-shape, and as management priorities reconfigure, looking for the best ways to enhance performance.

The new demands on organizations emphasize agility and nimbleness over bureaucracy, flat structures over pyramids, collaboration and partnership, knowledge-based work, internal and external networks, and new ways of motivating new types of employee over traditional approaches. Quite simply, the top-heavy bureaucracies of the past cannot survive. They are crumbling because they are too slow, they are weak at integrating the things that matter around the customers that matter, and frankly they are too expensive.

For example, Cadbury is a business struggling to re-shape itself to be able to compete more effectively. Cadbury has relatively low profit margins compared to its global competitors—Cadbury averages

10 per cent, compared to 18 per cent at Wrigley and Hershey. The low margins are linked to Cadbury's complex operating structure, with many brands and manufacturing sites. The organizational structure at Cadbury has become too complex with too many overlaps. Organizational costs, including sales and administration, account for 20 per cent of turnover, compared to 12 per cent at its rivals. Cadbury has spun off its drinks business and now has to find savings of $500 million a year from the remaining confectionery business, simply to survive.[39]

In short, there is a compelling argument that traditional ways of organizing cannot survive—they make companies too slow, too fat, too bureaucratic, and unable to respond effectively as the world of customers and competitors undergoes radical innovation. Organizations have to evolve—standing still is not an option. Nowhere is this more relevant at the moment than in the front-end of the organization where marketing and sales departments live.

Indeed, there is a compelling rationale that innovation in management thinking may be far more important than simply innovation in technology and products. It is giant steps in management that change how we all work, and which are directly connected to sustainable competitive advantage.[40] We believe that the continuing emergence of strategic customer management will be just such a 'giant step'.

Re-shaping and Repositioning Traditional Functions

Part of organizational evolution is that traditional specialist functions change in how they operate and in the level and type of influence they exert in the company. In some cases they may disappear altogether, in others they reappear in different guises.

There are lots of precedents for organizational evolution. In the 1960s, transport and warehousing was an important but tactical function moving things around. But things changed. There cannot be a company anywhere that does not now see the supply chain as a key component of its business strategy. In the same era, companies

---

[39] This illustration is based on: Laurence, Ben, 'Cadbury Sheds 5000 Jobs in Drastic Revamp', *Sunday Times*, 17 June 2007, Section 3, p. 1. Jenny Wiggins, 'Cadbury Sweet Talk on Confectionery Revival Fails to Move Sceptics', *Financial Times*, 20 June 2007, p. 27.

[40] Mol, Michael J. and Julian Birkenshaw, *Giant Steps in Management: Innovations That Change the Way We Work*, Harlow: FT-Prentice Hall, 2007.

had industrial relations departments, which developed into personnel managers providing a broader perspective on recruiting and developing people. Is there any boardroom now where human resource strategy is not seen as a key part of how we compete? At one time we had purchasing and supply departments, but once the potential for strategic purchasing to impact hugely on business performance became apparent, supplier relationship management became a permanent fixture on the boardroom agenda.

By contrast, sales and marketing seem to have spent a lot of the last two decades engaged in active interdepartmental warfare, while the rest of the world has moved on to more important things. While sales departments have obsessed over remuneration systems and marketing has pursued the holy grail of the perfect glossy brochure, big changes have taken place in what companies need their front-end organizations to deliver.

Smart companies have already started to evolve new ways of reshaping the front-end to meet the new demands that are faced, for example, in customer business development structures that focus on the opportunities provided by major customers and suppliers. Increasingly, we are seeing new job titles like Director of Strategic Customer Management and Strategic Customer Manager being adopted to indicate this type of change in the role of what was once sales.

For example, Proctor & Gamble under A. G. Lafley's leadership has transformed itself from the stodgy, slow-moving, inward-looking bureaucracy of the 1990s into a nimble, innovative, and aggressive competitor beating the rest. Part of that transformation has been the creation of Customer Business Development (CBD) organizations at the front of the business. The goal of CBD is to transform the old, narrow idea of buyer–seller relationships with customers into a multifunctional, collaborative approach designed to achieve mutual volume, profit, and market share objectives. CBD teams work with customers to develop the customer's plans and strategies to the advantage of both customer and P&G. CBD team members work collaboratively with experts from finance, management systems, customer service, and brand management to develop and implement business strategies that deliver sustainable competitive advantage for P&G brands.

Other companies have moved on way beyond traditional functional departments and their seemingly never-ending jurisdictional disputes, to organize around the key processes that impact on customer value.

For example, it is more than a decade since consumer goods companies like Kraft Foods pioneered the move away from traditional product and brand management approaches in order to place greater emphasis on customer management. Kraft organizes its teams around three core processes: the *consumer management team* replaced the brand management function to focus on customer segments; *customer process teams* replaced the sales function to serve retail accounts, and the *supply management team* manages the logistics function. A *strategic integration team* develops effective overall strategies and coordinates the other teams. Some traditional functions remain but their role is to coordinate activities across teams to ensure that shared learning takes place, to acquire and develop specialized skills, to deploy specialists to the cross-functional process teams, and to achieve scale economies.[41]

Leading edge examples underline that something new is developing from what used to be sales and marketing, and beyond even customer business development and process-based organization. For want of a better name, let us call this Strategic Customer Management[42] (and let us not forget what the supply chain people taught us about the importance of having the right name for something new). We show this proposed evolution in Figure 1.2. Then, we can focus on putting strategic customer management on the boardroom table along with the other key drivers of business strategy.

More Pressure to Change . . .

Anyway, apart from the natural tendency of organizations to evolve as priorities and strategies develop and change, there is another sword of Damocles hanging by a thread over traditional sales organizations. Think about it—we have 'total qualitied' and 'six sigma'ed' the heck out of internal operations; we have process reengineered ourselves to a standstill; we have all leaned and made our supply chains (fr)agile for stunning increases in efficiency; and we have constantly squeezed any

---

[41] Day, George S. 'Aligning the Organization to the Market', in Donald R. Lehman and Katherine E. Jocz (eds.), *Reflections on the Futures of Marketing*, Cambridge, MA: Marketing Science Institute, 1997, pp. 69–72.

[42] Some people react to this name by asking 'Do you mean the management of *strategic* customers, or the management of all customers *strategically*?' Part of the point of this book is to answer this question 'Yes, both of the above'. We will explain why shortly (Chapter 2).

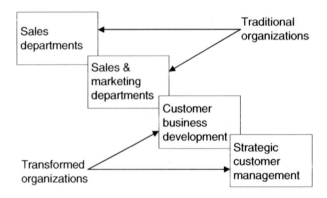

Fig. 1.2 Organizational evolution

advantage we can get out of the supplier base. So now, where do we look for the next generation of new models and increased efficiencies? It is going to be the black box surrounding how we connect with our customers, whatever label it currently has in the organization. I think that means us...

The Imperatives for the Strategic Sales Organization

What is happening here is nicely summarized by our colleagues:

Today's competitive environment demands a radically different approach. Specifically, the ability of firms to exploit the true potential of the sales organization requires that company executives adopt a new mindset about the role of the selling function within the firm, how the sales force is managed, and what salespeople are expected to produce. The sales function must serve as a dynamic source of value creation and innovation within the firm.   (The Sales Educators, 2006)[43]

---

[43] The Sales Educators, *Strategic Sales Leadership: BREAKthrough Thinking for BREAKthrough Results*, Mason, OH: Thomson, 2006.

Fulfilling that potential and delivering value creation and innovation to a company will require more than the conventional and traditional sales department. It requires a strategic sales organization.

We still have a lot to learn about the shape and operation of the genuinely strategic sales organization. On the basis of what we have learned so far, Figure 1.3 summarizes the imperatives and mandates for developing and evaluating the new strategic sales organization. This model provides the structure for this book; the structure deserves a brief explanation before we go further.[44]

The framework we propose in Figure 1.3 suggests the following imperatives for management focus in strategizing the sales organization:

- *Involvement*—placing the sales organization in the centre of the business and marketing strategy debate in companies and aligning sales operations with strategic direction. This means elevating sales above the tactical role of conducting the transactions to build the revenue demanded by business strategy, to becoming a partner in making the key business strategy decisions.

- *Intelligence*—building customer knowledge as a strategic resource critical both to strategy formulation and to building added-value strategies with major customers. Superior market sensing is becoming one of the most critical processes for building and enhancing strategic capabilities, which goes beyond marketing's obsession with surveys, to work on how managers really understand their customers and markets.

- *Integration*—establishing the cross-functional relationships necessary to lead processes which define, develop, and deliver superior value propositions to customers, and managing the interfaces between functions and business units impacting on service and value as it is perceived by customers. Total integration around customer value is a mandate but one which has proved elusive in the traditional functional organization.

- *Internal marketing*—using sales resources to 'sell' the customer across functional and divisional boundaries within the company and across organizational boundaries with partner companies, to achieve seamless value

---

[44] We are aware that alliteration is the last regrettable refuge of rogues, ruffians, and roustabouts, but the Marketing people have been going on about their '4Ps' so long we thought we better have more points than four and a different initial—so we have the '9Is'. Some object to this (yes, really) on the grounds that it is inappropriate because there is no 'I' in team, to which we have to respond, 'No, but there are several in "Irritating Idiot" '.

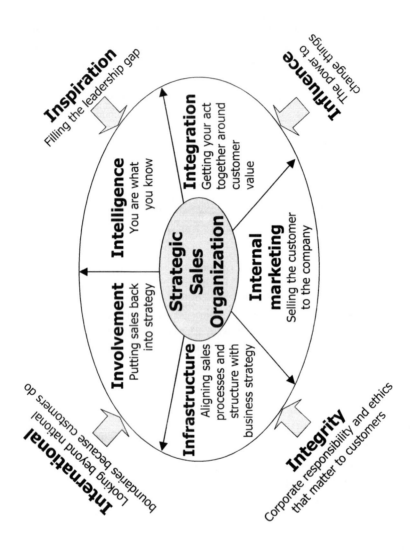

Fig. 1.3 Imperatives for the strategic sales organization

delivery for customers. Superior service and responsiveness to customer needs takes more than making speeches, it needs careful cultivation and management.

- *Infrastructure*—developing the structure and processes needed to manage sales and account management organizations to match customer relationship requirements and to build competitive advantage. Structures, compensation systems, evaluation systems, and training and development investments have to be designed to align with relationship and partnership, not the transactional focus of the past.

These challenges are the most immediate in assessing how to build the sales organization as an effective strategic force in a company. We discuss them in Part II of this book. However, there are also other broader drivers of change to which we should pay attention—not least in assessing if we are getting to where we should be or just going through the motions. We examine these broader issues in Part III of this book:

- *Inspiration*—part of the outcome should be to renew the ability of those who manage key external relationships with customers to inspire and provide leadership within the business.
- *Influence*—a test of whether we are taken seriously is the degree to which we exert influence over the company's strategic agenda and the key decisions which are made.
- *Integrity*—there has never been a time when scrutiny of the ethical and responsible behaviour of companies was greater, and when the cost of being judged unethical or irresponsible was higher. Managing relationships with customers, partners, and suppliers with integrity is a huge challenge, but not one that can be ignored. Increasingly, major customers cannot do business with people who they cannot trust, or whose corporate reputations carry a danger of contamination by association. This may be the highest priority in new types of buyer–seller relationship.[45]
- *International*—the globalization of markets, the emergence of global customers, and the spread of international competition mandates an international perspective on how we manage customer relationships in domestic and overseas markets.

These components of the strategic sales organization and its drivers provide the structure for this book—each gets its own chapter. This

[45] Galea, Christine, 'What Customers Really Want', *Sales & Marketing Management*, May 2006, p. 11.

provides a route-map through this book—whether you choose to start at the beginning or pick out the things that look most immediately relevant and actionable. However, in reality it is the overall effect and the links between the components that matter, so it may be useful to reduce things to a simple 'before-and-after' analysis.

Analysing the Changing Salesforce Role

Sometimes it helps to test things like these out against the reality you face. Figure 1.4 illustrates an approach you can take. The logic is that if we just think about salesforce size in headcount (although the skills base will also be important), and the salesforce role as we see it developing, then we may be looking at some routine activities, like basic order taking and processing which are likely to be *reduced*. In many situations, for example, employing people to undertake low-skill, repetitive tasks makes no sense when the technology does it better and cheaper.

For example, it is some years since insurance companies like Prudential, Sun Life of Canada, Friends Provident, and Britannic

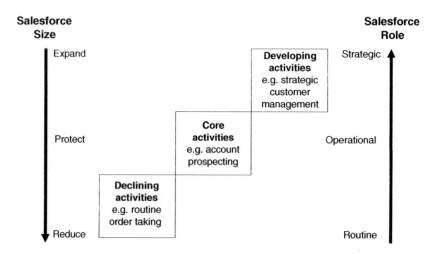

Fig. 1.4 Analysing the changing salesforce role

recognized that it was no longer economic to sell insurance and pensions to those on low and middle incomes through an on-the-road salesforce. Widespread salesforce downsizing followed that conclusion—the 'man from the Pru' was phased out after almost 150 years knocking on doors.[46]

On the other hand, Oracle has adopted a sales model where sales-people do not place orders—after a software demonstration they leave customers to place their own orders on the Web.[47] Nonetheless, the challenge for management is to match salesforce investment to competitive strategy, not to indulge in crude downsizing of sales operations.[48] Cisco, for example, has a successful strategy of using personal selling resources when a purchase is significant, complicated, and the decision is uncertain—typically the first sale to a customer or a new application—but leaving subsequent purchases to be made over the Internet.[49]

By contrast to declining sales activities, there are also likely to be core, operational salesforce roles and tasks which remain critical, and which should be protected from unthinking downsizing initiatives. Account prospecting and providing customer technical support are likely to be in this category for many of us. It is not a great idea to find out what the salesforce really adds to customer value by destroying that competitive advantage. One speciality industrial lubricants supplier learned this lesson the hard way. Large expenditure on CRM and the website provided the company with an alternative selling model to the 400 person salesforce. When launched, the new electronic sales model led to falling sales and profits. Worse, nearly a third of the salesforce resigned within the year (including 17 of the top 20 salespeople). The company had not bothered to ask its customers how they wanted to do business, and when they did customers identified this company's only real competitive advantage as the expertise of the salesforce and their ability to design solutions that solved technical

[46] English, Simon, 'Britannic Will Close Door on Sales Team', *Daily Telegraph*, 8 March 2001, p. 6.
[47] Clark, B. and Sean Callahan, 'Sales Staffs: Adapt or Die', *B to B*, 10 April 2000, p. 55.
[48] Olson, E. M., D. W. Cravens, and S. F. Slater, 'Competitiveness and Sales Management: A Marriage of Strategies', *Business Horizons*, March–April 2001, pp. 25–30.
[49] Royal. W., 'Death of Salesmen', *www.industryweek.com*, 17 May 1999, pp. 59–60.

problems for customers. Many of the best salespeople were by now working for the competition.[50]

Similarly, investors still wince at the memory of the botched sales-force reorganization at Xerox in 2001, which hastened the exit of the then CEO. Managers at Xerox are now a lot more cautious about judging the rate of change in the sales organization—move too quickly and you jeopardize customer relationships, move too slowly and you are overtaken by the competitors.[51]

Core, value-creating salesforce capabilities you protect and you may want to enhance.

For example, at technology company Logica, new CEO Andy Green is working to better integrate the disparate parts of the operation he has inherited, and to build the sales culture he needs to lift revenues to market-beating rates. Green was previously Logica's biggest cus-tomer at BT, so has a clear view of the company's sales approach. Part of his plan is to raid competitors to recruit around 60 key deal-makers and eventually have a force of 1,000 consultants to win new business.[52]

However, perhaps the most interesting issue in this type of analysis is what we can identify as new value-creating salesforce activities that are already emerging or exist as unused potentials in the busi-ness. For example, what *new activities* are likely to be required by the company and the customer, such as non-selling calls, information collection, working with partner organizations? What *emerging activ-ities* are already apparent—like interfunctional coordination, liaison with CRM, working with key account teams, and the like. And then there is the question of what *potential activities* may exist, not neces-sarily already apparent, but providing ways in which the salesforce can enhance customer value in new ways—for instance, in managing customer ordering profiles, liaison with direct channels, monitoring strategic account prospects and changes? The challenge here is to

---

[50] This illustration is adapted from: Friedman, Lawrence G., *Go To Market Strategy*, Woburn, MA: Butterworth-Heinemann Business Books, 2002.

[51] London, Simon, 'Xerox Runs Off a New Blueprint', *Financial Times*, 23 September 2005, p. 13.

[52] This illustration is based on: Palmer, Maija, 'Logica Set to Focus on Europe as Jobs Are Cut', *Financial Times*, 23 April 2008, p. 23.

build a case for the salesforce's new role in implementing market strategy, to more sophisticated and demanding customers, in a changing competitive environment, and with more complex channels to market.

This analysis is one you can undertake now, or postpone until you have progressed further through this book and developed more ideas for what the sales organization future should look like in your company. Whichever choice you make, we have provided a diagnostic worksheet structure as a basis for the analysis. This is shown in Appendix 1.1.

The worksheet just provides a simple mechanism for taking an overview of how the role of the salesforce in a company is likely to change in the future and to identify the opportunities for changing and enhancing the role it plays in the strategic development of the company. It is designed to provide a broad view as a basis for discussion and making strategic choices. It can easily be amended to make it fit better with a specific company's structure and approach. The worksheet structure follows the following logic.

Starting the Review. The *Company/Division* should be specified to identify which part of the business is under review. The *Time-span* should also be specified—how far into the future are you looking in this review?

Key Assumptions. It is worth making a note of any critical assumptions you are making about the company's growth, its market strategy, and any other issues which impact on your review of the salesforce role. These assumptions will have to be tested later and if they change, you will have to reconsider your conclusions.

Declining salesforce tasks/roles. Identify in broad terms the activities traditionally carried out by the salesforce that are of less importance— they are no longer required by customers, they are being replaced by other channels, they are superceded by CRM systems, and so on. Allowing for how much salesperson time was spent on these declining activities, the rate of growth of the business, and the rate of decline in the importance of these tasks, you need to make your best estimate of the change in salesforce headcount over the time span you have chosen (percentage change or number of people). You can then consider what are the major implications of your analysis of declining salesforce activities for training and development expenditure, redeployment of personnel, redundancies, recruitment and selection, reward and eval-uation systems, salesforce organization?

Core salesforce tasks/roles. Identify in broad terms the salesforce activities which remain central to how the company manages its relation-ships with customers, and which may need to be defended. Allowing for the rate of growth of the business, demands for core sales activities by customers and account management teams, you should make your best estimate of the change in salesforce headcount over the time span you have chosen (percentage change or number of people). You can then ask what are the major implications of your analysis of remaining core salesforce activities for training and development expenditure, recruitment and selection, reward and evaluation systems, salesforce organization?

New/potential salesforce tasks/roles. The most difficult part of your review is to identify the new and different types of activities that may be required of the salesforce in your planning horizon. This is probably the area most usefully discussed with customers, other executives across the business, and comparisons made with competitors. Then, allowing for the rate of growth of the business, what is your best estimate of the change in salesforce headcount over the time span you have chosen (percentage change or number of people) that would be required to implement each of the new types of activities you have identified? What are the major implications of your analysis of new types of salesforce activities for training and development expendi-ture, recruitment and selection, reward and evaluation systems, sales-force organization, interfunctional relationships?

This analysis may be the thing that sets you on the road towards developing the strategic sales organization that is capable of strate-gic customer management and creating superior customer value. The conclusions you reach may get richer if you track them through the remainder of this book.

The New Agenda

The new agenda is about strategic customer management not just tra-ditional sales or selling. The goal is to position the management of the customer portfolio and the design of relationship strategies for major customers as key issues driving business strategy and performance. Strategic customer management is the shift from sales as a tactical activity concerned only with implementing business and marketing strategy, to a strategic process that aligns corporate resources with customer needs and confronts the hard decisions about investment in customers and the risks in dependence on major customers.

Importantly, there are two sides to strategic customer management. The first relates to the strategic management of the customer portfolio—making investment choices between different types of customers to deliver the goals of marketing strategy, and also playing a role in shaping that strategy. The second component relates to the management of strategic customers—building relationships with the potentially dominant customers in the company's portfolio, some of which may be classified as strategic accounts and handled differently to the rest. These are important strategic decisions which impact directly on the profitability and risk profile of the company's business.

A strategic customer management approach will be distinguished by

- **The effective co-alignment of sales processes with business strategy**— the implementation of business strategy relies on the effective management of customer relationships—particularly with major customers—while the formulation of effective business strategy recognizes the resource provided by strategic sales capabilities.

- **Putting a customer perspective back into marketing and business strategy**—effective strategy increasingly relies on a profound understanding of customers and markets, yet the market sensing capability provided by the salesforce is frequently ignored by decision makers.[53] It will be harder and harder to survive without deep market knowledge which goes beyond platitudes and lip-service.

- **Managing the customer portfolio**—customers differ in their attractiveness, their prospects, and the risk they bring to the supplier business. The customer portfolio highlights the different relationship requirements and

---

[53] Fitzhugh, Ken L. M. and Nigel F. Piercy, 'Integrating Marketing Intelligence Sources: Reconsidering the Role of the Salesforce', *International Journal of Market Research*, Vol. 48 2006, pp. 38–60.

business opportunities with different groups and types of customers. Some of the most important decisions about customers relate to investment in meeting requirements and decisions not to invest. This is really not something you want to leave in the hands of a junior salesperson or brand manager.

- **Developing effective positioning with dominant customers**—it is characteristic of the customer portfolio that some customers are likely to be dominant in the market concerned. The dependence of a supplier on a dominant customer and the ways to survive in this situation are among the most critical issues we face. They belong on the boardroom table.

Strategic customer management makes explicit some of the most critical competitive and customer issues that companies face and which will shape their futures for better or worse.

But making the issues explicit is not enough on its own. Implementing a strategic customer management approach also demands a strategic sales organization, which deploys strategic sales capabilities. The chapters that follow are about building that new type of organization and enhancing its capabilities.

Diagnosing the Changing Saleforce Role

Company/Division:					
Key assumptions:			Time span:		

Declining tasks/roles:

Core tasks/roles:

New/potential tasks/roles:

Headcount/skills change:

Implications:

Headcount/skills change:

Implications:

Headcount/skills change:

Implications:

Headcount/skills change:

Implications:

Part II
Making the Sales Organization Strategic

2

Involvement: Putting Sales Back into Strategy

The first building block identified in our strategic sales model (Figure 1.3) is *involvement*. This means sales involvement in the generation and evaluation of marketing and business strategy, rather than just being a tactical operation responsible for implementing or executing strategies created by others. In other words, putting sales back into the business strategy process.

There are several compelling reasons why putting the sales voice back in the strategy debate makes sense. First, many of the most significant resource investment decisions actually hinge on the assumptions we make about the company's customer base—its customer portfolio. Second, the shape of the customer portfolio has a direct impact on the profit opportunities which are open to a company. Third, many of the most serious business risks companies face relate to the dependence they have on certain parts of the customer portfolio. Fourth, modern markets are increasingly characterized by fragmentation and granularity, so just looking at averages like market share and overall growth rates blinds you to the most important emerging trends, opportunities, and threats.

Putting the voice of sales back into the centre of the debate about competitiveness and business strategy recognizes that the most important 'unknowns' relate to customers, rather than to internal operations, systems, and processes, or to external promotional activities. In part, this is about filling the gap in the strategy debate created by the recent departure of marketing.

In fact, involvement of the sales organization in strategy has two aspects. The *first* strategic sales issue is concerned with developing a perspective on sales relationships which does not focus simply on the tactical management of transactional selling processes, but examines the different relationships that may be formed with different types of customers as the basis for long-term business development.[1] This implies a new appraisal of the activities and processes required to enhance and sustain value delivery to customers through the sales organization.

It is also increasingly the case that major customers require a highly specific value proposition built around 'unique value' for the customer. Nonetheless, different customers have different value requirements, for example, intrinsic value buyers, who want no more than transactional selling; extrinsic value buyers, who require consultative selling; and strategic value buyers, who demand enterprise selling.[2]

The *second* strategic sales issue is concerned with the role of sales and account management in interpreting the customer environment as a basis for strategic decisions. As the costs of dealing with major customers continue to increase, companies face major choices in where they choose to invest resources in developing a customer relationship, and where they choose not to invest. With large customers in particular, the risks in investment or disinvestment are high, and it is likely that the intelligence-gathering and market-sensing capabilities of the sales and account organization will play a growing role in influencing strategic decisions about resource allocation in the customer portfolio.

Strategic sales issues put the sales organization back into the strategy game. There are, however, a few things tied up in making this happen. The first relates to understanding what the strategy debate should be about. But the second and most significant way in to the debate

[1] Olson, Eric M., David W. Cravens, and Stanley F. Slater, 'Competitiveness and Sales Management: A Marriage of Strategies,' *Business Horizons,* March/April 2001, pp. 25–30.

[2] Rackham, Neil and John De Vincentis, *Rethinking the Salesforce: Redefining Selling to Create and Capture Customer Value,* New York: McGraw-Hill, 1999.

that matters is by placing the customer portfolio on the Boardroom table as the basis for strategic choices and investments. Inevitably, the customer portfolio analysis leads us into questions about dominant customers and the somewhat controversial application of strategic account management approaches. The key issue is about making strategic customer choices, and making them on a better-informed basis than often seems to be the case at present.

Putting a Handle on Business Strategy

Surprisingly, just clarifying what strategy is about is often the way in to the strategy process. The reason is that many management groups are not sure if they actually have a strategy or not. One recent commentary sadly reinforces this conclusion: 'It's a dirty little secret: Most executives cannot articulate the objective, scope, and advantage of their business in a simple statement. If they can't, neither can anyone else.'[3] This is alarming in the light of the evidence that most business successes come from careful strategic choices.[4] Companies that do not have a simple and clear statement of strategy are those most likely to fail in implementation of strategy, or worse they simply do not have a strategy which makes sense of what they are doing and where they are going.[5]

If one of the major challenges for managers is actually 'having a strategy' in the first place, then helping to clarify what it is, and should be, provides a pretty powerful logic for being part of the debate. Everywhere you go, people have plans and budgets. Most have neatly designed marketing and sales programmes. But, plans and programmes are not the same as strategy. In the complex situations we now face, the need for a strategic perspective on how we deal with our markets has become imperative.

---

[3] Collis, David J. and Michael G. Rukstad, 'Can You Say What Your Strategy Is?' *Harvard Business Review*, April 2008, pp. 82–90.

[4] Campbell, Andrew and Robert Park, *The Growth Gamble: When Managers Should Bet Big on New Businesses, and How They Can Avoid Expensive Failures*, London: Nicholas Brealey Publishing, 2005.

[5] Collis and Rukstad, 2008, op cit.

Fig. 2.1 Identifying strategic issues

But strategy has to be clear, understandable, and tell people where we are going and what will get us there. We should not confuse complexity with strategy. In fact, one of the most straightforward ways to deal with the question, 'Do we really have a strategy?' is to look for the externally oriented and integrated concept about how we will achieve our objectives and to seek out answers to five broad questions[6]:

1. *Competitive Arenas*—Where will we be active—in what sectors, markets, segments, technologies?
2. *Vehicles*—How will we get there—what products and services, value chains, or business model?
3. *Differentiators*—How will we win in the marketplace—what is our competitive advantage over alternatives faced by the buyer?
4. *Staging*—What will be our speed and sequence of competitive moves?
5. *Economic logic*—How will we obtain financial returns?

The model in Figure 2.1 provides a structure for identifying and evaluating the key questions to be asked about strategy.

[6] Adapted from: Hambrick, Donald C. and James W Frederickson, 'Are You Sure You Have A Strategy?', *Academy of Management Executive*, Vol. 15 No 4 2001, pp. 48–59.

Identifying Strategic Issues[7]

The Figure 2.1 model is a simplification, but is effective in flushing out major strategic questions and linking them together. It is really just a set of interrelated areas where questions should be asked.

Strategic thinking

How do we address the future for the business and look at how well our business model is standing up to the way the market is changing and new types of competitor? Thinking strategically about the business means more than writing plans and budgets. It is about questioning the way in which we do business and how we go to market. It requires a different perspective, separated from the day-to-day running of the business. Neglecting this management role risks what Donald Sull has called 'active inertia'—when we respond to changes in the market by accelerating activities that succeeded in the past. When the world changes—sometimes radically—a company trapped by active inertia will do more and more of the same things they always did. While there is an impression of purposeful activity, there is no strategy of change to deal with the new external realities.[8]

Market sensing and learning strategy

Underpinning effective marketing and business strategy is a superior market understanding—knowing where there is an unmet customer need, predicting where there are new value-creating opportunities, finding a competitive edge—based on insight and intelligence. Market-sensing capabilities and the development of effective market learning processes turn out to be key strategic resources in the turbulent and rapidly changing markets most of us now face. The critical questions are: 'What do we know that gives us an edge or advantage with the customer?' 'What do we know that everybody else does not?' 'How can we maintain that market understanding ability?'

[7] This section is based on: Piercy, Nigel F., *Market-Led Strategic Change: Transforming the Process of Going to Market*, 4th ed., Oxford: Butterworth Heinemann, 2009.

[8] Sull, Donald, *Why Good Companies Go Bad and How Great Managers Remake Them*, Boston, MA: Harvard Business School Press, 2005.

Capabilities for market sensing and learning are so closely aligned to
the emergence of the strategic sales organization, we devote the next
chapter to the issue of intelligence.

Strategic market choices and targets

The choice of where to compete is central to strategic decisions. Understanding the ways in which market boundaries are changing, new
sources of competition developing, and customer priorities changing
is fundamental to competing effectively. Choosing market targets—the
segments and niches of the market, or the customer types in which to
specialize—is a key strategic decision. The danger is that plans and
systems rely on fixed, unchanging market definitions that get out of
line with market realities, and segment and customer targets that were
right in the past but no longer work. The strategy challenge is to re-
think and redesign markets and targets, and then to write plans, not
the other way around.

Customer value strategy and positioning

Within the choices of market targets clear direction is needed as to
the value offered to each type of customer. Candidly, if you cannot
write it down, you probably do not have a value proposition for the
customer. Without a clear positioning in the customer's eyes regarding
the value you offer that matters to that customer and is better than
the alternatives—you are best a commodity supplier and will have to
operate on those terms (customers buy on price and technical specification). A strategy of superior value as perceived by the customer
and a clear and distinct positioning compared to the competition is
the basis for claiming a competitive advantage. This identifies the
need for the strategic sales organization to gather and analyse data to
demonstrate superior value products offer to customers, and to turn
salespeople into value merchants. If salespeople make vague promises
without hard data they are often forced to compete on price alone—
executives say that often salespeople have poor understanding of what
really creates value for customers and frequently play the role of value
spendthrifts giving value away through price concessions to make
the sale, rather than value merchants who sell profitable growth by
stressing the superior value of the firm's offerings. This way a supplier

with superior value is forced to compete as a commodity so does not get fair return for its superior value.[9]

Strategic relationships and networks

Increasingly, the ability to deliver superior value to chosen market targets relies on the management of strategic relationships internally and externally. Internal issues concern the buy-in to the strategy by employees and managers in the company. External issues relate to relationships with customers, with competitors, with contingent forces like recommenders and gatekeepers in the market, and with collaborators. In many cases now a network of alliances and collaboration networks underpin business strategy. Alliances and networks come with both advantages in flexibility and building bigger value propositions, but also risks of failure—the evidence is that many strategic alliances underperform and disappoint against expectations. The ability to manage effectively through this new form of organization is critical to strategy success.

Of course, radical new strategies frequently face both organizational barriers and implementation problems, and strategies which do not happen are not strategies at all—more unfulfilled aspirations. A strategic view of the business demands attention is given to how the organization itself has to be realigned with strategic direction, and how implementation barriers inside the company will be addressed. It may seem a long way from the world of customers and competition, but how we organize ourselves and manage initiatives through execution is also a strategic priority.

This approach indicates the scope and nature of the issues that should be confronted in the business strategy process. They are often issues with which managers in the business may be uncomfortable— they challenge familiar structures and comfortable ways of doing things. That is kind of the point.

Managers often avoid talking about strategy issues because they are potentially disruptive. The risk is maintaining the status quo until a competitor with a new business model comes along and takes the business away from you. The risk is forever playing 'catch-up' and never

---

[9] Anderson, James C., Nirmalya Kumar, and James A. Narus, *Value Merchants: Demonstrating and Documenting Superior Value in Business Markets*, Boston, MA: Harvard Business School Press, 2007.

taking the initiative, leading to a weakening competition position until the inevitable happens.

A priority for the strategic sales organization is participating in the business strategy generation process and bringing harsh market and competitive insights to the often complacent debate about strategy. Perhaps the best illustration of the business insights ignored by inwardly focused business strategy decisions is the impact of the customer portfolio.

The Customer Portfolio Is the Way into the Strategy Debate

The customer portfolio is a way of describing the mix of different types of customers that a business has. It is no more complex than that. However, the implications of the balance of the customer portfolio on business performance must be one of the most ignored issues when managers talk about business strategy and marketing.

Much of the momentum driving strategic customer management comes from recognizing the management of the customer portfolio and the design of relationship strategies for major customers as key issues driving business strategy and performance. Strategic customer management is the shift from sales as a tactical activity concerned only with implementing business and marketing strategy, to a strategic process that aligns corporate resources with customer needs and confronts the hard decisions about investment in customers and the risks in dependence.

Let's consider the different types of customers that are found in this type of portfolio analysis, so we can highlight the differences in relationship requirements (and hence cost to serve) between different customer types. Then, we can examine the most vexed issue highlighted by portfolio analysis: the impact of the dominant customer and the potential for partnership and close collaborative relationships with strategic customers.

A simple model for analysing the customer portfolio is shown in Figure 2.2.

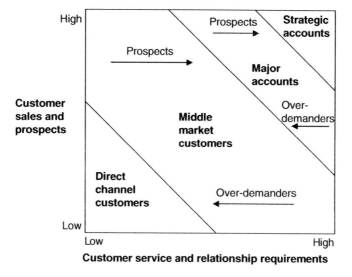

Fig. 2.2 The customer portfolio

Customer Types in the Portfolio

You can change the categories a bit to suit specific situations, but the generalized model in Figure 2.2 uses customer sales and prospects compared to customer service and relationship requirements to identify direct-channel customers, middle-market customers, major accounts, and strategic accounts. These different types of customers differ in important ways that strategic decision-makers need to understand. They differ not just in growth and profit prospects but also in investment demands (service and relationship requirements), and importantly they determine the level of business risk to which we are exposed. The overall portfolio can be considered as an investment matrix, where hard decisions should be confronted by decision-makers. This is really too important to be left to the salespeople in the field or junior marketing executives to decide (the default decision-makers on customer matters in many situations). The shape of the customer portfolio indicates your ability to grow, to make profit, and the level of business risk you are assuming (particularly in terms of the risk created by dependence on large customers).

Direct-Channel Customers

In most situations, the direct channel is the route to market for smaller accounts with low relationship/service requirements. Commonly, this will involve direct sales from the company website, but may also include telemarketing approaches and other routes to market that do not demand sales organization resources, such as using third-party intermediaries. The cost to serve should be low enough to offset the smaller orders placed by these accounts, and if investment of resources is managed carefully this type of business can be highly profitable.

In fact, some direct-channel business may be linked to other sales channels. For example, large customers may put routine, repeat business on the Web channel because it is cheap and convenient for them, even though they still require salesforce commitments when they are making larger, higher risk, less routine purchases.

Customer development strategy may mean some larger customers are progressively moved towards the direct channel because they are consuming more service/relationship resources than they justify. They may have justified salesforce resources in the past, but now they are over-demanders in terms of how much they want from us compared to what they buy. However, a strategic approach may also be about moving some customers from the direct channel to the middle market, based on their changing sales and profit prospects compared to the costs of serving the account.

Actually, in some cases, direct-channel customers do justify salesforce attention notwithstanding their web-based ordering. For example, in one case we examined, a sales manager looked at the ordering patterns in his direct-channel customers, and discovered medium-sized customers ordering on a haphazard and spasmodic basis. This was puzzling, because the product was a routine office supply, the customer demand for which was wholly predictable based on the customer's own sales. What our manager discovered was that some customers regarded the product as so trivial, they did not bother with strict stock control and just ordered small or large quantities whenever it occurred to someone to do so. It was fairly straightforward to visit such customers and offer them a better way of doing business—weekly deliveries of the product based on their sales forecasts. This is better service to the customer, but more significantly improves the seller's return on assets by reducing the stock needed to cover unpredictable customer ordering patterns. The sales manager did not sell anything but made an important difference to profitability.

Considerations like these illustrate the potential importance of shifting some salesforce resources from a short-term transactional selling focus to longer-term business development issues in line with business strategy.

Middle-Market Customers

In most portfolios, middle-market customers are the core of conventional and traditional sales. The middle market contains customers with varying sales prospects, but generally moderate to high relationship/customer service requirements. This is the territory which is most familiar to the conventional salesforce. It may be dominated by largely transactional business (though not necessarily, as demands for closer relationships spread through customers in the market). Often the middle market is the most profitable part of the portfolio—the cost to serve can be controlled, and each customer is likely to have only moderate ability to demand lower prices and better terms or customized value offers.

Customers in the middle market with promising potential may be moved into the major account area over time, where they receive a higher level of investment of sales and management resources. Correspondingly, middle-market customers with relationship/service requirements which are excessive compared to their potential may be moved towards the direct channel, to bring the cost to serve more closely into alignment with their value to the seller.

Major Customers

Major accounts are significantly different to the middle market. They are likely to be large in the supplier's terms (in other words, they buy a lot) and they have high relationship/service requirements (because they know they buy a lot from us, and can demand special treatment). However, they are not partners or collaborators or members of an alliance with the seller, they are customers in a conventional buyer–seller relationship. Naturally, major account size and prospects identifies the need to develop appropriate salesforce approaches to deliver value to these customers. However, it is likely that appropriate salesforce strategies will be, and should be, substantially different between major accounts and strategic customers.

Strategic Customers

Strategic accounts are different. They will be few in number. If these are strategic customers in the real sense, then collaborative and joint problem-solving approaches by the seller may be appropriate to win strategic supplier status. This is a different business model, and is no longer a conventional buyer–seller relationship. If we just call big customers 'strategic accounts' as a way of indicating that they are important, this is harmless, until and unless we make the mistake of confusing buyers with partners.

Strategic account management strategies and structures have been developed in many companies as a way of developing close, long-term, and collaborative relationships with the most important customers and meeting their needs in ways which the traditional salesforce did not.[10] Certainly, important questions surround the selection and management of relationships with strategic accounts, who may be the most expensive and least profitable customers to serve. Growing buyer concentration in many markets mandates collaborative relationships with strategic accounts as strategic suppliers, but the costs of partnership and the growing dependence involved underlines the need for careful choices and evaluation of performance.[11]

In fact, faced with the emergence of powerful and dominating customers in many markets, consultants and business schools who should know better have been quick to sell the idea of strategic account management as the new snake-oil to take away all the problems in dealing with large customers. The snake-oil cure does not usually work, it just costs you a lot of money. This has proved an expensive trap for many companies. In fact, we see this issue as so important and so potentially destructive for businesses, we will look in more detail at

[10] Homburg, Christian, John P Workman, and Ove Jensen, 'A Configurational Perspective on Key Account Management', *Journal of Marketing*, April 2002, pp. 38–60.

[11] Piercy, Nigel F. and Nikala Lane, (2006), 'The Hidden Weaknesses in Strategic Account Management Strategy', *Journal of Business Strategy*, Vol. 27 No. 1 2006, pp. 18–26.

the opportunities and the pathology of strategic account management in more detail below.

Importantly, the distinction between major accounts (conventional but large customers) and strategic accounts (collaborators or partners) underlines several strategic choices. Plans may include the movement of accounts between these categories—developing a closer relationship with a major account to nurture a new strategic account, or moving away from a close relationship that is ineffective to move a strategic account down to major account status.

Nonetheless, one aspect of escalating customer sophistication is that major customers are demanding the same service levels and relational investments as strategic customers—because they can. For example, food suppliers to Marks & Spencers (M&S) in 2008 experienced the retailer's 'Project Genesis' (renamed 'Project Genocide' by the suppliers concerned), which adds up to demands for bigger price discounts from its top suppliers—demanding up to 6.5 per cent off price from suppliers with 7 per cent margins who have given 5 per cent reductions in the previous two years. M&S thought it was simply clawing back money from suppliers that had benefited from growth. Suppliers concluded that M&S expected to pay as little as Tesco despite being a fraction of its size.[12]

Indeed, in the aerospace industry, avionics services supplier Thales has developed an approach to major customers it calls 'account management lite'. Introduced after the implementation of key account management across all strategic customers, 'account management lite' is presented to customers as a form of key account management which recognizes their importance to the seller, but the supplier's service and relationship investment is lower. The company describes this as a way of dealing with the 'next tier down' in their accounts, and providing a smooth transition to full key account management where appropriate.[13]

---

[12] Farndon, Lucy, ' "Brutal" M&S Turns Screw on Suppliers', *Daily Mail*, 5 February 2008, p. 66. Braithwaite, Tom, 'M&S Eyes Better Food Supplier Terms', *Financial Times*, 6 February 2008, p. 21. Braithwaite, Tom and Maggie Urry, 'A Taste of Change for M&S Food Suppliers', *Financial Times*, 6/7 June 2008, p. 15.

[13] Jago, Jason, 'Account Management Lite: Addressing the "Next Tier Down"', Presentation at the Sales and Strategic Customer Management network workshop, Warwick University, 30 May 2008.

Investment Within the Customer Portfolio

One strength of the mapping process in building a model of the customer portfolio is that it provides a screening device for identifying the most appropriate relationship to offer specific customers and the choices to be made in allocating scarce salesforce, account management, and other company resources, as well as evaluating the risks involved in over-dependence on a small number of very large accounts. Underlying the strategic sales issue is the question of developing the capability of the sales organization to deliver added-value in different ways to various categories of customers. It is unlikely that a traditional, transaction-focused salesforce will be able to deliver the added-value required by some customers. However, the deployment of expensive resources to develop added-value sales strategies for particular customers implies choices and investment in creating new types of salesforce resource and capability, which should be considered at a strategy level in an organization.

The customer portfolio identifies the case to be made for investing resources in moving customers from one type of relationship to another, and the gains to be made in re-shaping the portfolio. It also provides a logical framework for estimating both the quantity of sales volume that can be achieved with a given level of investment and the quality of the resulting sales volume (profitability and risk).

Dominant Customers—The Dark Side of Dependence

It is not news to any seller that one of the most troublesome issues for developing effective strategy in business-to-business companies is the impact of powerful customers and the demands that they can make on their suppliers—whether the consumer goods manufacturer dealing with very large retailers like Tesco and Wal-Mart, or the components manufacturer dealing with buyers like automotive companies.

The impact of dominant customers on suppliers may be profound. For example, mid-2006 Newport Networks, the telecommunications equipment company, saw its share value fall by 50 per cent, simply reflecting delays in the signing of a single contract with a large telecommunications company customer. The investment logic underpinning Newport's business model depended on this single contract with a dominant customer.[14] Success or failure with dominant customers impacts on investors as well as sellers.

One response to this sensitivity has been the growth in strategic (or key) account management approaches, to 'partner' with the most important customers. However, it is clear that some customers do not provide good partnership prospects—while they may be large, they are transactional customers, not collaborators. Like all 'one size fits all' solutions to important problems, strategic account management is achieving very mixed results.

If this is chosen as the approach to working with powerful, dominant customers, then that choice needs to be fully informed and carefully evaluated. Developing effective strategies to work with dominant customers requires more than a 'bolt-on' quick-fix from a strategic account management consultant. Sorry, life is not that easy.

Dominant Customer Strategy

Customer portfolio analysis provides a means for recognizing different types of customers in the company's portfolio, and their differing demands for value and relationship. Inevitably, some of the most important questions are raised about the largest and most influential customers—perhaps, the 20 per cent of customers who may account for 80 per cent (or more) of the supplier's business. It is important for strategic decision-makers to understand the basis for the different types of customer relationship which exist in the portfolio, and particularly the idea of a transition from traditional transactional relationships to much closer links between the seller and the most dominant buyers. Figure 2.3 summarizes some of the commonest business-to-business buyer–seller relationships with major and strategic accounts, and the critical differences between them.

Typically in the middle market, the conventional buyer–seller relationship is the most familiar—we sell things to customers. The links are usually between salespeople and purchasers, and the relationship may be purely transactional (depending largely on the importance

---

[14] Braithwaite, Tom, 'Newport Shares Tumble 50% After Contract Delays', *Financial Times*, 6 July 2006, p. 25.

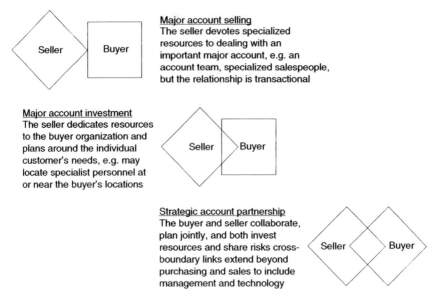

Fig. 2.3 Relationships with large customers

of the purchase to the customer, or the way in which the customer chooses to do business), or it may involve a higher-level or closer relationship being built between the buyer and the seller. This is the type of relationship which most traditional salesforces were created to manage. However, the existence of larger, more dominant customers requires different approaches.

Those approaches—developing closer and customized relationships with important customers—have substantial cost implications. Managing closer relationships with major customers involves active management by individuals and business functions. Closer customer relationships frequently expand interactions from sales and purchasing personnel to include people from diverse areas like engineering, manufacturing, marketing, finance, business planning, and R&D. This is not trivial in assessing the cost to serve the customer. These distinctions can be presented to management along the following lines.

Major account selling

With major customers the size and impact of a customer requires that sales and management efforts should be refocused to provide a dedicated approach to a particular customer. This may involve the appointment of an account manager, or a national account specialist, and the development of plans around this customer's specific needs. Nonetheless, the relationship remains largely a conventional buyer–seller format.

Major account investment

This takes things substantially further in terms of dedicated efforts around the major account. Substantial teams of people may now work around the single account and offerings may be substantially different for this customer compared to others—customized products and so on. Nonetheless, the resource commitment remains essentially one-sided. Proctor and Gamble's 200 person team for the Wal-Mart account is part of P&G's substantial investment in that customer. Correspondingly, while Dell Computers has a dedicated team for its major customer Boeing, this does not suggest that Boeing makes decisions about Dell's business. At the end of the day, these relationships remain buyer–seller transactions. The investment is essentially one-sided—it is made by the seller. It reflects the costs of doing business with powerful, demanding customers. They are not 'partners' or 'collaborators', they are customers.

Strategic account partnership

This is where the big difference and the big risk comes. This type of account relationship is based on collaboration and joint decision-making between the buyer and the seller. It is a two-sided relationship—both the buyer and the seller invest time and resources in the relationship. The impact of strategic account relationships and management merits more detailed attention, because it is potentially a deadly risk to the seller's business.

Knowing when to walk away

One of the distinguishing aspects of companies adopting a strategic customer management perspective will be making choices about where to invest in the customer portfolio, and also where not to—knowing when to walk away. It is not a familiar scenario for traditional sales managers pursuing volume-oriented targets. It will be increasingly common that we will have to stand up and say that big though it may be, a specific customer's business is not worth having and we are better to walk away. For example, as part of M&S' 'Project Genocide', Northern Foods was pressured to make large price cuts in the pasta ready-meals it made for M&S. Northern took the view that if M&S wanted cheap pasta they could go elsewhere—even though it meant closing their ready-meals factory in Lincolnshire. Northern's decision was not to accept unprofitable business under new terms. It was better to take the hit immediately than to become trapped in a continuing and unprofitable relationship.[15] There are a number of compelling reasons why knowing when to walk away and not make relational investments in a customer will be as important to effective business strategy as knowing where to invest in partnership. Perhaps the most compelling is the behaviour of some customers in their supplier relationships.

Customers who do not Play Nicely with the other Boys and Girls

One of the things people recognize more readily these days is that there really is such a thing as bad customers—some of whom you probably do not want to do business with if you can help it. Bad customers keep all the benefits of close supplier relationships for themselves, are difficult to work with, and sometimes just exploit their market power in a raw and brutal way to get what they want, whoever suffers in the process (because it will not be them).

Keeping All the Goodies for Themselves

The underlying theory of why developing closer relationships with customers—particularly large and powerful customers—is important is that everyone benefits. There is good research evidence that many customers have gained reduced costs, faster time-to-market, increased productivity, and enhanced product quality from closer relationships with suppliers.[16] Correspondingly, a lot of academics and practitioners

---

[15] Braithwaite, Tom and Maggie Urry, 'A Taste of Change for M&S Food Suppliers', *Financial Times*, 6/7 June 2008, p. 15.

[16] This has been reviewed in: Fink, Robert C., Linda F. Feldman, and Kenneth J. Hatten, 'Supplier Performance Improvements in Relational Exchanges', *Journal of Business and Industrial Marketing*, Vol. 22 No. 1 2007, pp. 29–40.

have claimed that suppliers gain because they have enhanced their customers' performance.[17]

However, what is also possible is that customers may demand closer supplier relationships to gain advantages for themselves, without any plan or intention of sharing resulting benefits with suppliers. Dominant customers can use their power over dependent partners to improve their own performance at the expense of that of weaker partners in the value chain. Research confirms that although customers may be achieving better performance through closer supplier relationships, suppliers do not necessarily reap reciprocal benefits.[18]

Somewhere our thinking needs to address the issue that investing in a closer relationship with a major customer may bring no performance gains, other than retaining the customer by giving in to its demands. That retention may be overly expensive, particularly if it is short-lived.

Being Difficult

Companies in the consumer goods field will be well aware of an old joke: '*Question*: What's the difference between Tesco and a terrorist? *Answer*: With a terrorist, you can negotiate.' Some customers are just plain difficult.

In some situations customer difficulty is built into the value chain anyway. For example, in 2008 Airbus and Boeing were looking at orders for around 7,000 new aircraft. They know, however, that some airlines have ordered more planes than they can afford. The wait for delivery of popular aircraft is more than six years, which is much longer than the planning horizon for most airlines. Airbus and Boeing know that some buyers who have ordered planes will renege or disappear before the planes are manufactured. They face the difficulty of predicting which orders in the book will really turn into deliveries. Getting it wrong carries the twin risks of either making too many planes and creating a glut or failing to meet orders on time and paying

---

[17] Cannon, Joe P. and Christian Homburg, 'Buyer–Seller Relationships and Customer Firm Costs', *Journal of Marketing*, Vol. 65 No. 1 2001, pp. 29–43.

[18] Fink, Robert C., Linda F. Feldman, and Kenneth J. Hatten, 'Supplier Performance Improvements in Relational Exchanges', *Journal of Business and Industrial Marketing*, Vol. 22 No. 1 2007, pp. 29–40.

large penalties to customers.[19] This business model creates a situation where customers are difficult.

In other cases, being difficult is how customers do business. Not everyone wants to play nicely. For example, consider the predilection of some customers to try and change the rules of the game after they have bought stuff from you: renegotiating prices, looking for cash contributions to their internal initiatives, imposing their corporate responsibility costs on suppliers, or inventing new liabilities and standards for suppliers after the event.

Renegotiating prices retrospectively is an increasingly common practice. For example, in 2008 Alliance Boots wrote to all its suppliers in the health, beauty, and over-the-counter medicine markets announcing unilateral changes in credit terms that would leave them waiting 105 days for payment—the move is not unconnected with the private equity owners needs to reduce the debt burden acquired in the purchase of Alliance Boots, but has left suppliers less than happy.[20]

Demanding suppliers provide *cash funding for customer initiatives* is also a neat trick. When companies like Tesco and Asda decide to get into 'price wars', their expectation is that suppliers will pick up the bill for this competitive initiative. Allegedly abusive e-mails and telephone calls were associated with attempts to coerce producers into picking up the costs of a Tesco/Asda price war in 2007. The implied or actual threat of being dropped as suppliers was used to suggest suppliers should accept terms which took their profit margins to zero or beyond. Allegedly farmers and other suppliers were so scared of losing contracts that they did not even dare to complain. It seems that as the weakest link in the consumer goods supply chain, suppliers get to pay for retailer initiatives like price wars.[21] Similarly, Woolworth displayed great disingenuity in January 2007, when it demanded retrospective discounts from its 700 suppliers, to cover the retailer's costs

[19] This illustration is based on: Lunsford, J. Lynn and Daniel Michaels, 'Jet-Order Boom Weighed Against a Dose of Realism', *Wall Street Journal*, 11–13 January 2008, pp. 1 and 28.

[20] Rigby, Elizabeth, 'Suppliers in Stand-Off with Alliance Boots', *Financial Times*, 31 March 2008, p. 20.

[21] Poulter, Sean, 'Supermarkets Forced to Hand Over "Bullying" Emails Sent to Suppliers', *Daily Mail*, 20 August 2007, p. 19.

(already incurred) in new store formats, product development, and marketing.[22]

Faced with escalating *environmental costs*, one interesting tactic among customers under pressure to display their environmental credentials and other signs of good corporate citizenship is simply to push the costs of such initiatives back down the value chain to let their suppliers pick up the tab. This seems to achieve a 'holier than thou' posture for the customer, with the costs picked up by the supplier. Dell, L'Oreal, PepsiCo, Hewlett-Packard, and Reckitt-Benckiser are all companies pressuring suppliers to measure and disclose their carbon footprint. Worthies such as Wal-Mart, Tesco, P&G, Unilever, Cadbury, and Imperial Tobacco also have an initiative to 'encourage' suppliers to measure and manage their greenhouse gas emissions, although they are seemingly unwilling to pay for such improvements.[23]

Customers Behaving Badly

In some situations, powerful customers go even further and just turn into thugs. There are few better examples than the British grocery market where powerful retailers like Tesco, Sainsbury, and Asda stand accused of outrageously bad behaviour towards their suppliers.

The Big 4 supermarkets in the UK–Tesco, Sainsbury, Asda, and Morrisons—hold nearly 80% of the UK grocery market. Tesco alone accounts for 31% of the market.[24] In some local areas Tesco has such market control that the areas are called 'Tesco Towns' subject to 'Tescopoly'. Supermarkets have been accused of abusing the power they have over their suppliers. Less than helpfully from a supplier perspective, the Competition Commission says its role is to protect consumers not suppliers.

[22] Leach, Andrew, 'Woolies in Shock Demand for Cash', *Financial Mail on Sunday*, 21 January 2007, p. 1.

[23] Fiona Harvey, 'Suppliers Pushed on Green Initiatives', *Financial Times*, 21 January 2008, p. 24.

[24] This illustration is based on: Jonathan Leake, 'Picky Stores Force Farmers to Dump Veg', *Sunday Times*, 17 July 2005, pp. 1–6. Lucy Farndon, 'ASDA Faces a Supplier Revolt Over Cash Demands', *Daily Mail*, 30 March 2006, p. 79. Richard Fletcher, 'Big Chains Surge as Suppliers Scrape By', *Sunday Times*, 4 June 2006, pp. 3–7. Teena Lyons and Patrick Tooher, 'Crackdown on Way for Sore Bullies', *Daily Mail*, 20 March 2005, p. 1. Joanna Blythman, 'The Big Stores Behave Like Medieval Barons', *The Mail on Sunday*, 4 November 2007, p. 4.

Supplier complaints about their treatment by UK supermarkets include the imposition of *listing fees*—huge lump-sum payments for placement of new products or just to get access to supermarket shelves; unreasonable *price pressure*—forcing prices down to unsustainable levels, through threatening and aggressive behaviour and bullying e-mails, and sometimes suspicious 'phantom bids' at online auctions which further drive down prices paid to suppliers; *changing contracts retrospectively*, for example, reneging on contract terms and demanding large cash payments to ensure future business—in 2006, Asda demanded £368 million from food and drink firms, including £45 million from Unilever alone, telling suppliers they would be classed as 'preferred', 'complacent', or 'underperforming' on the basis of their response—Kellogg's resistance led to Asda discounting their cornflakes (prompting other supermarkets to follow) and hitting Kellogg's profit margins; forcing suppliers to contribute to supermarket *marketing costs*, for example, paying for supermarket price wars, under threat of blacklisting; *unilaterally extending credit terms*—in 2005, Sainsbury tried to impose new terms on 1,900 suppliers so they would wait up to 49 days before being paid instead of 21 days; imposing *unreasonable product requirements* on suppliers—Britain's farmers are forced to throw away as much as a third of their fruit and vegetables because they fail supermarkets' cosmetic requirements—Tesco tests potatoes with a 'brightness meter' to see if the skin is shiny enough; *avoiding contracts*—more than two-thirds of suppliers have no formal contract, because the supermarkets will not agree terms (and accept being bound by them); *intervening in suppliers' businesses*—food producers are told to use specific carriers to deliver goods to supermarkets, to find that these carriers charge excessive freight rates, knowing that the producers have no choice; and using *category captains*—supermarkets avoid direct contact with fresh food producers so staying at arms length from production, with purchasing effectively subcontracted, avoiding links to the low wages and poor working conditions imposed on suppliers by low prices.

Amusingly, the CEO of Sainsbury has challenged suppliers who feel they have been badly treated to come forward with the evidence and make themselves known.[25] Yes, like that's going to happen? Most

[25] Harvey, Fiona, 'Sainsbury Chief Invites Evidence of Unfair Deals', *Financial Times*, 27 February 2007, p. 2.

suppliers committing commercial hari-kari are likely to want to do it in private. Unfortunately for the supermarkets, the Competition Commission appears to have found the 'smoking gun' in the form of e-mails between supermarkets and suppliers threatening black-listing for those who did not play along with retrospective price discounts.[26]

Some of these examples are extreme cases. We are trying to make a point here. Not all customers are oriented towards cooperation and collaboration for mutual benefit with their suppliers. This is probably the best context in which to examine strategic account management— 'partnering' with large, dominant customers—as the answer to the dominant customer problem.

Strategic Account Management

The growth in management attention given to Strategic Account Man-agement (SAM)[27] as a way of developing and nurturing relationships with a company's most important customers is unprecedented. While SAM gets little attention in the mainstream of marketing and business strategy, a Google search reveals hundreds of Web pages detailing managerial books about SAM, countless consultants eager to offer expensive advice on how to 'do' SAM, numerous training courses for executives, and a growing number of business school programmes in SAM in universities across the world.

The underlying concept is the shift from adversarial buyer–seller relationships towards collaborative or partnership-based relation-ships, with the company's most important customers. Apparently adversarial or conflictual relationships are bad and collaborative, cooperative relationships are good. As someone once said: 'the reason why something looks too good to be true is usually because it *is* too good to be true'.

Nonetheless, many major international companies have made SAM an important element of how they manage relationships with their

[26] Davey, Jenny, 'Supermarket "Bullies" Face Crackdown', *Sunday Times*, 7 October 2007, p. 3.
[27] For purposes of discussion we regard the terms Strategic Account Management and Key Account Management as interchangeable, and our commentary generally applies to what some designate as National Account Management and Global Account Management.

largest customers. For example, IMI plc is a major U.K. engineering group whose published strategy statement identifies SAM as a key theme in achieving its goal of 'leading global niche markets'. The company is investing heavily 'to enhance our ability to create and manage close customer relationships with our clients [and] provide IMI business managers with the skills to create and develop close and successful relationships with major customers . . . which places key account management among the central elements of IMI's business approach'.[28] IMI's investment in building a SAM system, training managers, establishing the IMI Academy at a prestigious business school to further work on SAM has been huge, but the results in the business are somewhat less so. But, the fact remains that for a growing number of companies, SAM is a deep-seated strategy for customer partnering, often on a global basis.

Similarly, in 2006 troubled telecommunications group Cable & Wireless announced plans to cut its customer base from 30,000 to just 3,000 key clients. The company was generating 96 per cent of its revenues and 98 per cent of its gross margin from the top 11 per cent of its customers. In the CEO's words, the rationale was to focus on big corporate customers and public institutions to become the 'Giorgio Armani' rather than the 'Top Shop' of telecoms.[29]

At the same time, many major buyers have adopted radical strategic supplier strategies, which focus on closer relationships with a smaller number of suppliers. In 2005, Ford Motor Company, as part of its downsizing exercise (they make too many cars), announced it was consolidating its supply base for its $90 billion components purchases from 2,000 suppliers to 1,000 globally. Moreover, the first seven 'key suppliers' constitute some 50 per cent of Ford's parts purchases, and will enjoy superior access to Ford's engineering resources and product planning. Ford will work closely with its key suppliers, giving them access to key business plans for new vehicles and committing to give them business.[30] Similarly, in 2007 in the European aerospace industry, Airbus was looking to cut its core network of 3,000 suppliers to about

[28] Quotation from 'IMI plc—Key Themes', www.imi.plc.uk/about.
[29] Palmer, Maija, 'C&W to Slash Staff and Customer Base', *Financial Times*, 1 March 2006, p. 1.
[30] Mackintosh, J. and B. Simon, 'Ford to Focus on Business from "Key Suppliers"', *Financial Times*, 30 September 2005, p. 32.

500, urging its smaller suppliers to form industrial clusters to reduce costs.[31]

In fact, on the one hand, a compelling case can be made for the attractiveness of SAM as a strategy of collaboration and partnership with major customers. However, there are several assumptions and propositions underpinning the case for SAM, which appear to have been largely ignored by the consultants and trainers selling SAM to companies. Balancing these issues is an important challenge for the strategic sales organization and business strategy decision-makers.

The Case for Strategic Account Management

A recent study suggests that strategic account management is one of the most fundamental changes in business organization,[32] and yet it remains one in which a sound research foundation to guide management's strategic decisions remains almost completely lacking.[33] Indeed, while there is a long stream of research in the areas of national and key account selling starting in the 1960s, this research has been largely descriptive and conceptual, and has not addressed the long-term impact of SAM on buyer–seller performance.[34] So, in spite of all the over-sell of SAM by consultants and academics (who make lots of money out of selling it), we do not have that much hard evidence about it achieving positive effects on supplier performance.

Nonetheless, the logic or rationale for SAM is that demands from large customers have caused suppliers to respond with dedicated organizational resources to concentrate on these 'key' or 'strategic' accounts, and to incorporate special value-adding activities (e.g. joint product development, business planning, consulting services) into

[31] Hollinger, Peggy, 'Suppliers Sound Alarm at Airbus Cuts', *Financial Times*, 16/17 June 2007, p. 21.

[32] Homburg, Christian, John P. Workman, and Ove Jensen, 'Changes in the Marketing Organization: The Movement Toward a Customer-Focused Organizational Structure', *Journal of the Academy of Marketing Science*, Vol. 28 (Fall) 2000, pp. 459–78.

[33] Homburg, Workman, and Jensen, 2002, op cit.

[34] Workman, John P., Christian Homburg, and Ove Jensen, 'Intraorganizational Determinants of Key Account Management Effectiveness', *Journal of the Academy of Marketing Science*, Vol. 31 No. 1 2003, pp. 3–21.

their offering to the customer.[35] Fundamental to the logic of SAM is the suggestion of an inevitable concentration effect whereby a small number of customers provide a disproportionately large share of a seller's sales and profits (the so-called 20:80 rule, suggesting 20% of customers provide 80% of sales). Almost as a natural consequence, suppliers frequently dedicate most of their resources to the core portfolio of buyers who represent the highest stakes and are identified as 'strategic accounts' or 'key accounts'.[36] This is the 'you have no choice anyway, so you might as well do it' school of thought on SAM.

Certainly, SAM is a strategic development which has become increasingly widespread in response to a variety of customer and market pressures, which may be summarized as: escalating levels of competition in most markets and consequently higher selling costs for suppliers; increased customer concentration resulting from merger and acquisition activity, as well as competitive attrition in many markets; growing customer emphasis on centralized strategic purchasing as a major contributor to enhancing the buyer's cost structure and building competitive success in their end-user markets; active strategies of supplier base reduction by larger buyers to reduce purchasing costs; and increasing exploitation by large customers of their position of strategic importance to their suppliers to gain lower prices and enhanced terms of trade.[37]

The key point is, however, that SAM is not seen simply as an organizational response that focuses on meeting growing demands from dominant customers, it is seen as progression towards a form of 'partnership' with those customers, characterized by joint decision-making and problem-solving, integrated business processes, and collaborative working across buyer–seller boundaries, described as a process of 'relational development'.[38] However, while everyone tells

[35] Dorsch, Michael J., Scott R. Swanson, and Scott W. Kelley, 'The Role of Relationship Quality in the Stratification of Vendors As Perceived by Customers', *Journal of the Academy of Marketing Science*, Vol. 26 No. 2 1998, pp. 128–42.

[36] Pardo, Catherine, 'Key Account Management in the Business to Business Field: The Key Account's Point of View', *Journal of Personal Selling & Sales Management*, Vol. 17 No. 4 1997, pp. 17–26.

[37] Capon, Noel, *Key Account Management and Planning*, New York: The Free Press, 2001.

[38] Millman, Tony and Kevin Wilson, 'Processual Issues in Key Account Management: Underpinning the Customer-Facing Organization', *Journal of Business & Industrial Marketing*, Vol. 14 No. 4 1989, pp. 328–37.

you about the strengths in effective strategic account relationships, decision-makers should also recognize the growing evidence that ineffective strategic account relationships may create a range of devastating strategic vulnerabilities for sellers.

The SAM Story the Consultants Don't Tell You

There are a number of potential flaws in the underlying logic for SAM, which may make it unattractive for sellers in many situations, and which should be made completely explicit in making strategic customer management choices. These flaws can create fatal strategic weaknesses for the seller.

Investing in Strategic Weakness

In some cases SAM involves the seller actively investing resources in the area of greatest strategic weakness. It is often highly unattractive to institutionalize dependency on major customers as a way of doing business. The SAM approach rests on the notion that the '20:80 rule' produces a situation for the seller which is attractive, or at least inevitable.

To the contrary, it can equally well be argued that any company which has reached a situation where a '20/80' position exists, that is, 80 per cent or more of profits and/or revenue come from 20 per cent or less of the customer base—has already witnessed the failure of its business model. The business model has failed because it has led to such a high degree of dependence on a small number of customers, that the company's strategic freedom of manoeuvre has been undermined, and much control of the supplier's business has effectively been ceded to its major customers. The eventual outcome for selling companies in this situation is likely to be falling prices, commoditization of their products, and progressively lower profits as major customers exert their market power.

A lot of managers dismiss this line of argument as pointless (possibly because of the amount of their companies' resources they have already thrown into SAM strategies and their need to protect that turf). They argue that in businesses like grocery there is no choice other than to deal with the major retailers who dominate the consumer marketplace, because there is no other route to market, and little choice other than to accept the terms they offer. Similarly, suppliers of automotive components point to the limited number of automobile manufacturers in the world, and producers of computer components argue that if you want Dell's business, then you do business on Dell's terms, robust though those terms may be. Such responses at least clarify that in many 'strategic account' situations, the real issue is less partnership and more about one party dictating terms to the other, which is not the concept of 'collaboration' normally advanced to justify SAM investments by suppliers. We are back to 'you have no choice anyway' as the rationale for SAM investments.

If you know from the outset that powerful customers will ultimately exploit that power to their own advantage, then their business carries a disproportionately higher risk than that of less powerful, less dominant customers, and it is less attractive as a result. If it is inevitable that major customers will demand more concessions and pay less, then it is likely they will also be substantially less profitable than other customers. There is little consistent empirical evidence, but there are suggestions that for many sellers, strategic or key accounts are the least profitable part of their business. So, now the logic for SAM looks like investing more and more effort and resource into the least profitable and highest risk part of the customer portfolio. Interesting.

Understanding the Balance of Power

However important strategic buyer–seller relationships are, it is almost inevitable that sooner or later the party in the supply chain enjoying the balance of power will use that power to its own advantage. For example, in spite of surging raw material costs in 2005, the pricing power of manufacturers continued to deteriorate. Producers were absorbing most cost increases and were unable to pass them fully through the supply chain, simply because powerful buyers would not permit it.[39] It is also illustrative that in the automotive components market, notwithstanding escalating steel and oil prices faced by producers, Volkswagen told its parts suppliers in 2005 it wanted 10 per cent cost savings over the following two years. At Chrysler, the CEO demanded an immediate 5 per cent price cut by suppliers, with a

[39] Cave, Frederick, 'Surging Costs Put More pressure on Manufacturers', *Financial Times*, 12 July 2005, p. 4.

further 10 per cent over the following three years.[40] They were not joking.

It is not surprising that as a result in sectors like automotive components, suppliers are actively seeking to diversify their customer bases and to change product portfolios to reduce their dependence on a small number of powerful accounts.[41] The issue is becoming one of staying close to strategic customers, but reaching out to other customers groups as a route to reduced dependency on a few, and enhanced profits as a result.[42] This question of managing buyer–seller dependencies may be one of the highest strategic priorities impacting on company survival—we will consider this issue further below.

The Real Buyer–Seller Relationship

This means that the most critical question in relationships with strategic accounts has become 'who is dependent on whom?'—in other words, who is calling the shots. Failure to grasp the simple issue of the direction of dependency is likely to blind the seller to a critical vulnerability of SAM, while at the same time souring relationships with the account in question—professional purchasers find it difficult to work with suppliers who misunderstand the nature of the relationship they really have with the buyer. Sellers with an exaggerated view of their strategic importance to a buyer have unrealistic expectations of the customer, with the potential for growing frustration because the customer does not behave in the way expected, and ultimately leading to conflict between the buyer and the seller.

Figure 2.4 illustrates a buyer perspective on supplier types—the professional purchaser distinguishes on the basis of market risk (lack of choice or substitutability) and impact (reduced costs or improved competitive advantage in the end-use marketplace).

For a start considering how buyers see suppliers underlines a very important point: the relationship that is on offer with the customer is

[40] Mackintosh, James, 'VW Takes a Hard Line With Parts Suppliers', *Financial Times*, 24 June 2005, p. 30.
[41] Simon, Bernard, 'Suppliers Reorder Priorities for Survival', *Financial Times*, 10 June 2005, p. 28.
[42] Witzel, Morgen, 'Big Spenders Are a Boon—But Don't Forget the Little Guy', *Financial Times*, 8 August 2005, p. 14.

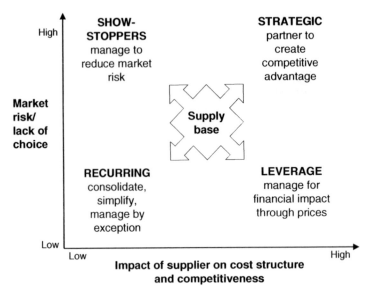

Fig. 2.4 How buyers see suppliers

defined and chosen by the customer, not the seller. This is how they decide where a supplier fits into their organization.

Show-stoppers are an annoyance and an irritation. They do not have much impact on the business, but they are difficult to replace. They might supply proprietary products not obtainable elsewhere. With suppliers who cannot easily be replaced, but have limited impact, the goal is to reduce the customer's risk exposure (e.g. to negotiate guaranteed supplies). *Recurring* supplier relationships exist with those who have limited impact on the customer's business, but who can also be replaced fairly easily, so market risk is not high. Suppliers with low impact on the customer's business, who can also be easily substituted, are likely to be treated as commodities, where the goal is to routinize transactions to reduce supply chain costs, and to manage by exception. Suppliers with significant impact on the buyer's business, but who can easily be replaced, are targets for *leverage*—pressure on price and terms. Only where a supplier cannot easily be substituted by a competitor, and has a major impact on the customer's business, is the customer likely to work towards a *strategic* supplier relationship. At any time, for most buyers it is likely that very few suppliers will have strategic importance. It is important to understand the relationship defined by the customer, before assuming that the buyer should be treated as a strategic account.

For example, at Kraft Foods a tool called Relationship Segmentation Analysis has been developed to determine the best supplier relationship type. The RSA is used by Kraft employees who are customers of a particular supplier. The group evaluates the supplier—and the potential value that might be realized through a relationship with that supplier—in 10 key areas. These areas are in two broad categories: economic value drivers (how financial value can be generated from the relationship) and compatibilities (the degree to which Kraft and the supplier organization fit across strategic, geographic, cultural, and other dimensions). The result of the assessment in the 10 key areas points to a supplier relationship which may range from a transactional relationship to a strategic alliance partnership.[43]

In effect, the situation with powerful customers is that they define the type of relationship on offer to a given supplier, and the issue is then whether that relationship fits with the seller's strategy.

The Risks of Dependence

A related point is that SAM exposes the seller to another type of risk, derived from the strategic account's own end-use markets. The closer the relationship becomes to strategic account/strategic supplier status, the higher this risk becomes for the supplier. Quite simply, if the key account's performance declines, or if its business fails, its strategic suppliers will suffer business losses which are likely to be substantial, and over which they have little control.

Consider the dilemma faced by tyre manufacturer Dunlop, and many other smaller suppliers, created by the 2005 collapse of MG Rover—it is believed some 15–20 per cent of Dunlop's UK business was lost with Rover's demise. Further, the value of Dunlop's investment in a long-term collaborative relationship based on new product development for Rover was also lost. The impact is equally serious for some 1,500 small car parts manufacturers who supplied Rover, both in lost business and in bad debts.[44] Focus on a strategic account creates

---

[43] Hughes, Jonathan, 'The Changing View of Supplier Segmentation', *Inside Supply Management*, October 2005, pp. 14–15.

[44] Quinn, James, 'Suppliers Turn the Screw on Rover', *Daily Mail*, 8 April 2005, p. 89.

a shared business risk for suppliers, which may be uncontrollable, unrecompensed, and unattractively high. Commitment to the relationship may easily blind us to the costs of the customer's failure.

The Paradox of Customer Attractiveness and Competitive Intensity

Fans of the SAM strategy argue this model should only be applied to the customers who are most 'attractive' to a particular supplier.[45] Setting aside the issue of how a company defines its criteria of attractiveness, the paradox is that the customers who are most attractive to one supplier will probably at the same time be the most attractive to its competitors. While there will be situations of 'fit' which make a customer attractive to one supplier and unattractive to others, this is likely to be the exception rather than the rule. Accordingly, the most 'attractive' customers for a SAM strategy are also likely to be those where competitive intensity is highest and consequently where the ability of the customer to substitute one supplier for another is highest. The likelihood seems that competitive intensity will deny strategic supplier status for any seller and place all in the routinized, commodity supplier category. The most 'attractive' customers become the least 'attractive' through processes of competitive convergence of suppliers on the same customers as potential strategic accounts.

The Dubious Case for Strategic Account Investment

This brings us to another critical question—if strategic accounts are less profitable for a supplier and impose higher levels of risk on the supplier's business, then how is it possible to make a case for increasing dependence on such accounts, and to invest in SAM systems to further reinforce the dependence of the company on low-profit, high-risk business? There may be no choice, certainly in the short term, other than to meet the requirements of dominant customers for special treatment, but to regard this element of the business as the highest investment priority for the longer term is highly questionable. Indeed, the more rational course might be to find ways of ring-fencing such customers and diverting resources to develop more profitable parts of the customer portfolio.

[45] Capon, Noel, 2001, op cit.

SAM strategy also carries the substantial opportunity cost that management focus on strategic accounts reduces the attention given to other customers, who in reality offer higher margins and lower risk. Indeed, there is a significant danger that having invested in SAM with a customer, even as the account becomes progressively less profitable because of excess demands, inertia and reluctance to admit failure may easily cause the supplier to cling to the key account relationship regardless of disappearing margins.

There is a strong, and for some companies urgent, argument that investment priorities should be reconsidered in many customer relationships, with an emphasis on long-term profitability and balanced risk exposure, and less on the short-term characteristics of existing markets. The logic is that if the business model has failed, then the issue becomes one of searching and developing a new business model, not persisting with the old model until commercial failure ensues. The goal is to invest in strength and enhanced future earnings, not to invest in positions of weakness and to maintain the status quo, only to enjoy progressively reduced earnings.

Understanding Customer Relationship Requirements

The European purchasing manager with a leading engineering company observed to us that: 'I love it when a supplier tells me I am a key account—I make a lot of fuss of them. However, most times all I really do is to get concessions on price and terms. I almost feel guilty, it is so easy, but it's my job.'[46] He said that on average it took suppliers about three years to wise up to what was happening. Underpinning the weakness of SAM strategy in potentially mismanaging critical inter-organizational dependencies is the observation that suppliers frequently tend to have exaggerated views about the relationship that major customers want to have with their suppliers.

SAM stands no chance of success unless there is a close match between seller and buyer relationship requirements. Consider the model in Figure 2.5. Where there are similar relationship requirements from buyer and seller, their strategies are aligned (the 45° line in the model). However, there is a mismatch when the customer

---

[46] Quoted in: Piercy, Nigel F. and Nikala Lane, 'The Underlying Vulnerabilities in Key Account Management Strategies', *European Management Journal*, Vol. 24 No. 2–3 2006, pp. 151–82.

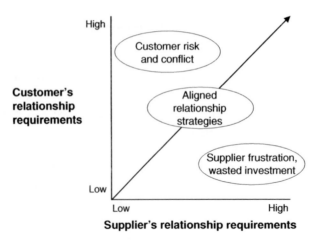

Fig. 2.5 Buyer and seller relationships

wants more relational investment than the supplier is prepared to give—perhaps this customer does not warrant a larger relationship investment by the supplier. The choice of the supplier not to invest causes conflict with the customer and potentially places the business at risk. On the other hand, supplier frustration and wasted investment results for the supplier attempting to build close relationships with customers who mainly want efficient transactions—from the buyer perspective the supplier is not important enough to justify strategic supplier status, or this may simply not be how this company does business with its suppliers. Only where there is continuous alignment between buyer and seller relationship requirements is there potential for effective SAM. The problem facing suppliers seems to be recognizing how rare alignment may be in practice, as well as how transitory.

Distinguishing Large (Major) Customers from Strategic Accounts

The tendency among sellers is to equate large customers with strategic accounts. It probably should not be, but it is. We commented earlier on the importance of distinguishing major accounts from strategic accounts in the customer portfolio. This is where getting it wrong really hurts. The danger of not distinguishing these types of customer is threefold: first, confusing the major account with the real strategic account prospect, leading to unproductive investments in the relationship; second, diverting attention from developing new and profitable major accounts growing out of the traditional middle market; and third, neglecting the productivity enhancements available by moving over-demanding customers from the traditional middle market to the direct channel. Identifying major customers wrongly as strategic accounts is capable of undermining the management of the whole portfolio of accounts being serviced by the seller, with likely further negative effects on overall performance and profitability.

What is more, some major customers may be relatively unattractive because they offer little profit or future growth. The fact that such customers may presently be large buyers does not alter this fact. On these grounds, simply being a large customer does not justify supplier relationship investments like SAM. There is no logic in building stronger relationships with unattractive customers, particularly if this reduces opportunities to invest more productively elsewhere. As noted earlier, in many ways, the large low-profit customer should encourage ring-fencing to minimize additional investment to the lowest level that retains the business, and the diversion of resources to more profitable applications elsewhere in the business.

Understanding the Reality of Customer Loyalty

Much of the attraction of SAM lies in the promise that collaborative relationships with strategic customers will enhance the retention of that business, that is, strategic accounts will reciprocate by offering loyalty to their long-term strategic suppliers. This promise may not be fulfilled. As Chainsaw Al said many years ago—'if you want loyalty, buy a dog'. Customer loyalty seems to be in very short supply.

Consider the textile and clothing suppliers who believed their long-term relationship with Marks & Spencer was secure, only to discover that when their customer was under pressure, purchasing transferred to cheaper off-shore sources. Examine the US situation for clothing manufacturers for whom Wal-Mart is a 'key account' —Wal-Mart is now the eighth largest purchaser of Chinese products at incredibly low prices, which seems to matter more than long-term relationships with domestic suppliers. Alternatively, view the Dell Inc. situation—a company renowned for its strategic account strategy—acting almost as an out-sourced IT department for major customers. Dell Inc. does not extend the same philosophy to its suppliers—a company remains a Dell supplier only as long as it has better technology than the rest.

Indeed, we saw earlier recent research suggests that while relational exchanges between suppliers and customers frequently benefit customers in performance improvements, generally the customers concerned do not reward suppliers with a higher share of their expenditure or long-term contractual commitments.[47] The mutual benefit and long-term relationship building implicit in strategic account management approaches may have been grossly exaggerated.

If SAM is seen as a model of collaboration that has many similarities with strategic alliances (both involve agreement for partnership and joint decision-making, with no transfer of ownership), then it is perhaps worth considering the evidence that the majority of strategic alliances fail, and in the view of many executives do not deliver the benefits they promised. The success of alliances seems to depend on conditions of mutuality and symmetry between partners. Those conditions do not appear to exist in many SAM situations.

Underestimating How Fast Things Change

Even if a customer is willing and eager to offer a seller the status of a strategic supplier and is treated as a strategic account, with all the additional investment that this is likely to require, some sellers believe that strategic relationships with these accounts will be stable and long-term (otherwise the seller investment makes little sense).

The more likely truth is that as a seller's own strategy changes, the importance of a particular supplier will change—possibly dramatically and quickly. As the recorded music business transforms to one based on Internet downloads instead of physical products, strategic suppliers will be those with expertise in the new technology, not those offering CDs and support for the old technology.

In fact, supplier switching may increasingly be an explicit element of a customer's business strategy. For example, in 2005 Apple announced it was teaming up with Intel to provide the components suitable for new generations of Apple products, effectively bringing

---

[47] Fink, Robert C., Linda F. Edelman, and Kenneth J. Hatten, 'Supplier Performance Improvements in Relational Exchanges', *Journal of Business and Industrial Marketing*, Vol. 22 No. 1 2007, pp. 29–40.

an unexpected end to long-term supplier relationships with IBM and Freescale (formerly Motorola).[48] Apple's goal is to build on the momentum created by its iPod digital music player and to meet the lower prices demanded in the mass consumer market. Also in the consumer marketplace, Dixons, the electrical retailer, ceased selling video recorders in favour of DVD players at the end of 2004 and film-based cameras in favour of digital cameras in 2005. Dixon's strategy follows trends in the consumer marketplace notwithstanding disruption to established suppler relationships.[49] Supplier switching may be an inevitable consequence of strategic change. As strategic priorities change, so does the identity of the suppliers now regarded as strategic.

The reality is that the strategic supplier relationship for many suppliers will be temporary and transitory, as customers develop their own market strategies and adopt new technologies. This leaves the supplier investing heavily in the strategic account relationship, only to see that relationship disappear as the customer moves on. Customers rarely offer recompense to a supplier to cover the costs of dismantling a redundant SAM system—you are on your own with that one.

Even more traumatic is the sudden collapse of a strategic supplier relationship. Changes in customer businesses may end relationships that have taken years to build—perhaps the strategic account is taken over and the acquiring company imposes its own supplier arrangements on the acquired business; possibly there is a change in supply strategy from the top of the customer organization, for example, the move from single sourcing to multiple-sourcing; sometimes the customer learns technology and process from its strategic supplier, enabling it to undertake production of the product in-house; or, sometimes customer personnel move on and their replacements do not have a close relationship with the supplier and maybe do not want one. The collapse of a strategic account relationship will have a major negative impact on sales volume, which may not have been predicted. The end of a SAM relationship may impose additional and substantial costs—adjusting operations capacity to allow for short-term volume

[48] This illustration is based on: Morrison, Scott and Richard Waters, 'Time Comes to "Think Different" ', *Financial Times*, 7 June 2005, p. 25. Witzel, Morgan, 'An Alliance that Can Supply a Competitive Edge', *Financial Times*, 13 June 2005, p. 14.
[49] Rigby, Elizabeth and Jenny Wiggins, 'Dixons Closes Shutters in Film Cameras', *Financial Times*, 9 August 2005, p. 5.

reduction, disentangling integrated systems, rebuilding processes previously shared with the key account, reallocating or removing personnel previously dedicated to the key account, putting in place new
arrangements to retain whatever residual business there may be in the
account.

For example, in 2008 computer giant Apple dropped chip-maker
Wolfson Microelectronics as its chip supplier for new iPod models.
Apple's iPod account was worth 12 per cent of Wolfson's sales. There
was no acrimony—Wolfson continues as a supplier of chips for the
iPhone. Nonetheless, on the day Wolfson's shares collapsed by 30
per cent. The reason was simply Apple's intention to source from a
cheaper supplier—Wolfson's US rival Cirrhus Logic.

Actually the failure of a strategic account relationship may be very
public and create an additional type of vulnerability for the selling
company. If a company's shares are written down because of the collapse of business with a strategic account, then the supplier becomes
vulnerable to a predator—perhaps even the customer in question, who
has the opportunity to in-source the product by buying the supplier;
possibly a competitor; or, possibly a stalker from outside the sector.
The point is that the cost of a failed key account relationship may
not simply be losing the customer, it may be losing the company
as well.

Consider the experiences of Marconi in its strategic relationship
with British Telecom. Marconi was the rump of the former GEC and
through the 1990s focused investment heavily on the telecommunications sector. Marconi was one of British Telecom's largest suppliers
of network equipment for several decades. By 2004 BT represented a
quarter of Marconi's total sales—as much as the next nine customers
put together. Notwithstanding being described as a 'terrific partner'
by the chief executive of BT Wholesale, in 2005 Marconi was shut out
of BT's £10 billion '21st Century Network' project. BT's decision was
based on price, not technology or relationships, and Marconi could not
equal the prices of overseas competitors from eight countries ranging
from France to China. Under BT pressure, Marconi had even lowered
prices to a level that would have represented substantial losses in its
UK operation, but it was not enough to satisfy BT. With the loss of
a quarter of its sales base, shares falling 60 per cent in value, and
substantial job losses in prospect, Marconi's experience underlines

the risks of over-reliance on one customer, and the critical error of believing that BT would be a loyal partner. The loss of the BT business fundamentally weakened Marconi's ability to compete globally in new areas like Internet Protocol networks. Within months of the BT decision, it was clear that investors were looking for Marconi to sell the business or merge to survive. Marconi's Chinese joint venture partner, Huawei, gained two parts of the BT contract, and ironically Marconi's technology may be available to BT through this low price channel. In 2006 the main Marconi business was sold to Ericcson, leaving Marconi only a smaller services business working on maintenance of legacy systems.[50]

Making a Balanced Case for Strategic Account Management

What we have tried to do here is to contrast the apparently compelling case for strategic account management (SAM) models that develop collaborative and integrative relationships with major or dominant customers, with the serious flaws in the underlying assumptions of those models and the potentially damaging traps for the unwary. In many situations, it appears that the adoption of SAM models is based on the suspect logic that the best use of a company's resources is to invest heavily in that part of the business (the largest most dominant customers) which has the lowest margins and the highest business risk.

Defenders of the SAM model would argue that this scenario reflects not the weakness of the model, but poor choice of key accounts by companies. There is some merit in such a response. However, since the apparent reality is that companies choose as strategic accounts those customers to which they sell most, or respond to the demands of large customers for special treatment, then suggesting that the weaknesses inherent in the SAM model can be overcome by better choice

---

[50] This illustration is based on: Ashton, James, 'Marconi Up For Grabs', *Daily Mail*, 4 May 2005, p. 64. Brummer, Alex, 'Marconi Crisis Is a Disaster for UK PLC', *Daily Mail*, 11 May 2005, p. 67. Durman, Paul and Dan Box, 'Cut Off', *Sunday Times*, 1 May 2005, pp. 3–5. Grande, Carlos, 'Marconi's Technology Fails the Price Test', *Financial Times*, 4 May 2005, p. 23.

of strategic accounts seems somewhat unrealistic in many practical situations.

One logic is that the search should be for alternative strategies that avoid the trap of high dependence on a small number of powerful dominant accounts. Some will probably suggest that this is a search doomed to failure—the most powerful customers control markets and are unlikely to surrender this control willingly. Yet, on the other hand, consider the potential disruption of the status quo in a market by the introduction of a new business model. For example, consumer and business computer users have voiced numerous complaints over the years about the product functionality of Microsoft offerings, and struggled in vain against the massive Microsoft market share in areas like operating systems and server software. In 2005, we saw the dramatic impact of Linux software—available free or cheaply—developed through a peer-to-peer network, in a business model that appears uninvolved with concerns like profitability. Microsoft increasingly looks like a company with a mid-life crisis that has no effective response to Linux. However, more interesting yet is the fact that much of the Linux revolution has been driven and facilitated by IBM, Sun Microsystems, and Dell, who are dramatically reducing their dependence on the old adversaries at Microsoft. Actively managing dependence between the buyer and the seller may be one way out of the trap.

It is interesting that 2006 saw the Proctor & Gamble/Gillette merger to create the world's largest consumer brands group. The combined portfolio of brands provides a much stronger hand in dealing with major retailers.[51] However, the merger also represents a fundamental change to P&G's business model. The goal is to serve not only the world's most affluent 1 billion consumers in developed countries, but also the world's 6 billion consumers, with a new focus on lower-income consumers in such markets as China and India. In developing these emerging markets, P&G is deliberately not partnering with global retailers like Wal-Mart, Tesco, and Carrefour. Instead, in China P&G will offer Gillette access to a huge distribution system staffed by an army of individual Chinese entrepreneurs—what P&G

---

[51] Quinn, James, 'Gillette Deal to Put P&G Ahead By a Close Shave', *Daily Mail*, 29 January 2005, p. 105.

calls a 'down the trade' system ending up with a one-person kiosk in a small village selling shampoo and toothpaste. The effect should be that stable growth in Asian markets will reduce the combined company's dependence on mature markets dominated by powerful retailers.[52]

New business models that will be effective in avoiding the dominant customer trap will probably share some of the following characteristics:

- reducing critical dependencies and risks by developing alternative routes to market—consider the example of the automotive manufacturers developing direct-channel strategies to take back control of the value chain and reduce dependencies on independent distributors;
- developing alternative product offerings to rebuild brand strength as a counter to the power of the largest customers;
- emphasizing the need for high returns to justify taking on high risk business, not the other way around;
- reducing strategic vulnerabilities created by excessive levels of dependence on a small number of customers or distributors;
- clarifying the difference between major accounts and strategic accounts and developing appropriate ways of managing these different types of relationships profitably;
- actively rejecting business from some sources because the customer is unattractive in terms of profitability and risk, even if the business on offer is large;
- managing customer accounts as a portfolio (see Figure 2.2) using criteria of attractiveness and prospective performance, not simply customer size.

There are situations when SAM is an effective strategy to manage relationships with major buyers and to develop collaboration and partnership rather than adversarial transactions. However, careful management consideration needs to be given to understanding under what conditions this is true, and whether these are truly the conditions they face. There is potential insight in evaluating the customer portfolio and its changing composition, and to consider not simply the quantity of business offered by the largest accounts, but also the quality of that business. The quality of business with major accounts

[52] Grant, Jeremy, 'Mr Daley's Mission: To Reach 6Bn Shoppers and Make Money', *Financial Times*, 15 July 2005, p. 32.

includes the profitability of the business, and also the business risk involved, the impact of increased dependence on a small number of customers, and the opportunities given up. A balanced evaluation of this kind provides the basis for a more informed decision, but may also be the trigger for the search for strategic alternatives that may avoid the down-side of dependence on powerful key accounts. This balanced evaluation and search for new business models appears urgently needed in many organizations. Gaining this strategic insight and applying it to choices made is a potentially major contribution of a strategic sales approach.

Managing Strategic Dependence

It is likely that in a world dominated by collaboration, alliances, and networks, the systematic management of dependencies on other organizations will become even more important rather than less. Evaluating the full implications of strategic dependence on certain customers and the relative freedom of manoeuvre in dealing with others looks to be high on the strategic sales organization agenda. Importantly, dependence is something that can be managed relative to a customer's power. The power of dominant customers to dictate terms to suppliers is not inevitable.

In fact, dependencies can reverse or be reversed. For example, Gate Gourmet makes meals for airlines; primarily it is the sole supplier to BA in the UK. BA represents 80 per cent of Gate Gourmet's sales at Heathrow. Throughout the 2000s, BA used its dominant position to force down supplier prices—for Gate Gourmet this meant big steps down in price in 2002 and 2003, with further small steps down each year until 2008. By 2004, Gate Gourmet's losses on its Heathrow operation had reached £25 million a year and were worsening, with daily losses of £500,000–£1 million in 2005 at Heathrow. However, in 2005 Gate Gourmet found itself with new owners, who quickly became involved in cutting costs and reforming working practices, resulting in strikes by Gate Gourmet workers followed by sympathy strikes by BA employees—paralysing BA's flight operations at its global hub for more than 24 hours, stranding around 1,10,000 passengers and costing BA around £40 million.

Faced with possible financial collapse, Gate Gourmet threatened to put the company into administration unless BA offered a more generous catering contract. Of course, what became clear is that no other caterer was big enough to supply the food and drink BA needs for the 550 flights that leave Heathrow each day. BA agreed to pay an additional £10 million to Gate Gourmet catering, conditional on the employee dispute being resolved. Gate Gourmet's stance then became that BA should pay the costs of resolving the dispute.[53]

It is apparent that at some point the direction of dependency changed—when push came to shove, the issue changed from being about BA as dominant customer and became about Gate Gourmet as dominant supplier. The change in dependency was expensive for BA. The same flip in direction of dependency explains why automakers like Ford and GM are now faced with running components factories—which is the last thing they want to do. It is because after years of price reductions the components supplier held their hands up and said 'you want it at that price, you do it, here's the keys to the factory, we're in Chapter 11'. Managing strategic dependencies has become a major challenge in buyer–seller relationships.

Responses to adverse dependencies may include long-term strategic shifts to counter-balance customer power, to reduce dependencies, or to avoid situations where critical dependencies impact negatively.

Balancing Customer Power

The scenario of aggressive, all-powerful customers we have seen in some situations changes dramatically when suppliers have something to balance against the power of the customer. For example, Northern Foods makes Goodfella's Pizzas, Fox's biscuits, and thousands of different types of sandwiches, salads, ready-meals, and puddings that appear as retailer own-label products. Impressive financial performance is built on high quality, a determination to focus on products where the company has something unique to offer, and a clear view that if customers will not pay what the company thinks it should get,

---

[53] This illustration is based on: Done, K. 'BA Caterer Sends Out Offers on Redundancy', *Financial Times*, 27/28 August 2006, p. 2. 'Gate Gourmet Prepares for Shutdown in UK', *Financial Times*, 22 August 2005, p. 2. 'Gate Gourmet Dispute Likely to Hot Up As Chief Remains Unbowed', *Financial Times*, 1 September 2005, p. 2. O'Connell, D., 'Digs Dinner', *Sunday Times*, 21 August 2005, pp. 3–5.

they will stop and do something else. Northern pins customers down to penalties for any delays they cause, failing to take up agreed sales volume, or making recipe changes. Having products which are important to retailer customers and not available elsewhere changes the balance of power.[54] However, when push changes to shove, Northern is prepared to make tough decisions and to walk away from unattractive business.[55]

Similarly, Corning's record of creating new technologies in the glass business has given the company an enviable degree of power over its customers. Since starting in 1851, Corning has been a technology leader in many key areas from lightbulbs to television sets, and has been one of the most successful technology-led innovators in the world. Technological superiority in materials engineering puts Corning in a position where it can pursue novel business strategies like extracting 'down payments' from customers to shield itself from market fluctuations. Corning deploys technology to create competitive advantage that makes customers happy to lock in supplies of products they cannot source elsewhere.[56]

Reducing Dependencies

As we mentioned earlier, perhaps the best-known example of a dependency reduction strategy is IBM's war against Microsoft, and the latter's domination of computer and server operating systems. IBM has championed the rise of the Linux open-source operating system enthusiastically to hurt Microsoft: IBM offers open source software versions of some of its low-end middleware software; IBM research labs have 600 programmers spending all their time improving Linux; the company has organized a 'patent commons' —giving away over 500 software patents in 2005, with value at least $10 million, to be used free by anyone working on an open-source projects; and IBM contributed management software to the Apache Geronimo project—a

[54] Laurance, Ben, 'Northern Foods Goes Upmarket', *Sunday Times*, 14 October 2007, pp. 3–17.

[55] Urry, Maggie, 'Northern Mothballs Plant', *Financial Times*, 14 May 2008, p. 21. Rigby, Elizabeth, 'M&S Faces Challenge of Retaining Exclusive Label', *Financial Times*, 14 May 2008, p. 21.

[56] Marsh, Peter, 'A Careful Giant Behind the Glass', *Financial Times*, 30 September 2005, p. 14.

collaboration of programmers aiming to create an open-source version of the software most businesses use to run their most demanding applications. Through a strategy of openness and collaboration, IBM is breaking the whole sector free from Microsoft's previous domination.[57]

Avoiding Dependency

We saw earlier (p. 77) that part of the P&G/Gillette strategy for long-term development of the business in emerging markets is to develop new types of distribution channel that avoid the types of dependencies that brand owners have on dominant retailers like Wal-Mart, Tesco, and Carrefour in the developed countries. In other sectors too, major companies are making strenuous efforts to find ways of establishing new business models that avoid dependencies on powerful intermediaries—the 2000s have seen companies like Apple and Sony opening their own retail outlets to be closer to consumers but also to avoid dependencies on major consumer electronics retailers like Best Buy and Circuit City.

For example, Nespresso, a subsidiary of Nestlé, is establishing 'coffee boutiques'. Located at prestigious addresses like New York's Madison Avenue and London's Beauchamp Place, the boutiques are lined with dark wood panelling, discreetly lit, with plush interiors. Nespresso previously sold coffee capsules for espresso machine by mail-order (and online) to members of the 'Nespresso Club', and then started selling branded coffee machines. Nespresso plans further retail expansion—taking the brand into hotels, restaurants, offices, and first-class airline lounges. The goal is to enable an increasing number of people to experience the brand first-hand. The brand experience is hoped to lead to purchase of the coffee machines and accessories. The strategic logic for such moves is that branded consumer goods companies are often at the mercy of third-party retailers when it comes to the marketing and placement of their products. The goal is to move beyond selling a 'product in a box' to offering a superior 'service experience'.

---

[57] Waters, Richard, 'Big Blue Looks to be More in the Pink After Changing Tack', *Financial Times*, 28 February 2007, p. 30.

Nespresso's objective is to become a lifestyle brand and this is reflected in its new channel strategy.[58]

The logic of the customer portfolio is in part to make more explicit the consequences of critical dependencies on major customers. This provides a basis for making explicit decisions about the acceptable level of customer risk to have in the business, and to develop ways of balancing customer power, reducing and avoiding undesirable and damaging dependencies. Many of the dependencies most critical to businesses are those in the marketplace—on customers and collaborators—and this is likely to escalate. In turn this identifies a key strategic sales role, which appears to be largely neglected in many businesses at present. This is a powerful way into the strategy process at most companies.

Making Strategic Customer Choices

Choice concerns not simply selecting strategic customers with which to attempt to build partnerships. It is also about adopting a strategic perspective on customer investments in other parts of the customer portfolio. For most of us, the second of these issues is probably the more important one.

One approach to screening the customer portfolio is shown in Figure 2.6—although this can be made more sophisticated if need be. The screening can be done for all large customers where the distinctions between middle-market, major, and strategic accounts is not clear (and the analysis may help make this clearer), or it can be done for strategic, major, and middle-market accounts in turn. It can also be done for the direct channel. The goal is to uncover the weaknesses in the portfolio from business risk and dependence on certain customers, hidden inside our choices of the most attractive customers and our investment in building a strong position with them.

This model suggests first evaluating customers in terms of the *business risk* involved in dealing with them. Risk is not just about

---

[58] Wiggins, Jenny and Haig Simonian, 'How to Serve a Bespoke Cup of Coffee', *Financial Times*, 3 April 2007, p. 10.

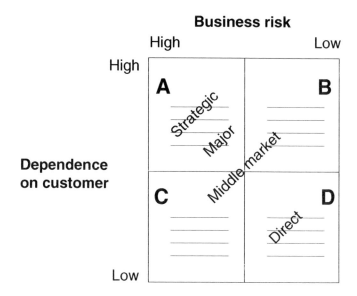

Fig. 2.6 Screening the customer portfolio

the dangers of losing the customer. It should include all aspects of the way in which the customer relationship could damage the supplier business if it went wrong. The evaluation of business risk in this sense might be easier if you go back through the factors we have discussed in this chapter concerning relationships with major and strategic customers.

Dependence on the customer may be related to calculations of risk, but is easiest to assess as the percentage of total sales accounted for by each customer. Even so, dependence may involve other factors that give the customer power over the supplier—such as the retailer or distributor who controls access to a market, or technology links which may be difficult to replace.

The process of evaluating business risk and dependence by customer identifies the risk/dependence categories shown in the first stage of the Figure 2.6 model. The categories are: A—customers with the highest levels of business risk and also a high degree of dependence for the seller, many of which are likely to be customers from the major and strategic account parts of the portfolio; B—customers on which the seller has a high degree of dependence, but where business risk is seen as comparatively lower, probably dominated by middle-market accounts; C—customers where although business risk is high, seller dependence on these customers is comparatively lower, which is also likely to be mainly middle-market customers; and D—customers where both business risk and seller dependence are relatively low, probably populated largely by smaller middle-market customers and direct-channel customers.

At this stage it should be possible to take a view on the balance of the customer portfolio and whether this is desirable and acceptable to the company. Excessive reliance on category A customers for sales volume indicates high strategic vulnerability—our dependence is high and yet these are the customers showing the highest levels of business risk. At the very least, we should be looking for high levels of profitability to compensate for the risk being accepted. Conversely, category D customers are more secure and less potentially damaging, but we have to ask whether the levels of profit and sales growth they offer will meet company goals. Category B customers are high in dependence characteristics, but appear low risk. The danger here is that as they grow, they may move into category A. Category C customers are high risk, but dependence is low, so they may be attractive if profits match the risk level, and they do not expose the business to a high level of vulnerability.

The second stage of the analysis suggested in Figure 2.6 is concerned with assessing the attractiveness of customers to the business, and the strength of the position we can take with them, but incorporating our analysis of business risk and customer dependence to identify both problems and opportunities.

For a start it is worth giving some thought to the criteria you want to use to judge the attractiveness of a customer. These are not the same for all companies, but depend on the specific business' strengths and weaknesses. Most times, profit and growth prospects will feature high on the list of criteria, though even then the weighting is likely to differ between companies, and should be tied down to specific numbers. Beyond that criteria—and the direction of evaluation will vary according to what is judged most important by a specific management team. For example, one company might place a high weight on stability in customer sales, while another might be better set up to handle volatile sales. Some companies will likely place great weight on the prestige of the customer as a reference site which will attract other customers, while others will value highly the extent to which a customer provides a strategic platform to cross-sell over time. There is great advantage in making the criteria of attractiveness quite explicit— even to the extent of placing quantitative weights on the criteria to show their relative importance. With this task completed customers can be systematically evaluated on the basis of how attractive they are to the supplier business.

A similar logic applies to identifying the criteria which make the business position we have with the customer strong or weak. Typically this will include factors like the share of wallet we take with the customer, the strength of the relationship established, and the 'fit' between our characteristics and those of the customer (such as culture, way of doing business, communications, mutual interests). The list will also likely be substantially different between companies. It is also worth making the criteria fully explicit and putting quantitative weights on them, leading up to a systematic assessment of the strength of the position we have (or anticipate) with each customer.

The attractiveness of the customer compared to the business position we take provides the basis for quantitatively identifying several categories of customer: *core*—where we have a strong position with customers who are very attractive to us; *targets*—customers who are very attractive, but where our business and competitive position is relatively weak; *maintenance*—we have a strong position but these customers are not particularly attractive to us, perhaps because the prospects are not good, or the cost to serve is too high; *cash flow*— these customers are not very attractive and we have not built a strong position, and they are only in the portfolio for the positive cash flow they generate (as long as they do).

Conventional investment logic suggests that core customers should attract the resources needed to maintain our strong position and to protect these customers from competitive inroads. Targets may be candidates for additional investment of resources if there are good prospects of building a stronger position and a closer relationship, because these customers meet our criteria of attractiveness. Maintenance customers only justify investment if their business provides profit and we need resources to protect that flow, because these customers are not attractive to us as long-term business. Cash-flow customers are essentially marginal and we keep them in the portfolio only as long as they produce a positive cash flow for minimal investment— they are not long-term prospects either.

However, our analysis of business risk and customer dependence adds a new insight to the conventional evaluation of customer attractiveness and business position. Within each of the categories— core, targets, maintenance, and cash-flow customers—we can identify which are A (high risk/high dependence—mainly strategic and major accounts), B (low risk/high dependence—mainly middle-market accounts), C (high risk/low dependence—mainly middle-market accounts), and D (low risk/low dependence— mainly middle-market and direct-channel customers).

This now provides a basis for asking questions about the underlying investment attractiveness of different customers or customer groups, informed not just by how attractive the customer appears to be and the strength of the relationship we have with them but also the impact the customer has on our business risk and our dependence characteristics. For example, in the customers identified as core business: how vulnerable are we if our core is dominated by category A customers; should we be looking at shifting resources from category A which represents high risk and dependence to category B where risk is lower; should we be looking at more investment in category C customers to lower our overall customer dependence; are category D customers in the core of the business receiving sufficient support, given that they show low risk and do not adversely affect our dependence ration, but are currently mainly left to the direct channel?

This questioning can be carried out systematically in each of the attractiveness/business position cells. By adding insight into business risk and customer dependence to the usual perspective taken in making strategic choices, the outcomes are likely to be considerably different.

A key input of the strategic sales perspective to the debate about business strategy and the investment of resources is to emphasize customers as assets and liabilities which should be assessed in those terms, not just in how much we think they will buy. The shift is from thinking just about the quantity of sales to emphasizing the quality of sales produced by different customers.

Building the New Agenda

Probably the most important element of the truly strategic sales organization is the perspective brought to the design and generation of business strategy and the investments associated with it. In this chapter, we have underlined the important contribution of clarifying what business strategy is actually about and what issues should be addressed. To the conventional debate we bring the perspective of the customer portfolio and what it suggests about differences between customers in the type of level of investment they require and justify. This led us inevitably to the issue of dominant customers. We tried to take a balanced case on the value and contribution of strategic account management as a response to dominant customer demands, and how attractive this investment really is. However, a broader perspective suggests that increasingly the issue is becoming the strategic management of dependencies and exploring ways to balance seller dependence on powerful customers or to reduce and avoid critical marketplace dependencies. It is long overdue that the debate on business strategy in companies should address these questions. Lastly, we packed these themes together by combining the analysis of business risk and customer dependence with the more usual assessment of customer attractiveness and relationship/position strength, to generate new insights and possible quite different conclusions about the type and level of investment we should be making in different parts of the customer portfolio.

The next stage of the agenda turns to the issue of intelligence—what do we know and learn from the marketplace—and the role of strategic sales in enhancing and exploiting superior market-sensing capabilities.

3

Intelligence: You Are What You Know

The second building block in developing the strategic sales organization is intelligence—knowledge and understanding of the market that underpins the ability to identify value-creating opportunities for the business (Figure 1.3).

This is based on two pieces of logic. First, we live in a world where intense market knowledge and superior understanding underpins competitive advantage. At its simplest, wherever you go, it appears when you look at the winners that 'those who know more, make more'. (We do not have a fancy business school term for this characteristic yet, but we probably soon will have.)

Second, too much information inside companies is about themselves (e.g. market research studies of brands and market share) and is essentially out-of-date by the time anyone gets it because it is historical (e.g. CRM system data on past sales to existing customers is not a great basis for insight into the future). If we accept that 'you are what you know' has replaced the idea that 'you are what you make', then we have just put a handle on the most fantastic opportunity. By virtue of its deep links into the marketplace, the strategic sales organization can impact on business performance by enhancing management understanding of how markets operate and how they are changing based on real intelligence. The challenge is bringing customer issues into the boardroom in a way which marketing departments have largely failed to do—a survey of large US companies show that their boards spend less than 10 per cent of their time discussing customer-related issues.[1]

For example, it is incredible to realize that Enterprise Rent-A-Car has its origins in an amazingly simple insight uncovered by a smart sales organization. Enterprise is now the largest US car rental and leasing business. Enterprise's primary focus is on car rentals to consumers who need a replacement vehicle as a result of an accident, mechanical repairs, or theft, or who require a car for a special occasion like a short business trip. While Avis and Hertz were already established in the airport rental market, Enterprise specialized in a different niche: short-term leases through insurance adjusters for people whose car was temporarily off the road. This was an untapped market niche. Enterprise got into short-term rental in 1964 in response to a customer request to a sales office for a temporary replacement car, not a long-term lease, while his own car was being repaired. As a result, the salesforce started to call on insurance companies and repair garages to prospect for temporary replacement deals. (Incidentally, then and now they took doughnuts with them because smart salespeople know what it takes to be more popular than the other guy!) The salespeople found that insurance offices and garages *hated* making car rental arrangements for customers—because it was extra unpaid work and they then had to give the customer a lift to the rental company. Enterprise provided both services and has built a billion-dollar rental business with more than 25 years of uninterrupted profitability. It is a mistake to underestimate the power of simple market insights that identify new ways of offering superior value to customers (or to underestimate the importance of doughnuts).

First, let us consider what it takes to develop a higher 'market IQ' through superior market sensing capabilities, and then some specific points where the intelligence capabilities of the strategic sales organization impact: underlining changing market definitions and the implications, highlighting changing market structures and sales channels and what they mean for business strategy, building market pictures to show how market change creates strategic opportunities, and providing customer insight when managers talk about their strengths and

---

[1] McGovern, Gail J., David Court, John A. Quelch, and Blair Crawford, 'Bringing Customers into the Boardroom', *Harvard Business Review*, November 2004, pp. 70–80.

weaknesses and the opportunities and threats in the market. These techniques provide the structure to go from simply having great information to identifying implications and opportunities to be addressed. Being ignored is no longer an option, there is just too much at stake.

However, then we can turn to the second and equally significant aspect of intelligence for the strategic sales organization—the impact of market intelligence on building added-value in dealing with major customers.

Developing a Higher Market IQ

One neat view of the market knowledge challenge has been described as raising a company's 'market IQ'.[2] In fact, many companies show signs of a low market IQ: they do not look closely enough at their customers and so they miss the important opportunities, leaving them to benefit competitors; they look only at the slice of the market where they currently sell, blinding themselves to growth in new segments of the customer base; they base conclusions solely on current transactions data—looking at past successes with existing customers and ignoring failures that have lost customers or failed to attract profitable business; and they take a piecemeal approach to market information, which produces little value in identifying untapped customers and new markets. The goal is instead to think more broadly.

For example, research by the *Business Management Performance Forum* underlines the fact that typically 'companies are failing to respond to fast-changing markets because they are unable to understand and adjust to what their customers want . . . businesses are struggling to meet the demands of increasingly competitive international markets and sophisticated clients'. Typically companies take a 'rear view mirror' approach to their markets looking backwards not forwards, and fail to 'read' their markets as a result.[3]

[2] Duncan, Calvin P., Constance M. O'Hare, and John M. Matthews, 'Raising Your Market IQ', *Wall Street Journal*, 3 December 2007, p. R4.
[3] Guerrera, Francesco, 'US Groups Fail to Understand Customer Needs', *Financial Times*, 5 June 2006, p. 27.

Sometimes, higher market IQ may come from surprising places. Nelson Peltz is best-known as an activist investor, buying companies and forcing management to change their ways. Importantly, when he buys into a company he frequently looks to change the sales pitch. In fact, he spends hours touring supermarkets, malls, and fast-food restaurants with his 10 (middle-aged) children, looking for ideas. In 2007, he took a stake in Tiffany, the luxury retail jeweller in the United States. The insights he brought from outside the business based on his understanding of the market were as follows: Tiffany had become too reliant on gift giving and was missing the opportunity to attract women shopping for themselves; the appeal was too narrow and the stores needed to sell watches other than Tiffany's own; there was an opportunity for smaller stores that do not carry engagement rings, to promote more self-purchases by people on their own.[4] Market IQ shapes strategies, but is not necessarily 'scientific'.

It follows that the signs of a low market IQ in a company are

1. a focus largely on current customers—normally using internal data which say nothing about non-customers or lost customers or potential new customers,

2. managers basing their strategies on information that is shared by all rivals—executives reject the chance to develop their own thorough and independent view of a market and rely on things like published reports, leading to timid strategies that mirror those of competitors,

3. reliance on qualititative market research—instead of looking for hard data and evidence on which to base decisions, and

4. a pattern of taking a piecemeal approach—characterized by narrow, one-time studies—which are expensive and never integrated.

If that sounds at all like your company, then you have just identified an important opportunity for the strategic sales organization—to assist the business in becoming more competitive and strategically effective by becoming better at market sensing, or building superior market understanding.

[4] This illustration is based on Kapner, Suzanne, 'Nelson Peltz, Activist Marketer', *Fortune*, 21 July 2008, p. 22.

Market Sensing Capabilities

In fact, one of the defining characteristics of agile fast-moving businesses is that they show a high level of strategic sensitivity—they have a high level of awareness of what is happening around them and what is going to happen next. Fast, nimble companies are very good at scanning for information and insight.[5] There is a strong argument that one of the key attributes of leading companies is that they are fact-obsessed.[6] Fact-based management and evidence-based management are approaches which allow managers to challenge corporate decision-making assumptions and stereotypes and look for new knowledge and its implications—breaking free of the 'dangerous half-truths and total nonsense' to which managers all too often cling.[7]

Indeed, it can be argued that the only way companies can take risk out of the business is by paying closer attention to how customers are changing and how markets are developing. For example, a characteristic of successful companies like Toyota, Coach, Samsung, and Target is that they are more 'risk-shapers' than 'risk-takers' because of their superior market knowledge. Adrian Slywotsky summarizes the challenge of becoming a knowledge-intense organization: 'The best countermeasure for defeating customer risk is creating and applying proprietary information about your customers...It's answering the question: what do we know about customers that others don't? And then using that information to make and keep profitable customers for life'.[8]

However, effective market sensing and superior market knowledge is not simply about doing more market research (as quite a few companies have learned the hard way to the financial benefit of their market research agencies, if not to themselves). The difference

[5] Doz, Yves and Mikko Kosonen, *Fast Strategy: How Strategic Agility Will Help You Stay Ahead of the Game*, Wharton School Publishing, 2007.

[6] Davenport, Thomas H. and Jeanne G. Harris, *Competing on Analytics: the New Science of Winning*, Boston, MA: Harvard Business School Press, 2007.

[7] Pfeffer, Jeffrey and Robert I. Sutton, *Hard Facts: Dangerous Half-Truths & Total Nonsense*, Boston, MA: Harvard Business School Press, 2006.

[8] Slywotsky, Adrian with Karl Weber, *The Upside: From Risk Taking to Risk Shaping: How to Turn Your Greatest Threat Into Your Biggest Opportunity*, New York: Crown Business, 2007.

between market sensing and marketing research is that market
sensing describes the processes in the organization which develop
enhanced management understanding about the external world, while
marketing research is mainly concerned with techniques of data collection and reporting—surveys, observation studies, market experiments, and so on. The difference is between process (understanding)
and technology (collecting data through formal techniques). There is,
however, good evidence that one major stimulus for market sensing
is marketing research results—it is not so much that one is superior to the other, more that they are different. Market sensing is
concerned with a broader view of market intelligence and the inter-
pretation of the evidence to gain new insights and identify new
opportunities.

Actually, some commentators do go further, and blame the shortcomings of marketing research for the decline of marketing's corporate
influence: 'Most marketing research has degenerated into an overused
set of tools and techniques, often selected on the basis of a low-cost
supplier. Research has become commoditized, just like the toilet paper
aisle at Wal-Mart...Marketing research has wrapped itself in a set
of beliefs and methodologies that are rooted in refuted behaviorist
psychological concepts.'[9] That is an extreme view, but it is a good
challenge to the belief that 'doing a bit of market research' is the
answer to all our strategic problems.

Increasingly, real market understanding comes not from the formal research studies marketing departments like to conduct and
buy. For example, General Electric has developed its competitive
position in the plastic fibres business—providing material for high
value products like fire-retardant jackets and bulletproof vests—on
the basis of a single new insight, which caused the company to
change its strategy. GE thought that the fibres industry was a commodity business based on obtaining the cheapest materials. What it
found instead was an artisan-based industry where customers wanted
to collaborate from the earliest stages to develop high-performance
materials—these are people with curiosity who like to get their hands
dirty. GE now shares prototypes with customers, by-passing executives, and working closely with engineers on technical questions.

---

[9] Schultz, Don E., 'MR Deserves Blame for Marketing's Decline', *Marketing News*, 15
February 2005, p. 7.

A considerable advantage has been achieved in access to a new market.[10]

Similarly, Intel grappled with the ethnography of the use of computers by children in China. For two-and-a-half years they observed Chinese families—examining their lives and values. The insights and understanding gained have shaped the company's strategy for this market in interesting ways. In the United States the conventional parents' belief is that a child should be bought a computer in the early stage of his or her development—exposing the child to computing at the earliest age. In China, parents believe the opposite—they want children to learn Mandarin, and the computer is a distraction from this. This insight led Intel designers to launch a PC aimed at the Chinese home educational market, which has a touch-sensitive screen that allows users to write in Mandarin, tracing the order in which the character is being written (correct stroke order being an important part of the learning process). Chinese parents also had misgivings about allowing children unlimited Internet access. Locks and keys are important symbols of authority in China. Instead of installing a software-based key on the PC, Intel included a physical locking mechanism, visible elsewhere in the room, and reassuring to parents.[11]

The point is that the difference between market sensing and conventional market research or information systems is that our focus is on managers' *understanding* of the market. Understanding is not the same as information. It is about developing new ways of looking at the outside world, to improve the way in which we develop our strategies and deliver our programmes. This is not something to be taken lightly. What we are building up to is no less than a challenge to the organization's culture. This challenge in the status quo is a key responsibility of the strategic sales organization, because that is where the market and competitive insight is likely to reside.

The problem is that *telling* people what their problems are, and by implication to get their act together, has proved to be a singularly ineffective approach to winning peoples' commitment and achieving effective strategy implementation. This is for a number of reasons concerned with how organizations work. The challenge is to manage

[10] Ante, Spencer E., 'The Science of Desire', *BusinessWeek*, 5 June 2006, pp. 98–106.
[11] Thomas, Kim, 'Anthropologists Get to the Bottom of Customers' Needs', *Financial Times*, 24 August 2005, p. 9.

the *process* of market sensing, not simply the providing of information and conclusions.

The important questions to ask in understanding whether the strategic sales organization is fulfilling its intelligence function are simple: what do we know; in particular, what do we know that is not obvious to every rival in this business—what do we know that they do not? Where does this superior insight create us a competitive advantage, an edge, a difference that matters, a way of delivering value better and to higher levels than the competition? And while you are at it—if you believe you have learned more than the others and you have the basis for building competitive advantage from that market knowledge— how do you plan to sustain that learning advantage as a basis for how you compete long term?

However, in most situations, nothing is for nothing. There are costs involved in fully leveraging the sales organization's unique capability to capture intelligence and enhance a company's market sensing process. It takes processes to capture and communicate new insights— it often needs management support to re-engage salespeople who have become accustomed to having their insights ignored. It needs to be prioritized in how the salesforce is managed and motivated. It means diverting resources from other opportunities. The direct and opportunity costs have to be justified in comparison with the benefits to the company of energizing the prime source of marketplace intelligence. Intelligence also has to be packaged and presented so it cannot be ignored.

Let us illustrate those benefits by considering some of the most important applications of superior market intelligence gained by fully leveraging the strategic sales organization's capabilities.

Changing Market Definitions

One of the advantages of developing superior market sensing resources is understanding faster and better fundamental changes in the shape and scope of the market, and responding more effectively. Traditional marketing research and analysis does not achieve this, and yet there can be few things more important to developing effective

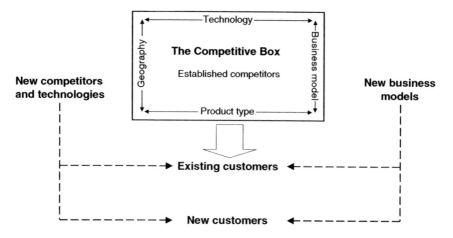

Fig. 3.1 Changing market definitions

business strategy. The dilemma, and one way to present it to managers, is shown in Figure 3.1.

If you have a fixed and changing view of the products and customers that constitute the 'market', then you are probably sitting inside the competitive box shown in Figure 3.1. You will not be lonely. Established competitors who do essentially similar things to you for essentially the same customer base will probably be there to keep you company. Our competitive box is defined by things like the geographic boundaries of the 'market', the types of products we sell, the type of technology we deploy, and the business model we operate. Usually everyone inside the box is pretty much the same in how they see these things. Our idea of competition is restricted to marginal changes in price and specifications compared to the other players inside the competitive box.

People who spend their lives writing plans have to have a competitive box. If you cannot define a market precisely in this way, then it is difficult to measure things like market share, or to run analytical models of market value and trends, or statistically identify segments within the market. These things are all of paramount importance to people who write plans and do great PowerPoint presentations.

The trouble is what actually kills you is outside the competitive box, not your friendly rivals inside the box. It is the things we ignore which are the ones that have the potential to put us out of business.

The challenge is identifying new competitors, often bringing new technologies into the marketplace, and the development of new business models that meet customer needs better than the old ones. These threats not only attack the existing customer base but they also create new demand and dominate new customers as they come into the market.

One major contribution from those who are out in the marketplace, meeting customers, tracking competitor behaviour, and identifying new market trends, is to provide early warning of the type of competitive changes that are happening outside the box, and to refuse to allow these factors to be ignored. There are many examples of executives focusing internally on the excellence of their products and services, and being displaced by new types of competition and competitors with new business models. Many of them did not see the change coming, and if they did—they chose to ignore it.

There are few better illustrations than the music business. While the world moved on to music downloaded from the Internet and Apple launched the iPod/iTunes product to monetize digital download, traditional recorded music companies like EMI were still using their marketing and sales resources to pile recorded music CDs into retail stores (many of which were returned and trashed). The next wave of disruption is not simply from a superior technology, but from new business models like that pioneered by concert organizer LiveNation. The LiveNation model recognizes that the money in music is no longer in recordings, it is in concerts, merchandize, and other artist-related products like computer games—it does not matter if you give the music away for nothing, the money lies elsewhere. This is why artists as diverse as Madonna, U2, and Jay-Zee have signed with the concert promoter instead of the traditional recorded music company.

In the computer and technology business, a revolution of similar proportions is unfolding through 'cloud computing' pioneered by companies like Google, Amazon.com, and Salesforce.com. The cloud concept provides a way for computer users to buy their computing power and access to software from the grid provided by the giant data centres that now exist. The analogy is that buying information processing capabilities should be like buying electricity from the national grid—few companies cling to the idea of maintaining their own electricity generation capabilities. As this model takes hold of the corporate computing market, it will fundamentally undermine the business models of conventional computer and software sellers like Dell, Intel, and Microsoft (who used to control this market). The survivors will be those who can adapt their business models to add value in a completely re-shaped marketplace.

The point is the need is for strategic insight into market change, rather than the measurement of what used to be—which is what traditional marketing research tends to be. The strategic sales organization should use its access to intelligence to foster that insight and provide a market-based perspective on the challenges facing strategy decision-makers. The model in Figure 3.1 provides a structure for presenting this issue—identifying the familiar players inside the competitive box, but also tracking new competitors and technologies which are moving in, and the potential for new business models to meet customer needs.

Then at a finer level of detail, once market parameters are agreed, there is the question of the sales channels and structures within the market and how they are changing or can be re-shaped to create competitive advantage—demanding another input from the strategic sales organization.

Changing Market Structure

Another benefit of leveraging sales organization intelligence capabilities is in opening peoples' eyes to the structure of the market and how it is evolving. It should not be true, but it generally is—it is amazing how often a simple, graphical mapping of sales channels opens peoples' eyes to how their market works and how it is changing.

As an illustration, Figure 3.2 shows a map of market structure for air conditioning units in the UK (the figures are hypothetical to avoid breaching confidentiality). It simply shows for a single year, the production and imports of air conditioning units (120,000 units) and the destination of these units (commercial building companies and domestic/small business customers). The model shows the different direct and intermediary-based sales channels in this market,

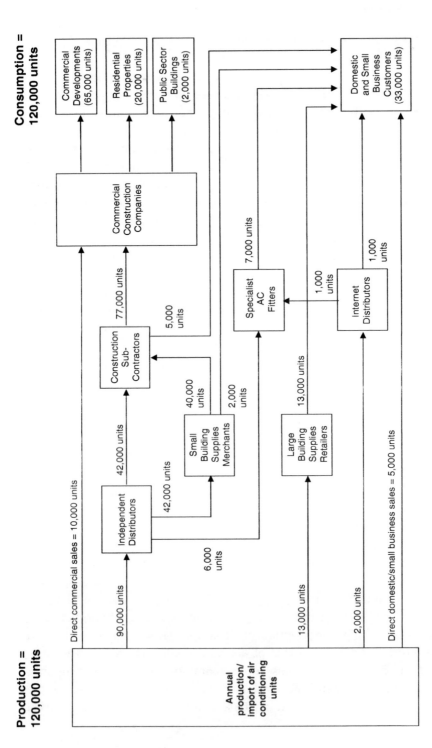

Fig. 3.2 Understanding market structure and trends

and their relative size. In most cases models like this are very easy to produce.[12]

Then it gets interesting. Sometimes very interesting. For many internally focused executives, this is likely to be the first time it has occurred to them that distributors and large retailers are not end-user customers, and should not be treated as such. Nor are the commercial construction companies end-users—their demand will depend wholly on the type and amount of development work they have in hand. That insight alone is a breakthrough in many situations. But then there are a number of questions to raise about our strategy for going to market: for each sales channel, what is our share of the business compared to competitors? For each sales channel, what is our average revenue per unit, compared to the rest (and if the data exist—what is our profitability in each sales channel)? How competitive are we in different sales channels—where are our strengths and weaknesses compared to the rest? Which sales channels are growing and which are declining—and where does that leave our go-to-market strategy? What are the bottlenecks in important sales channels and are there ways of overcoming them (e.g. in this model Independent Distributors and Large Building Supplies Retailers are responsible for 85% of the flow of products to the end users, suggesting the desirability of developing alternatives); are some sales channels strong in some product types—for example, do specialist fitters specify higher priced models than small customers would select for themselves from a retailer? And what are the possibilities for new sales channels and models developing—should we be leading this change or be prepared to respond when competitors do? In some cases, shifts in the relative importance and accessibility of sales channels may have a profound impact on strategic choices faced.

For example, in common with most other major drugs companies, Glaxo SmithKlein is being forced to redesign its primary sales channels. Traditional approaches to selling medicines to doctors have become less effective—doctors are resistant to what they see as excessive drug company promotion. Glaxo has launched and monitored the

---

[12] Actually, there is the complication of allowing for changing stock levels in the market which means that the input and output figures may not balance, but this does not usually make a huge difference to the picture being built and the purposes for which it is going to be used.

effect of 15 different sales models in 13 countries. As a result, there will be fewer salespeople selling primary care products in established markets like North America and western Europe, and more highly skilled employees selling vaccines and secondary care drugs, most notably for cancer, and expansion in the emerging markets. The pilot studies indicated better or equal results compared to traditional approaches, but with 20–40 per cent fewer salespeople. Similarly, Novartis in the United States is reorganizing its salesforce in some areas to pay less attention to the doctor and more attention to the powerful parties who pay for the drugs—such as health insurance companies. In both cases, salesforce numbers are reducing, but this is not simply about downsizing, it is about developing the new business models that will be effective in new types of market reality.[13]

Our stance on this is that business strategy should be informed and shaped by the realities of the structure of the market and the sales channels within it, and particularly the dynamics of how sales channels are evolving, because this indicates where the opportunities and threats exist in the market. This is something that a strategic sales perspective brings to the strategy debate, which amazingly often has not been there before.

Building New Market Pictures for Strategy Making

There is also a priority in enhancing 'market IQ' for integrating information so it can be interpreted better. One way of approaching this is to build managers pictures of their markets using the structure shown in Figure 3.3.

The approach is simple and accessible to managers. The goal is simply to provide a structure to articulate what they know about changes outside the company, and to identify the most critical gaps in that knowledge. It provides a picture of what is good and bad about the

---

[13] This illustration is based on Jack, Andrew, 'Garnier Taking the Painful Medicine', *Financial Times*, 25 October 2007, p. 19. Whalen, Jean, 'Novartis to Focus on Influence Insurers Wield Over Doctors', *Wall Street Journal*, 14 December 2007, p. A.12.

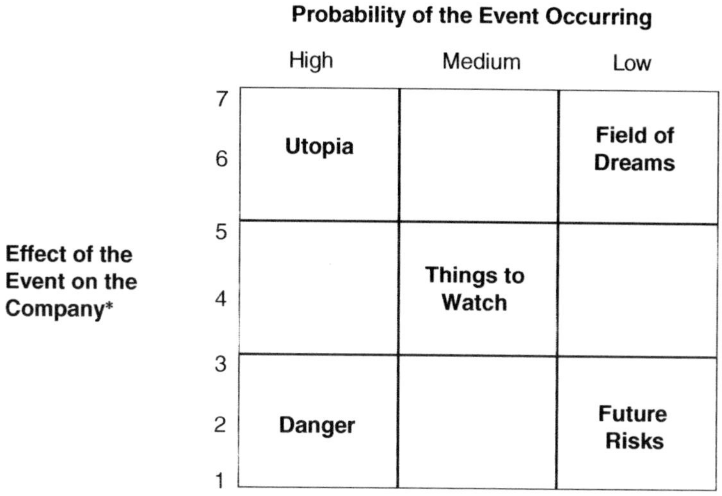

Probability of the Event Occurring

	High	Medium	Low
7			
6	**Utopia**		**Field of Dreams**
5			
4		**Things to Watch**	
3			
2	**Danger**		**Future Risks**
1			

Effect of the Event on the Company*

*1=Disaster, 2=Very bad, 3=Bad, 4=Neutral, 5=Good, 6=Very good, 7=Ideal

Fig. 3.3 Building market pictures

market in question. It is surprising how infrequently this integration of 'what we know' is done, or done well, and it provides another opportunity for the strategic sales initiative.

The task is to brainstorm the events in the chosen part of the company's environment which might take place or which are currently developing. The most important events are listed (and also mnemonic codes for ease of reference). However, the framework also requires that we identify specific effects on the company if this event takes place. If we cannot do this—the event is too broad and should be defined more narrowly, or it is unimportant to our analysis. Then, we need to do two further things: assess the current view of the *probability* of the event happening (initially a subjective 'guesstimate' which we may want to test and evaluate further) and the *likely effect* of the event on the business if it does happen (the suggested scale runs from 1 = Disaster to 7 = Ideal, and again this is something on which we may want to take an initial view which can be refined at a later stage). We should try to build a full view of the most important aspects of the environment as they impact on the company. The events (or their codes) are then entered on the model in Figure 3.3—positioned by the scores we have placed on the probability of each event occurring and the effect of the event if it does occur. The broad categories are categorized into *utopia*—events with a very good effect which are very likely to occur; *field of dreams*—events which are highly desirable but seem unlikely to happen the way things are at the moment; *danger*—events which are very threatening to the company and which are very likely to happen; *future risks*—undesirable events that seem unlikely to happen, but which we may want to monitor in case they become more likely; and *things to watch*—where we do not see the probability as very high and the impact is relatively neutral, but where monitoring is needed in case either of these changes.

What we now have is a model of the outside world, based on our market sensing and understanding, which we can use to test the robustness of proposed market and business strategies, identify information gaps, and evaluate market attractiveness.

Now we have a picture which provides us with the basis for working with strategic decision-makers on interpreting the outside world. There are three questions to stress and demand attention. Given that the model is a picture of the things happening outside which we regard as most important to the survival and prosperity of the company, then we need responses to the following questions:

- We have identified the changes in this market which are potentially very advantageous for our performance in this market, and which are likely to happen (utopia in the model)—the question is, *where, explicitly and realistically are we exploiting those factors in our business strategy?*
- We have also identified the changes in this market which are potentially major threats, and which are also likely to happen (danger in the model)—the question is: *where, explicitly and realistically are we defending against these changes in our business strategy?*
- If it has been done properly then the model we have produced shows the things that are most important to our position in this market—the question is *are we monitoring and evaluating these factors?*

It is amazing how often executives have to admit that their plans and strategies do not address the real changes in the marketplace where they intend to operate—this is the moment when new thinking about strategies may become possible for the first time, because managers are confronted with their own logic. Even more surprising are situations where managers are forced to admit that their information systems do not focus on the things that really matter to their performance—the systems report the figures and statistics that are easiest to report and that have always been reported.

Customer-oriented SWOT Analysis

Directly related to new insight into markets by building pictures for managers is taking a different view on the SWOT analysis that managers appear to use everywhere.[14] SWOT analysis is an incredibly simple approach to evaluating a company's strategic position when planning, by identifying the company's strengths and weaknesses and comparing these to opportunities and threats in the market. The major attraction of SWOT analysis is that it is familiar and easily understandable by users.

However, in practice, the use of this tool has generally become sloppy and unfocused. SWOT analysis is frequently done extremely badly, but that does not mean it *has* to be the way the technique is used. Notwithstanding general disillusionment with SWOT analysis (because it is done so badly), it *can* be made to work, and real strategic insights *can* be generated and used.

There are a number of very straightforward guidelines to achieve these goals, that is, we keep the technique because we know how to do it, but we change the rules. The 'rules' we propose for using SWOT to produce insightful results are (a) focused SWOTs; (b) shared vision; (c) customer orientation; (d) environmental analysis; and (e) structured strategy generation.

Focused SWOTs

The more carefully we define the area to be evaluated with a SWOT analysis, the more productive the analysis is likely to be. By focusing on a particular issue, and excluding non-relevant material, we can overcome the bland, meaningless generalizations that executives frequently produce if asked to take a global view of their businesses'

---

[14] For the uninitiated, SWOT stands for nothing more complicated than 'Strengths, Weaknesses, Opportunities, and Threats'. It is probably the single most common tool used by strategy planners.

strengths and weaknesses. Pick a single important issue, customer, or market and focus on it.

Shared Visions

Because of its apparent simplicity and ease of communication, SWOT analysis is an excellent vehicle in working with groups of executives. There is little or no barrier created through executives having to learn complex analytical techniques (or succumbing to the temptation to leave it to the 'experts'). Advantages of using SWOT as a structure for looking at an important issue include the following: pooling of ideas and information from a number of sources produces richer results; the SWOT analysis provides a concrete mechanism for expressing team consensus about important issues; and it flushes out potentially harmful disagreements

Customer Orientation

But, now we get to the real crunch point. The way we can use the SWOT technique in a particularly powerful form is summarized in Figure 3.4, and this is where the important difference comes. The first requirement is that in evaluating our strengths and weaknesses, we can *only* include those resources or capabilities which would be

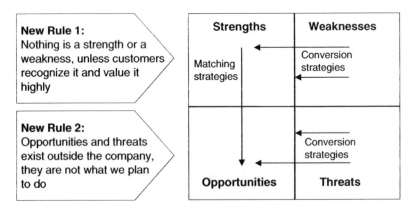

Fig. 3.4 New rules for customer-oriented SWOT analysis

recognized and valued by the *customer* with whom we are concerned. This helps us to get past the 'motherhood' statements often produced as a list of strengths: service, quality, an established firm, and so on— because we have to define what we believe is *seen* by the customer and is *valued* by him or her.

For example, our 'great private medical scheme' for employees is *not* a strength for these purposes. It is only relevant if we can say that customers would recognize that we treat our employees well, and this in turn has payoffs in how they deal with customers and the establishment of long-term relationships. Applying this rule is often a considerable discipline on executives, and in the event of disputes which cannot be resolved about what is a strength and what is not—the joy is that we may actually test our claims with *customers*.

Forcing executives to confront the difference between what *they* think is important and what *customers* think is important is a substantial contribution. We can, in a very practical way, force users of the technique to identify the critical success factors in their business, their customers' needs, and hence factors influencing customer relationships. In one company, for example, what executives told us was their strength of 'technical service excellence' turned out to mean to customers that this was a company that sent out PhD-level engineers to *prove* that products had been abused in use, and that warranties did not apply.

Similarly, in working with a secondary retail bank, the key strength identified by banking executives was 'relationship banking', that is, the availability of skilled, professionally qualified branch managers to meet and deal personally with customers. This may be true for affluent, high-income customers, but in fact, in the market segments providing critical niches for this company (mainly lower-income consumers and heavy credit users), it was found that the *last* thing such customers normally wanted was frequent meetings with the bank manager. In some ways the bank's most critical problem was actually to keep the branch managers *away* from the customers!

One problem which regularly emerges is that executives claim that the same thing can be listed as a strength and a weakness. This is not true; it simply means that we have not gone far enough in our analysis. What we need to do here is to ask the question: which aspects of these characteristics are strengths and which are weaknesses? For instance, a common 'motherhood' statement is that 'we are an old established firm'. Indeed, that quality may produce certain strengths (providing stability in supply, being trustworthy, being highly experienced), as well as certain weaknesses (being inflexible, being old-fashioned, lacking in innovation). However, it is the strengths and weaknesses that matter, not the overall characteristic. People often say things like 'we are a large supplier', which is our greatest strength and our greatest weakness. In fact, the strengths may be things like comprehensive product range and technical expertise, or high stability that reassures the customer, while the weaknesses may be things like being bureaucratic and slow, being off-hand with customers, and being poor at sustaining personal contacts. Again, it is not being big which matters, but what that means to different customers in terms of what they get from us compared to the alternatives.

Environmental Analysis

The same discipline is required to view the Opportunities and Threats in the environment relevant to our point of focus—the specific market, customer, issue, etc. This turns our attention to the lower half of the model in Figure 3.4. Here the goal is to list those things in the relevant environment which make it attractive or unattractive to us, and our search for ideas should be as thorough and widely informed as possible. The major difficulty here is that executives tend to jump the gun and put their strategies and tactics down as Opportunities in a kind of self-fulfilling prophesy.

The way out of this trap is the insistence that Opportunities and Threats exist *only* in the outside world—the things we propose to do about them are our *strategies*. For example, it may be suggested that price-cutting is an Opportunity. This is *not* an Opportunity in a SWOT analysis—it is a price tactic which we might adopt. We would *only* accept the desirability of price-cutting if, for example, our size gave us greater cost economies than our competitors, and there was an identified, external market Opportunity in terms of there being a price-sensitive segment of the market, or the need to meet a competitor's threatened entry to the market with low prices. The rule is that Opportunities exist independently of our policies and actions—the actions we plan are our tactics and strategies.

Structured Strategy Testing and Generation

When we are able to complete all four cells of the SWOT matrix, and we have ranked each item in each category in terms of importance, then the matrix acts automatically as a generator and tester of strategies, as shown in Figure 3.4: *matching strategies*—our central focus is on matching our strengths to opportunities in the outside world, following the logic that strengths which do not match any known opportunity are of little immediate value (however proud of them we may be), while highly ranked opportunities for which we have no strengths are food for further thought; *conversion strategies*—more difficult is the design of appropriate responses to highly ranked weaknesses and threats. Here the goal is ideally to convert these factors into strengths and opportunities. In some cases this may be relatively straightforward—a weakness in sales coverage may mean adding to the salesforce, a threat from a competitor may be bought-off by collaboration or merger or neutralized by an advertising campaign, but in other cases we may be unable to think sensibly about converting or neutralizing these factors. In the latter case these factors remain the limiting problems in this business and determine how attractive it is to us; *creative strategies*—finally, we have to recognize that going through this analytical process often simply generates new, creative ideas for how to develop the business. Good ideas should never be discarded simply because they are unusual. Whatever recording we are doing, we should have a box especially for creative ideas that may not fit elsewhere in the model.

These guidelines are incredibly simple to apply, but the disciplines imposed are very severe. Used in this way, SWOT analysis gives us a mechanism for putting our knowledge about the customer marketplace and competitive change directly into the strategy building process. We can replace vague generalizations about customers and competitors with specific insights in a way which forces internally oriented executives and planners to address the implications of this reality. This is a potential powerful tool in getting the strategic sales organization heard in the strategy debate.

Although these are very simple tools, they provide a practical framework for leveraging the market learning and sensing capabilities—or market intelligence capabilities—of the strategic sales organization to impact and enrich the strategy decision-making process. They provide a way forward for the strategic sales initiative.

However, importantly there is another side to the intelligence issue as well—its impact on customer relationships and the ability of the seller to add value for the customer.

Changing the Focus

Superior intelligence resources are also closely related to competitiveness as well as to better strategy-building. For example, one clear and repeated demand by corporate buyers is that suppliers should demonstrate deep knowledge of the customer's business, such that they can identify needs and opportunities before the buyer does.[15] Customers are increasingly unwilling to spend time talking to suppliers who do not understand the business, and very grumpy about sellers who see it as the customer's job to educate the seller's salespeople.

In the buyer's eyes, the deployment of superior knowledge and expertise has become a defining characteristic of the world class sales organization. The buyer logic is straightforward: if the seller cannot bring added-value to the relationship by identifying new opportunities for the buyer to gain competitive advantage in the end-use marketplace, then the seller is no more than a commodity supplier, and can be treated as such (the product is likely to be bought only on price and technical specification).

This underlines the need for a revolutionary change in focus in the way sales organizations interact with major customers. Consider the transition shown in the simple value chain in Figure 3.5. The traditional sales focus was primarily on the manufacturer's need to convert product and service into cash flow. That was what you got

[15] H. R. Chally, *The Chally World Class Sales Excellence Research Report*, Dayton, OH: The H. R. Chally Group, 2006.

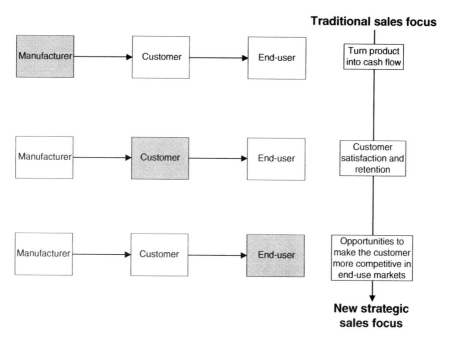

Fig. 3.5 Changing focus in strategic sales

paid for. Metrics were about sales volume and selling costs. When marketing arrived in the scene the focus shifted from seller need (for cash flow) to buyer needs (and metrics incorporated things like customer satisfaction, share of wallet, and customer retention). We coped—not least because lot of customer satisfaction was actually down to supply chain efficiencies anyway, however excited everyone got about being more 'market oriented' and all the rest of that marketing stuff.

This is not where we find ourselves now. In the overwhelming number of situations faced by sellers now, major customers demand that the seller displays not simply a superior understanding of the customer's own organization but detailed and insightful knowledge of the customer's end-use markets and the customer's strategies. If you cannot offer the customer ways of becoming more efficient and more competitive in the end-use market, you are a commodity at best, and possibly as far as the customer is concerned, you are a waste of space. The strategic sales role is becoming one of deploying end-use market knowledge to enhance the customer's competitive position and cost efficiency.

Even in the consumer goods sector, retailers continue to report that their suppliers perform inadequately in the key areas which help differentiate them (the retailers) to the consumer, such as consumer insight development. Major retailers emphasize that trade relationships are no longer based on buyer–seller roles, and characterize the best-in-class supplier as one that has a firm understanding of the retailer's position, strategy, and ambitions in the marketplace—they require consumer market insight from their suppliers.[16]

Successful business models like those at companies as diverse as Dell Inc. in computers, Johnsons Controls in automotive controls, and Kraft in groceries display this type of end-use market perspective in their strategic sales relationships. Dell does not talk to Boeing about personal computers—they are boring and trivial to people selling aircraft—the conversation is about Boeing's changing needs for different types of information processing capabilities as the aircraft business develops. Johnson Controls did not win the Ford F Series truck business by talking to Ford about their car seats and electric switches—Ford knows more about that stuff than anyone else anyway. Their conversation was about the truck driver and his or her use of the vehicle, and how Johnson Controls products could enhance the driver experience and give Ford a competitive edge. Kraft does not talk to retailers like Krogers and Safeway about their biscuits. The conversation is about how Kraft can leverage its market knowledge to enhance the value of the retailer's snack category store-by-store, based on its extensive market information on consumer characteristics. That is how you dominate the biscuit business with very, very ordinary biscuits.

Customers evaluate their suppliers on the seller's success in enhancing the customer's competitive position, and increasingly expect proof of this achievement. The challenge to suppliers from an increasing proportion of their customers is to understand the customer's business and the customer's end-use markets and to leverage that knowledge to create competitive advantage for the customer. The alternative is

---

[16] *The Strategic Agenda for Customer Management in the Consumer Products Industry,* New York: IBM Institute for Business Value Executive Brief, 2005.

to face growing commoditization and declining margins. Meeting this challenge is a central element of strategic sales choices. The corresponding challenge for the strategic sales organization is to develop, deploy, and sustain new skills and capabilities in market sensing.

The Search Is for Big Ideas

Intelligence is an urgent issue for many of us. We are in an era when big ideas change markets and revolutionize industries. Big ideas have more impact than hot metal in creating new opportunities. Big ideas will change business models, redefine customer relationships, and create new ways of competing better. Most 'big ideas' will come from outside the company. They will come from relationships with collaborators, customers, and others. They will come from the external world of market relationships, which is the domain of the strategic sales organization.

At the heart of radical innovation is the search for 'big ideas', rather than settling for 'small ideas'. To stay relevant and to succeed, companies need bold innovative strategies. But this relies on the ability to create and resource 'big ideas', and to overcome inertia, narrow-mindedness, and risk aversion that provide barriers to true innovation—'big think strategy'.[17]

For example, 2007 saw the launch of the iPhone by Apple—the cutest mobile phone in the world, albeit based on out-of-date technology—with mixed sales results. On the face of things, hardly a 'big idea'—you might ask whether the world actually needs another mobile phone, but it is an obvious extension of the iPod and iTunes music business, and there is the prospect of competing against the Blackberry in the business market. In fact, as the underlying iPhone strategy unfolds, it starts to look like a very big idea indeed. By allowing software manufacturers to create programs custom-built for the iPhone—freed by the iPhone's breakthrough touch screen from the constraints of fixed buttons and small screens—the goal is to allow the iPhone to develop into the 'third great platform' for software makers,

[17] Schmitt, Bernd H., *Big Think Strategy: How to Leverage Bold Ideas and Leave Small Thinking Behind*, Boston, MA: Harvard Business School Press, 2007.

after the personal computer and the Internet. It may not work, but it is certainly a 'big idea'.[18]

A single big idea can change everything. Federal Express is a $31 billion logistics giant. When Fred Smith founded the business 36 years ago, it was based on a single revolutionary concept. Traditional parcel deliveries were made point-to-point—because it was just common sense to do it this way. Smith's concept was the 'hub and spoke' idea like a bicycle wheel, that he first articulated in a piece of college homework. He proved mathematically that the fastest, cheapest way of delivering parcels was to fly them from the points at the end of each spoke to a central hub where they could be sorted, and put on different aircraft and transported with others sharing similar destinations. Instead of (say) 9,900 couriers connecting 100 points, you have 99 connected to 1 central point—more efficient by a factor of 100. All the rest of the global FedEx business stems from the power of that single idea.[19]

Increasingly, competitive strength lies in new ideas not simply new products and routes to market. Imitating competitors' strategies is unlikely to develop the radical new ideas that can change industries. Leadership may be about more than simply market share (by definition just a benchmark of our sales compared to competitors in the existing market). It may be about new types of market power other than that achieved by size and volume.

One of the most influential places to look for big ideas is the marketplace populated by customers, competitors, collaborators, and intermediaries. An emphasis on the strategic role of market intelligence is central to the emergence of the truly strategic sales organization.

Building the New Agenda

Part of the expanding role of the strategic sales organization in developing business strategy is based on the potential for leveraging

---

[18] Allison, Kevin, 'Apple Unveils iPhone Grand Plan', *Financial Times*, 10 March 2008, p. 23.
[19] Baer, Justin and Francesco Guerra, 'The Man Who Reinvented the Wheel', *Financial Times*, 2 December 2007, p. 18.

superior market intelligence to drive both management insight and market understanding, and also as a route to meeting major customer demands for added-value based on market knowledge.

However, actually delivering that added-value to customers and keeping ahead of the competition is likely to involve getting a handle on the organizational factors and processes that impact on customer value. We turn our attention next to the priorities for integration and internal marketing by the strategic sales organization.

4

Integration: Getting Your Act Together Around Customer Value

It is pretty clear that just about everywhere you go turbulent and demanding markets are creating new types of challenges for managers in supplier organizations. So far, so obvious. As we have already seen, powerful customers increasingly demand that sellers provide problem-solving and creative thinking about their business. They require the commitment of, and access to, the supplier's total operation. Indeed, one European executive recently described this as 'the convergence of strategic management, change management and process management, all critical elements of transforming the sales function to meet today's customer requirements'.[1] This pretty much identifies the challenge of integration around customer value.

However, it is also clear that where suppliers have developed programmes of value creation around major customers, they have been plagued by problems of 'organizational drag'—often the seller's organizational functions are not aligned around processes of creating and

---

[1] Seidenschwartz, W., 'A Model for Customer Enthusiasm: Connecting the Customer With Internal Processes', Presentation at Strategic Account Management Association Conference, February, Paris, 2005.

delivering customer value.[2] Major retailers across the world emphasize supplier organizational structure and culture as key obstacles to
improving customer management effectiveness.[3]

The trouble is that it appears that traditional 'command and control'
company organizations seem to have been established and designed
precisely to prevent us from integrating and coordinating things
around the customer. Rigid, hierarchical organizations do not permit
the merging of systems, activities, people, or anything much else.
People and what they do have been put in boxes, and the boxes have
been put in divisions, and lines have been drawn between them—
those lines have become a straitjacket preventing movement, change,
or integration, and resisting the challenges of those who try to achieve
these things.

Success in the new marketplace increasingly demands the careful
and systematic integration of a company's entire set of capabilities
into a seamless system that delivers superior customer value—what
we have called elsewhere 'total integrated marketing'.[4] Our logic is
based on the observation that superior performing companies seem
to share one simple yet vital characteristic: they get their act together
around the things that matter most to their customers, and they make a
totally integrated offer of superior value in customer terms. The model
in Figure 4.1 provides a framework for concentrating management
attention on the actual and potential contributions of functional units
and departments on delivering superior value to customers, and consequently how to improve the integration of these activities.

Integration Around Customer Value Processes

The logic of the Figure 4.1 model is that however they are organized,
companies have essentially three sets of processes: those to identify

[2] Koerner, LaVan, 'Conducting an Organizational Assessment of Your SAM Programme', Presentation at Strategic Account Management Association Conference,
Paris, 2005.

[3] *The Strategic Agenda for Customer Management in the Consumer Products Industry*,
New York: IBM Institute for Business Value Executive Brief, 2005.

[4] Hulbert, James Mac, Noel Capon, and Nigel F. Piercy, *Total Integrated Marketing:
Breaking the Bounds of the Function*, New York: The Free Press, 2003; London: Kogan
Page, 2005.

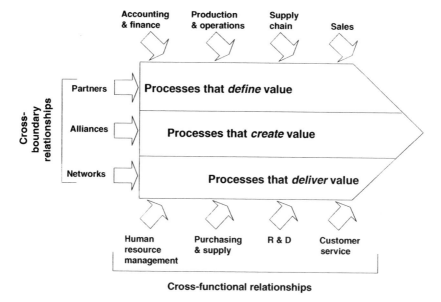

Fig. 4.1 Integration around value processes

and define customer value, those that create a value offering, and those that deliver value to the customer.[5] Figure 4.1 shows these processes of value definition, creation, and delivery as making up the horizontal process of going to market and the creation of customer value.

In fact, although this type of approach is increasingly influential in designing market-led organizations,[6] it is unlikely that the processes will be labeled in this generic way. For example, processes to define value may be named Customer Relationship Management or Marketing Information Systems, processes to create value may be called New Product Development or Brand Development, while processes that deliver value may be recognized as Distribution Management or Customer Service. The specific organizational labels matter less than

[5] Webster, Frederick E., 'The Future Role of Marketing in the Organization', in Donald R. Lehmann and Katherine E. Jocz (eds.), *Reflections on the Futures of Marketing*, Cambridge, MA: Marketing Science Institute, 1997, pp. 39–66.

[6] For a full discussion of the importance of the market-led organization, see: Cravens, David W. and Nigel F. Piercy, *Strategic Marketing*, 9th ed., McGraw Hill/Irwin, 2009, Chapter 14.

the recognition of the need to provide leadership and coordination for the organizational activities that impact on the value received by customers. The important point is that value processes become the focus of our resources (people, technology, funds), our capabilities (skills, competencies, and abilities), and strategic relationships (partnerships, collaborations, cross-functional integration). The creation and delivery of superior customer value becomes the arena in which we deploy creativity, innovation, and sometimes the reinvention of the model of how we do business.

However, what the model also underlines is that integration depends on a whole range of specialist inputs from different functions and from external partner organizations—members of alliances and networks of collaborators. There are two sets of relationships impacting on integration: cross-functional relationships with other departments and cross-boundary relationships with partners.

It is likely that one of the most critical roles of the strategic sales organization will be in managing processes of customer value definition, development, and delivery that cut across functional interfaces and organizational boundaries to build real customer focus. Many of the barriers to developing and delivering superior customer value come from the characteristics of supplier organizations. The challenge of strategic customer management mandates effective approaches to cross-functional integration around value processes. Rather than managing only the interface with the customer, the strategic salesforce must cope with a range of interfaces with internal functions and departments, and increasingly partner organizations, to deliver value seamlessly to customers.

For example, when Sam Palmisano took over as CEO at IBM, he conducted a painful overhaul of the 38,000 person salesforce.[7] In the 1990s salespeople representing the various IBM business units were essentially on their own—looking for good opportunities to sell individual products or services. Palmisano has 'reintegrated' IBM in front of customers by bringing together specialists from computers, software, consulting, and even research into teams that meet with customers to help solve their business problems and develop new business strategies.

---

[7] This illustration is based on: Hamm, Steve, 'Beyond Blue', *BusinessWeek*, 18 April 2005, pp. 36–42. Hamm, Steve, 'Big Blue Goes for the Big Win', *BusinessWeek*, 10 March 2008, pp. 63–5.

People who do not work well with others get replaced. Collaborating with customers, suppliers, and even rivals is part of his plan to invent new technologies to create new markets.

However, notwithstanding management claims to the contrary, it looks like un-integration is more common than integration in many companies as they face up to the demands of getting their act together around customer value. We start by looking at some of the consequences of un-integration. Then we look at a total integrated marketing approach and the issues involved in managing cross-functional, interfaces for integration. Our thinking also has to incorporate the challenges of cross-boundary relationships.

The Consequences of Un-integration

Un-integration is where functions, divisions, and business units ignore the impact of their strategies and actions on others. It leads to bad results and sometimes major problems which can become business disasters. Functional specialisms, complex corporate divisionalization, and multi-leveled bureaucracies have often been at the centre of problems in delivering consistent, superior value to customers. Often un-integration is simply because internal functions have different goals and performance metrics, and sometimes it is just silly. Some examples are illustrative of some of the silliness resulting from un-integration.

Sales and Supply Chain Management

In one company, the Sales Director found that his major customer was ordering a product sporadically, as and when stock control indicated the need to re-order. He realized that if the customer could be persuaded to adopt continuous replenishment, he could substantially reduce the stock he needed to cover the sporadic orders. This is an increasingly common situation in repeat purchase situations and the customer was happy to cooperate. Two days into the new continuous replenishment system, the very unhappy customer phoned to say he was almost out-of-stock of product and on the point of taking his business elsewhere. The Sales Director raced to the distribution depot to find out what had happened. The answer was simple—the distribution system prioritized large orders. The smallest orders were lowest priority and often not picked by the end of the day. By definition, continuous replenishment produces the smallest orders ...

Sales and Operations

In a leading clothing company, the sales manager was told to increase sales targets for salespeople and not to worry about production capacity, which was none of his concern. Urged on by his sales manager, a salesperson pulled off a major deal with a national retailer. The factory cannot deliver. The customer is furious. The salesperson is demotivated. The sales manager is tearing his hair out ...

Sales and the Accounts Department

Many salespeople report that one of the most negative impacts on customer relationships can come from the Accounts Department. The internal employees in accounts who operate credit control, invoicing, and payments, and handle account queries can inadvertently undo large investments of salesforce resource spent in building a customer relationship and winning an order, simply because no one has ever provided them with any information about the company's sales strategy or customer preferences.

Sales and Human Resource Management

The quality and skills of the people who deliver service and manage relationships with customers directly reflect HR strategy—which determines how they are selected, trained, evaluated, and rewarded. If HR managers are not party to marketing and sales strategy, how can they recruit and train people appropriately to implement the strategy? Yet, in many companies this appears to be what HR specialists are expected to do. It is hardly surprising that they work with out-of-date person profiles and skills requirements.[8]

[8] Adapted from: Lane, Nikala and Nigel Piercy, 'Strategic Customer Management: Designing a Profitable Future for Your Sales Organization', *European Management Journal*, Vol. 22 No. 6 2004, pp. 659–68.

Sales and Marketing

Failing to link sales operations with marketing campaigns has led to many famous debacles—the stockouts caused by aggressive sales campaigns that were never mentioned when sales forecasts were done. In the music industry, EMI, for many years, put huge pressure on salespeople to get as many music CDs into retail stores as possible— which resulted in around 35 million discarded CDs each year. Under new management, EMI has centralized sales, marketing, and administration, in part to improve coordination and integration.[9]

The consequences of weak integration can be massive. In the late-1990s aircraft manufacturer Boeing tried to expand production of planes so quickly that suppliers were unable to make parts rapidly enough. Unfinished planes stacked up in factories, forcing managers to close production for a month to allow the over-strained supply chain to catch up. The result was a rare year-end loss and $2.6 billion in charges against earnings over two years for Boeing. Underpinning the crisis was the fact that the salesforce had struck deals to sell hundreds of aircraft at fire-sale prices because financial executives had not shared information about how much it cost to make one, and sales targets were related to volume. Salespeople did deals on an implied assumption that the factories had infinite capacity to make planes, because no one had communicated with them about production capacity. Now Boeing has a high-level management group that must approve major aircraft orders. This group includes engineers and accountants and makes sure factories can deliver work on the promised timetable and that suppliers can deliver parts on time. Nonetheless, in 2008 Boeing's innovative 787 aircraft— the Dreamliner—was the fastest selling new airliner in history, but slow off the assembly line and plagued with supply chain delays. The cost of selling more aircraft than you can make is huge penalty payments to disgruntled airline customers.[10]

[9] Arnold, Martin, Andrew Edgecliffe-Johnson, 'EMI Chief Confident of Ability to Call a New Tune', *Financial Times*, 14 January 2008, p. 19.

[10] This illustration is based on: Lunsford, J. Lynn, 'Gradual Ascent: Burned by Last Boom, Boeing Curbs Its Pace; It Uses New Restraint to Juggle Jet Orders; Avoiding "Bunny Holes"', *Wall Street Journal*, 26 March 2007, p. A.1. Lunsford, J. Lynn, and Daniel Michaels, 'More Delays Likely for Boeing's Dreamliner', *Wall Street Journal*, 16 January 2008, p. 3.

Actually, to look on the bright side, sometimes, customers are more than happy for suppliers to show signs of un-integration. One Marketing Director recently explained to us why he wanted to kill his Sales Manager. The company had imported 20,000 DVD players from the Far East for £15 a machine. The plan was to sell these to small stores and chains with a wholesale price of £25, and a recommended retail price of £50, offering good margins to the supplier and the trade. So far, so good. However, Mr. Numpty the Sales Manager was delighted to report that he had been able to sell 10,000 players in a single deal to one of UK's largest supermarket chains—let us call them BigCo—for £17.50 a player, allowing the supermarket to sell them for £20. He was pleased with himself. He became less pleased when the Marketing Director pointed out that the remaining 10,000 machines were unsaleable, to anyone other than BigCo. Why would any independent retailer buy the machines for a wholesale price of £25, when BigCo was retailing them for £20? The Marketing Director says the worst of it was knowing that someone at BigCo was grinning and saying 'do you think they have had that conversation yet—shall we make the call?' Sure enough, when the call came, BigCo offered £10 a player for the remaining 10,000 machines. He had to accept—losing £25,000 on the overall deal. That is why he wants to kill Mr. Numpty his Sales Manager. Not getting your act together may be expensive, even if sometimes smart customers rather like it.

If un-integration costs us money and leads to poor performance with the customer, then it follows that we need something better.

The Pursuit of Total Integrated Marketing[11]

Powerful customers and innovations in how we go to market have a clear implication: we have to focus on integrating and coordinating everything in the company that goes towards identifying, meeting, and delivering the customer's value requirements: total integrated marketing.

---

[11] This section is based on: Hulbert, James Mac, Noel Capon, and Nigel F. Piercy, *Total Integrated Marketing: Breaking the Bounds of the Function*, New York: The Free Press, 2003; London: Kogan Page, 2005.

The Overwhelming Priority of Integration

There is not much new in suggesting that getting the real job done, that is, delivering superior value to customers—requires working with other functions better and more effectively. The trouble is the fact that people have to keep saying it, kind of suggests we may not be too good at doing it. What all this suggests is that integration is actually now one of the main challenges in strategic sales.

Companies have generally not been very good at managing across functional or organizational boundaries. Clearly working across functions suggests the potential for *conflict* (which needs to be managed) but also the prospect of shared interests and *partnership* (which should be exploited). Exact priorities for inter-functional partnerships will depend on the situation faced and the strategy in question, but examples of critical cross-functional relationships for the strategic sales organization include *finance/accounting*—viewing customers as assets with impact on shareholder value provides a basis for avoiding traditional conflicts in resource allocation, and lining internal systems up with customer value imperatives (see discussion of the customer portfolio); *operations*—the challenge is matching internal capabilities in operations and supply chain management, for example, in speed, flexibility, quality management, operational systems—with market opportunities; *marketing*—in many situations the salesforce represents the ability of the company to implement marketing strategy, which is constrained by lack of 'buy-in', and traditional sales management practices which do not support strategic change (more about this later in the chapter); *R&D*—the challenge is building structures to link innovation and research capabilities with market opportunities; *customer service*—customer service operations may represent the most important point of contact between a customer and the company and impact directly on customer perceptions of value, mandating alignment with strategic initiatives; and *human resource management*—the key issue may be building competitive advantage through the quality of the people in the company, with major implications for aligning processes of recruitment, selection, training, development, evaluation, and reward with business strategy requirements.

Many successful companies display the characteristics of cross-functional effectiveness. In fact, this capability may be one of the key attributes of the market-led company of the future.

Achieving Totally Integrated Marketing

There is no perfect solution that fits all situations to achieve better integration across functions. Some perspectives on achieving total integration are considered briefly below.

Customer-centric Perspective

A real customer focus is about aligning everyone on the organization around the same customer commitment and market focus—everyone from the CEO to the telephone salesperson. This is about achieving a customer-centric philosophy for the whole company to be embraced by everyone, and needs the support of knowledge management, relationship management, and supply chain management. Put another way, if everyone knows what the brand stands for, it helps determine investment and new product priorities, the choice of business partners, distribution strategies, the risks worth taking, the areas to 'lean', and so on. If that is the ideal, then the issue remains—what are the tools we can use to get there?

Leadership and Vision

For a totally integrated marketing effort to be effective, then the core strategy of the organization needs to be the driver of all the functional activities that affect the customer. Increasingly, customers will accept nothing less than totally integrated marketing (about which they could care less) to deliver them superior value (about which they care quite a lot). This may turn out to be a defining characteristic of effective company leadership (see Chapter 7 for more thoughts on leadership and the strategic sales organization).

Communicating Out of the Silo

A start is to look at how well, how regularly, and how effectively we have built channels of communication between the front-end of the business (sales, marketing, customer service) and the rest of the company. The paradox is that executives who pride themselves on skills and expertise in communicating with customers often seem unable to flex those same skills and expertise inside the company.

Collaborative Relationships Inside the Company

Integration based on building collaborative relationships is mainly about informal processes, based on trust, mutual respect, and information sharing, the joint ownership of decisions and collective responsibility for outcomes.[12] Some people suggest that what we really need to do is to build alliances and use the same skills inside the organization in partnering, as we have tried to do outside the organization in inter-company and supply chain alliances.

Formal Mechanisms for Integration

A lot has been written about formal mechanisms for integration, although the evidence of what works in different situations is mixed.[13] The types of mechanisms for achieving integration include the following: *relocation and design of facilities*—mainly concerned with using spatial proximity to encourage communication and exchange of information between people and to reduce conflicts; *personnel movement*—including joint training programmes with other functions, job rotation, and so on, with a goal of helping people understand and allow for the language, goals, perspectives, problems, and priorities of other functions; *rewards*—some suggest changing reward systems to pay people for achieving higher level goals not just functional objectives to provide managers with incentives to interact more with other functions and bring their goals into line; *formalization of procedures*—others take the approach that centralized control over procedures and systems is the route to achieving better integration across functions—for example, project investment proposal documentation that requires coordinated input from marketing, finance, operations, and IT is one way to encourage working together around a common goal; *social orientation*—yet others suggest that part of the problem may be solved by providing people in the organization to interact in a social, non-work-related setting, as a way to let them understand each other better

[12] Ellinger, Alexander E., 'Improving Marketing/Logistics Cross-Functional Collaboration in the Supply Chain', *Industrial Marketing Management*, Vol. 29 2000, pp. 85–96.
[13] Maltz, Elliot and Ajay K. Kohli, 'Reducing Marketing's Conflict With Other Functions: the Differential Effects of Integrating Mechanisms', *Journal of the Academy of Marketing Science*, (Fall) 2000, pp. 479–92.

and want to avoid conflicts; *project budgeting*—another approach is
to centralize control over financial resources so that they are chan-
nelled to the project and its team, not to functional departmental
managers.

Cross-functional Teams

One established and possibly overused tool is the use of teams drawing members from diverse functions and levels in the company. The
main idea is to pool the talent needed to solve a problem or manage a
project all the way through—focusing on the goals of the organization
not the department or function—but the subsidiary benefits are reducing barriers between functions and the team members acting as 'trans-
lators' and mediators in interfunctional relationships on a longer-term
basis. An extreme example is Toyota, where teams of designers, engineers, product planners, workers, and suppliers are required to work
face-to-face, in the process Toyota calls *obeya*—literally 'big room'.
This dramatically cuts the time it takes to get from drawing board to
showroom. It took only 19 months to develop the 2003 Solara—well
below the industry average of about 3 years.[14]

   Some companies even include suppliers, distributors, and customers in this type of team, to achieve integration across the organization's boundaries, as well as between functions inside the organization. The danger, of course, is that teams become a battleground for
turf control, power plays, and budget fights.

Organization Structure

Some major approaches to improving cross-functional integration
bring us back to the issue of structure—and the management dic-
tum 'if all else fails, let's reorganize'. Noel Capon and Mac Hulbert
describe some of these approaches as follows: *inclusion organizations*—sharing marketing responsibilities rather than putting them
in a department; *business process organizations*—one outcome of the
re-engineering movement has been the attempt to organize around
business processes by some companies, so the company retains functional structures but much of the work is done by cross-functional

<hr>

[14] Kerwin, Kathleen, Christopher Palmeri, and Paul Magnusson, 'Can Anything
Stop Toyota?', *BusinessWeek*, 17 November 2003, pp. 62–70.

process-based teams; *customer management organizations*—although it is a mixture of structural change and information technology, the current trend towards Customer Relationship Management systems is a form of this approach to integration. The problem with approaching the integration issue through structural change alone is that we may achieve no more than conformity, not genuine commitment across the company, and people will just keep their heads down until the latest management fad has run its course.[15]

Internal Marketing

One of the key tasks in the future may be internal marketing— marketing the customer, the strategy, and the marketing process to all parts of the organization. Increasingly, this responsibility may extend to developing and sustaining relationships with alliance partners and other organizations in the network, because they also impact on the value that we deliver to the customer. We will develop a practical framework for internal marketing strategy later (see Chapter 5).

Process Focus

Many organizations are moving away from reliance on functional organizations—departments staffed by 'specialists'—to reorganize around processes, such as innovation, customer support, and so on. In part, this reflects the weaknesses of functional organizations, and also the need to respond faster and more effectively to change—this demands that we work 'in parallel' not 'in sequence'. Strategic sales and marketing may have a number of specific skills to bring to the process party—identifying innovation opportunities; brand building capabilities; and experience in building networks and partnerships that can work together to deliver superior value.

A key characteristic of new types of organization is an emphasis on managing organizational process, rather than an emphasis on structure.[16] The logic is that traditional, vertical organizational hierarchies have been the norm in the past and led to functional

---

[15] Capon, Noel and James M. Hulbert, *Marketing Management in the 21st Century*, New Jersey: Prentice-Hall, 2000.

[16] Day, George S., 'Aligning the Organization to the Market', in *Reflections on the Futures of Marketing*, Donald R. Lehman and Katherine E. Jocz (eds.), Cambridge, MA: Marketing Science Institute, 1997, pp. 69–72.

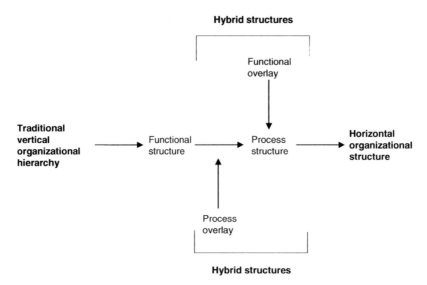

Fig. 4.2 Changing organizational imperatives, (adapted from Day 1997)

organizational structures. However, numerous pressures are pushing towards an emphasis on process-based structures leading in time to the completely horizontal organizational structure. However, in this progression hybrid structures are likely: overlaying processes onto functional organizations and later building a functional overlay to complement a process-based structure.[17] At the time of this research, a study of 73 companies by the Boston Consulting Group placed 32 per cent in the hierarchy, 38 per cent in the process overlay, and 30 per cent in the functional overlay form. No horizontal structures were reported. The prevailing organizational forms appear to be the hybrid overlay structures.

As suggested in Figure 4.2, the structures of large established companies are moving toward horizontal business processes while retaining integrating functions (planning, human resources) and specialist functions (research and development, operations). The processes are major clusters of strategically important activities such as new product development, order generation and fulfillment, and value/supply chain management. As companies adopt process structures, various

---

[17] Day, 1997, op cit.

organizational changes occur including fewer levels and fewer managers, greater emphasis on building distinctive capabilities using multifunctional teams, customer value-driven processes and capabilities, and continuously changing organizations that reflect market and competitive environment changes.[18] (See Chapter 1, pp. 20–1, for our review of the Proctor & Gamble and Kraft approaches to process focus.)

Our description of value processes in Figure 4.1 provides a working model for examining the move from functional specializations (sales, marketing, operations, and so on) to a process focus (value definition, value creation, and value delivery). This approach is probably the best hope we have of building the seamless value being demanded by customers.

However, getting the act together inside the company is only part of the challenge. Managing relationships with partners outside the company is also a high priority for many of us.

Working Across Organizational Boundaries

C. K. Prahalad and M. S. Krishnan[19] have recently described the fundamental transformation of business taking place in industry after industry. In their view, the transformation is being driven by two factors. First, the age of mass production is over and customers demand unique value: 'value is shifting from products to solutions and experiences', and relationships are taking over as the central element of exchange. Second, no single business is likely to be big enough to cope with complex and diverse customer demands. In turn this underlines the importance of alliances and networks to deliver customer value— constellations of suppliers that can be configured in different ways to meet different customer needs. Succeeding will involve giving us flexible business models and managing through new collaborative networks.

---

[18] Day, 1997, op cit.
[19] Prahalad, C. K. and M. S. Krishnan, *The New Age of Innovation: Driving Co-Created Value Through Global Networks*, New York: McGraw-Hill Professional, 2008.

For example, already more than a third of Proctor & Gamble's new products come from external alliances. Similarly, IBM has transformed into a borderless organization working globally with partners to enhance the value of offerings to customers on a worldwide basis. IBM is a highly internationalized business. It has over 50,000 employees in India—IBM's second biggest operation outside the United States. The company has moved its head of procurement from New York to Shenzen in China.[20]

IBM's Chairman and CEO, Samuel Palmisano, has defined a vision for the globally integrated enterprise (GIE), as the twenty-first century successor to the multinational corporation. Palmisano argues that businesses are changing in fundamental ways—structurally, operationally, and culturally—in response to imperatives for globalization and the impact of new technology. The emerging GIE is a company that shapes its strategy, management, and operations in pursuit of a new goal: the integration of production and value delivery worldwide. Shared business practices and connected business activities make it possible for companies to transfer work from in-house operations to outside specialists. Global integration forces companies to choose where they want work performed geographically, and whether they want it performed in-house or by an external partner. The centre of the GIE is global collaboration both with commercial partners and with governments.

Similarly, John Hagel and John Seely-Brown argue that lowered barriers to international trade and technological developments suggest companies must concentrate their areas of expertise, while collaborating globally with others specializing in different activities. The goal is to find ways of working with suppliers not simply to cut costs but to collaborate on product innovation. Li & Fung is a Hong Kong-based clothing supplier that Hagel and Seely-Brown describe as a 'process orchestrator'. The company produces goods for Western companies drawing on a network of 7,500 partners—yarn from Korea, dyed in Thailand, woven in Taiwan, cut in Bangladesh, assembled in Mexico, with a zipper from Japan. Importantly, these companies are partners to Li & Fung rather than simply suppliers. By operating as

---

[20] This illustration is based on: 'Globalization's Offspring', *Economist.com* 4 April 2007. Samuel J. Palmisamo, 'The Globally Integrated Enterprise', *Foreign Affairs*, Vol. 85 No. 3, pp. 127–38.

a network, the partners help each other innovate in both design and manufacture.[21]

Working with partners to create enhanced customer value creates a need for flexible yet effective integration of inputs to deliver seamless value to customers. While building effective customer relationships has always depended on understanding and predicting customer needs, the additional role is to work with a set of providers of different parts of the value offering—some internal and some external to the company—to construct and deliver a coherent value offering to the customer.

Nonetheless, the problems of working with external partners means that this is not always the best route to customer superior value. Rolls-Royce runs a global service network providing a real-time support and maintenance service to airlines operating planes with Rolls-Royce engines—there are more than 50,000 Rolls-Royce engines flying and the support extends decades after the original purchase. As recently as the late-1980s conventional wisdom was for aero-engine makers to licence out much support and maintenance and their aftermarket business was restricted to spare parts and distress repairs. To align the interests of airlines with its own, Rolls-Royce now runs its own operations centres, in a move which has revolutionalized the industry. By 2008, support and maintenance was generating 55 per cent of Rolls Royce revenues.[22] Partnership strategies should not be a knee-jerk reaction to all complex customer and market situations.

Similarly, many European producers are moving outsourced production back closer to home because of disappointing results in working with overseas partners in emerging markets. Managing across organizational and national boundaries is frequently not straightforward.[23]

However, in many market situations it is clear that complex networks of partnerships will be the way in which business is done.

---

[21] John Hagel III and John Seely-Brown, *The Only Sustainable Edge: Why Business Strategy Depends on Productive Friction and Dynamic Specialization*, Boston, MA: Harvard Business School Press, 2005.

[22] This illustration is based on: Pfeifer, Sylvia, 'Rolls Royce Reaps the Rewards of Client Care', *Financial Times*, 2 June 2008, p. 22.

[23] Milne, Richard, 'Homesick Producers Lose Taste for Going Overseas', *Financial Times*, 5 June 2008, p. 24.

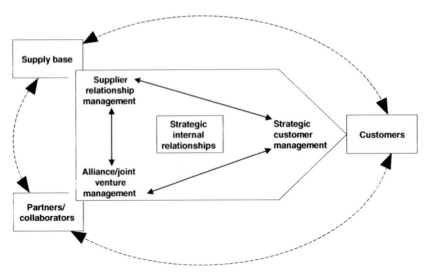

Fig. 4.3 Strategic internal relationships

The transition to working across traditional organizational boundaries identifies a new and possibly complex integration challenge.
Responding effectively to that challenge is, in part, a strategic sales
responsibility.

It is likely that the strategic internal relationships which will be
vital to achieving effective integration in networked companies will
be between the organizational units and processes that manage key
external relationships, in the way suggested in Figure 4.3. As customer
demands for more complex value offerings grow, the ability to work
collaboratively to create solutions will emphasize the need for close
coordination between suppliers, partners, and sellers. The management of that coordination will require the effective management of
relationships between those responsible for strategic customer management, those who manage relationships with suppliers, and those
who are tasked with the management of alliance and joint venture
relationships with external organizations. In many companies these
strategic internal relationships may be the core of the value creating
processes described in Figure 4.1. These strategic internal relationships
will often have to cope with complex markets where there are also
links between our suppliers and our partners and between them and
our customers.

The Particular Problems of Integrating Sales and Marketing

It is impossible to talk about cross-functional integration without at least mentioning the marketing/sales interface. Integration problems between marketing and sales may become far less significant with the emergence of the strategic sales organization. But for many companies right now, getting marketing and sales to work together remains a challenge. It is sad that this is true, but it is.

The Marketing/Sales Interface

Positioning sales as an increasingly strategic function concerned with delivering competitive advantage to the organization and aligned with business strategy appears the way forward, but this still leaves unresolved the issue of the relationship between marketing and sales. Unproductive conflicts between marketing and sales provide a significant barrier to the development of the strategic sales organization, and consequently to the implementation of strategic customer management.

Surprisingly little serious research attention has been given to the relationship within the marketing area between marketing and sales. Yet for many companies this relationship remains highly problematic. Frederick Webster observes 'The relationship between sales and marketing functions has persisted as one of the major sources of organizational conflict',[24] while others note that 'The marketing-sales relationship, whilst strongly interdependent, is reported as neither collaborative nor harmonious'.[25] Sales and marketing integration remains a high priority on the management agenda.[26]

[24] Webster, Frederick E. (1997), 'The Future Role of Marketing in the Organization', in Donald R. Lehmann and Katherine E. Jocz (eds.), *Reflections on the Futures of Marketing*, Cambridge, MA: Marketing Science Institute, pp. 39–66.
[25] Dewsnap, Belinda and Jobber, David, 'The Sales-Marketing Interface in Consumer Packaged-Goods Companies: A Conceptual Framework', *Journal of Personal Selling & Sales Management*, Vol. 20 No. 2 2000, pp. 109–19.
[26] Rouzies, Dominique, Erin Anderson, Asjay K. Kohli, Ronald E. Michaels, Barton A. Weitz, and Andris. A. Zoltners, 'Sales and Marketing Integration: A Proposed Framework', *Journal of Personal Selling & Sales Management*, Vol. 25 No. 2 2005, pp. 113–22.

Traditionally, there was sound logic for marketing and sales to be separate and different because the functions they perform are different.[27] However, the new market conditions and strategic sales role place considerable importance on cross-functional collaboration and cooperation, which aligns poorly with the traditional need for functional separation of marketing and sales based on task specialization.

What is far from well understood is what conflicts or elements of conflict actually have negative consequences for business performance and which do not.[28] While marketing and sales exist alongside each other as business functions, there are likely to be fundamental differences between them in perspective and priorities. However, in examining the coordination of these differentiated functions, Frank Cespedes highlights an important paradox: 'the solution is *not* to eliminate differences among these groups',[29] but that 'paradoxically, there is virtue in *separating* and distinguishing functional roles in order to improve the cross-functional coordination needed'.[30] His suggestion is that differences between marketing and sales may actually provide a much-needed breadth of perspective and richness of market understanding because of the differences between the functions. As collaboration and cooperation between marketing and sales grows in importance, this paradox provides an important insight—teamwork and joint-working has to accommodate differences in perspective and understanding, and to focus on enhanced business performance not simply smooth team operation or harmonious interrelationships.

Does the Marketing/Sales Interface Really Matter?

To other functions in the business the marketing and sales functions look alike—they are both focused on the customer and the market—but aligning sales and marketing has proved difficult in practice and is likely to be even more difficult in the future. The importance of the

[27] Shapiro, Benson P., *Creating the Customer-Centric Team: Coordinating Sales & Marketing*, Harvard Business School, Note 9-999-006, 2002.

[28] Deshpande, Rohit and Webster, Frederick E., 'Organizational Culture and Marketing: Defining the Research Agenda', *Journal of Marketing*, Vol. 53 January 1989, pp. 3–15.

[29] Cespedes, Frank V., 'Beyond Teamwork: How the Wise Can Synchronize', *Marketing Management*, Vol. 5 No. 1 1996, pp. 25–37.

[30] Cespedes, Frank V., *Concurrent Marketing: Integrating Product, Sales and Service*, Cambridge, MA: Harvard Business School Press, 1995.

issue is quite simply that poor cooperation between marketing and sales will lead to inconsistent and weak strategy, coupled with flawed and inefficient implementation.[31]

In the days when the customer base was homogeneous, simple, and dominated by mid-sized accounts, marketing operated as a strategic function concentrating on product strategy, segmentation, and competitive positioning, while sales executed the strategy in the field, selling to end-users and distributors. The easy separation of sales and marketing has come to an end in markets dominated by very large accounts with sophisticated buying teams, and multi-channel strategies to reach medium and small accounts. With the largest accounts, marketing and sales need to make joint decisions to achieve an integrated offer that meets the standards required by purchasers who can dictate many terms to their suppliers. With multi-channelling (e.g. an Internet channel, telesales, direct marketing, and personal selling working alongside each other), effectiveness and profitability also require shared sales and marketing decisions on channel strategy and execution.[32]

The escalating customer power we have described, often resulting from buyer concentration, in both industrial and consumer goods business-to-business marketing, indicates that the salesforce can no longer passively accept and execute plans produced by marketing. Strategic account managers, product/brand managers, category specialists, and advertising executives need to work jointly to protect profits and enhance volume. Marketing executives need to acquire new understanding of individual customers, key account needs, and the sales task (see Chapter 1).

While relatively little empirical evidence is available, executive opinion and anecdote suggests the relationship between marketing and sales remains problematic in many companies, with conflict surrounding such issues as the division of responsibilities and demarcation lines, ownership of customer information, competition for resources, control of price, and the short-term orientation of sales versus the long-term orientation of marketing. Differences in reward systems (volume-based in sales and margin-based in marketing), information needs (geographically and customer based in sales and product/brand oriented in marketing), and competencies underline

---

[31] Shapiro, 2002, op cit.   [32] Shapiro, 2002, op cit.

the potential for conflict rather than collaboration between marketing and sales.[33]

Underpinning the potential for market/sales conflict is what has been described as the existence of different 'mindsets' in marketing and sales—different perspectives on issues and approaches for addressing problems—which have been described as *customer versus product*—focus and rewards for sales are based on customers and territories, while marketing champions products and brands; *personal relationships versus analysis*—sales may be more 'people-oriented' and relationship-focused, while marketing emphasizes aggregations of data and abstractions; *continuous daily activity versus sporadic projects*—sales is driven by constant daily tasks, while marketing is organized around longer-term projects; *field versus office*—sales is under immediate customer and budget pressures, while marketing may be removed from this environment; *results versus process*—sales lives by fast, direct results from its selling efforts, while marketing activities are less easily linked to short-term results, so may emphasize process and intermediate outcomes; and *short-term orientation versus long-term orientation*—sales emphasizes month-to-month sales results, while marketing concentrates on long-term competitive position.[34] Such differences in 'mindset' provide the context in which marketing–sales collaboration must be achieved, but may provide important practical barriers.

The Signs of Poor Marketing/Sales Integration

Research suggests that sales managers frequently do not set sales objectives consistent with the strategy developed by marketing executives for a product, through poor communications and incompatibility between marketing and sales goals. They note also attempts by marketing executives to mislead sales managers about product

[33] For example, see: Cespedes, Frank V., 'Coordinating Sales and Marketing in Consumer Goods Firms', *Journal of Consumer Marketing*, Vol. 10 No. 2 1993, pp. 37–55. Cespedes, Frank V., 'Industrial Marketing: Managing New Requirements', *Sloan Management Review*, (Spring) 1994, pp. 45–60. Montgomery, David B. and Webster, Frederick E., 'Marketing's Interfunctional Interfaces: The MSI Workshop on Management of Corporate Fault Zones', *Journal of Market-Focused Management*, Vol. 2 1997, pp. 7–26. Dewsnap, Belinda and Jobber, David, 'The Sales-Marketing Interface in Consumer Packaged Goods Companies: A Conceptual Framework', *Journal of Personal Selling & Sales Management*, Vol. 2 2000, pp. 109–19.

[34] Rouzies et al., 2005, op cit.

performance in attempts to manipulate their behaviour. Unsurprisingly, the result is feelings of distrust and resentment towards marketing on the part of sales managers. Often changes in marketing strategy do not lead to consistent modification of sales operations.[35]

Can it be Done?

The answer appears to be sometimes 'yes', sometimes 'no'—it all depends...A fascinating piece of recent research in Germany offers some interesting insights into the realities of the marketing/sales interface.[36] These researchers took measures of information sharing between marketing and sales, structural linkages, relative power, orientation, and knowledge/expertise and clustered companies marketing and sales organizations. They uncovered the following groupings:

Ivory Tower, where the marketing role is an isolated caller for customer orientation, while sales is about product-driven selling. The sales unit is product-focused and has a short-term focus, and has an operational rather than strategic mindset. Marketing has a high consumer focus and a medium-term time orientation. However, marketing is isolated by its lack of product and market knowledge. There is little information sharing or joint planning between marketing and sales. The research suggested this form was common in financial services and the engineering industry. The quality of cooperation between marketing and sales, market performance, and profitability are low.

Brand-focused professionals, where marketing is the expert in a leading role, and sales is a congenial counterpart of marketing. These companies show high levels of formalization, joint planning, team work, and information sharing. Both marketing and strategy have high levels of market and product orientation and long-term orientation, and cooperation between them is structured and professional. This form is common in consumer packaged goods industries characterized

[35] Strahle, W. M., Spiro, R. L., and Acito, F., 'Marketing and Sales: Strategic Alignment and Functional Implementation', *Journal of Personal Selling & Sales Management*, Vol. 16 (Winter) 1996, pp. 1–20. Colletti, J. A. and Chonko, L. B., 'Change Management Initiatives: Moving Sales Organizations from Obsolescence to High Performance', *Journal of Personal Selling & Sales Management*, Vol. 17 (Spring) 1997, pp. 1–30.
[36] Homburg, Christian, Ove Jensen, and Harley Krohmer, 'Configurations of Marketing and Sales: A Taxonomy', *Journal of Marketing*, Vol. 72 No. 2 2008, pp. 133–54.

by a strategic focus on brands and by powerful brand managers. Cooperation quality, market performance, and profitability are high. High levels of information sharing, knowledge, and structural linkages appear to pay off for this group.

Sales rules where marketing provides operational support to the dominant product-expert role of sales. Sales is powerful and knowledgeable compared to marketing. Marketing is little more than an appendage to sales with a very limited role. This form was common in the machinery and automotive industries. Other examples were project-based businesses with very small customer numbers. Cooperation quality, market performance, and profitability are low. Low structural linkages and unilateral power concentration do not appear to pay off.

Marketing-driven devil's advocacy where marketing is the long-term product voice, while sales is the shorter-term customer voice. Sales has a short-term operational focus while marketing has a long-term strategic focus. Marketing is high in product orientation and product knowledge, and may be technical and inward-looking. This form of dominant product-focused marketing is typical in the chemicals and electronics industries. Cooperation quality is low, as would be expected with clashing orientations. By contrasting alternatives, 'devil's advocacy' produces good market performance. However, profitability is low.

Sales-driven symbiosis where marketing is the market expert and sales is dominant as the product expert. Both marketing and sales are highly customer-focused and team work is high. Cooperation is structured. This form was typical for utilities businesses. In terms of cooperation quality, market performance, and profitability, this group was second only to the 'brand professionals'.

Overall, the most successful marketing/sales relationships were characterized by a high use of structural linkages, high market knowledge in marketing, and a longer-term orientation in sales. They also showed a clear but not extreme power distribution between marketing and sales. The less successful marketing/sales relationships were associated with low levels of information sharing, fewer structural linkages, lower knowledge, and more extreme power distribution.

So, another interesting question for us to consider is which of these stereotypes sounds most like our own organization, and perhaps more importantly what form of marketing/sales interface would be most supportive to the strategic sales organization? The research suggests that to understand and shape the marketing/sales relationship we should examine information sharing between the functions, structural linkages (joint planning, team work, formalization), power of each function over market-related activities, orientation (customer vs. product, short-term vs. long-term), and knowledge (market and product).

Aligning Sales and Marketing Processes More Effectively

There are no 'quick-fixes' to achieve superior marketing/sales alignment. Benson Shapiro notes that the prerequisites are a common understanding of the need for integration, and that both sales and marketing focus on the productive sharing of power, information, and resources, but also warns: 'There are many approaches to improving integration. They work best when they themselves are well integrated (big surprise!) . . . the stress will be on "mixing and matching" the individual elements of coordination to get a robust, efficient program.'[37] The components are not much different to those we considered earlier in looking at the search for total integrated marketing.

In some important ways the issue has moved on from building more productive collaborative relationships between marketing and sales functions. The priority has become integrating the marketing and sales processes that impact on the delivery of superior value to customers, whoever owns them in the organization. The way forward probably lies in the process-based perspective we described earlier.

Importantly, organizational transformation, of the type we are discussing here, even when mandated by external pressures and change in business strategy, may be perceived as unwelcome and undesirable by those who believe their interests to be threatened. Such perceptions may unleash 'counter-implementation strategy'—attempts by executives to block and avoid change. It is important that the advent of the strategic sales organization should be positioned as an enhancement of marketing processes to impact positively on business performance, not as some form of attack by sales on the position of the marketing department. This suggests that developing an effective and constructive communications interface between marketing and sales remains a high priority. Frankly, if we cannot even align the customer-facing

[37] Shapiro, 2002, op cit.

parts of the organization, then the strategic sales organization and its strategic customer management role looks a long way off.

Cross-functional Synergies: Managing Critical Interfaces

Whether we are talking about working across several functions to achieve integration, working across organizational boundaries with partners, or focusing closer to home on the relationship between sales and marketing, we are talking about managing critical interfaces between different groups of people.

One approach which some executives have found useful in planning how to do this, and in articulating the problems they face, is illustrated in Figure 4.4 in the context of cross-functional relationships. The logic is simple. When you look at most issues that involve change, you can find out who matters to you in getting the change implemented, and you know broadly if they are on your side or not. In other words, looking at individuals, subunits, departments, or partners—are they important to the issue, what is the quality of the relationship we have with them?

This suggests the world falls into four groups: *partners*—closely involved and important to the issue we are trying to resolve and a good quality relationship means they are on our side; *friends*—we have

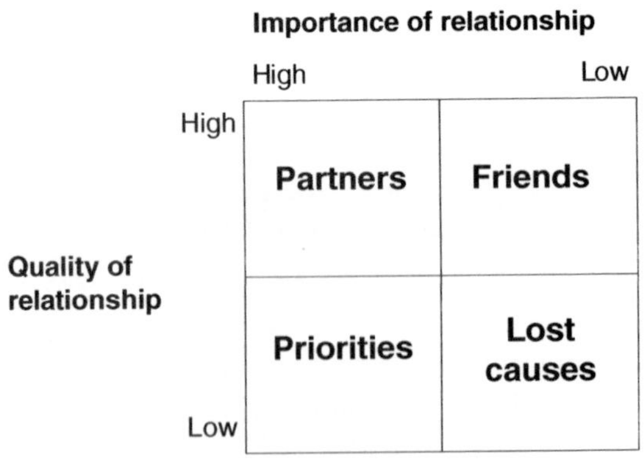

Importance of relationship

	High	Low
High	**Partners**	**Friends**
Low	**Priorities**	**Lost causes**

Quality of relationship

Fig. 4.4 Key cross-functional relationships

a good quality relationship, but they are not directly involved in the issue we are trying to deal with; *priorities*—we cannot claim to have a good relationship with them, but they are highly important to the issue we have to resolve, which makes them priorities for attention; and *lost causes*—they do not currently matter to the decision with which we are concerned, and we do not have a good relationship with them, so they are unlikely to support us whatever we want to do.

This then turns our planning for managing key cross-functional interfaces into a series of questions about how we exploit the relationship we have with partners and reinforce that relationship because it matters to what we are trying to do. How do we focus on winning the support of the priorities and building a stronger relationship with them, because they are central to the issue at stake? Are there opportunities for getting friends more closely involved in the issue, so the strong relationship we have with them becomes useful? Are there any risks that the lost causes will become more closely involved in the issue and threaten what we are trying to achieve? Although it is not a sophisticated analysis, it has proved useful in clarifying what needs to be done to drive customer-related initiatives through cross-functional relationships.

For example, in one company the barrier to extending the relationship with a major customer was the poor quality of technical service being provided to support product maintenance. Complaints by the salespeople about the technical service department had produced little useful effect. In fact, the real barrier was that technical service personnel were evaluated and rewarded for dealing with customer issues quickly—their metrics emphasized speed of handling queries and minimizing costs in coping with customer complaints. It was clear that pleading with them to offer more time and to spend more money on a customer was pointless—it was not in their best interests. However, the resolution of the issue meant exploiting the strong relationship between marketing/sales and human resource management—*friends*. While HRM had no direct involvement in technical service, they were the right people to re-examine performance metrics and evaluation systems to bring technical service performance closer in line with customer requirements. It took a while but they got there.

In another company, a key account manager (KAM) faced the dilemma that while he was investing in building a long-term relationship with the customer, the production director was determined to sell a beta-version of a new software product to the customer, whatever the KAM thought about it. The problem with beta-versions of complex software products is that they tend not to work, so the KAM did not think much of this ploy. However, he lacked the organizational authority to refuse to allow the new product to his customer. Investigation suggested that the real problem was not the product, but the fact that the production director had spent two years developing the product and was desperate to get a positive cash flow as quickly as possible to meet his targets. The KAM's way out of this trap was to exploit his close partnership with the salesforce. With the production director's agreement he arranged for the salesforce to sell the new beta-version product into small accounts—they were enthusiastic customers because software is a fashion product and they got to have it a year earlier than the big players (though unhappily it did not work properly). The key account was protected from a beta-version product, the production director got his cash-flow, and the salesforce won industry awards for taking the new product to small accounts.

In another case, also in a high-technology business, the problem was that a vertical marketing strategy of sales focus on different customer groups had run into obstruction by senior technical management who were resistant to the idea of customizing products and service levels around customer groups. Technical managers were the *priorities* but they had no real relationship history with sales and account management (other than a mild degree of antagonism to 'selling' in a world of 'science'). To move forward, account managers were able to work with *partners* in marketing services and *friends* in training and development to create and fund a small series of technical seminars for customers to be presented by technical managers. The social interaction between technical specialists from supplier and buyer organizations went a long way to overcoming the resistance to customer-led change in products and services. As someone pointed out, when you end up with R&D specialists berating account managers for not doing a better job for their new buddies in the customer organization, you know you have shifted something.

It is surprising how often the simple truth is that doing a better job with the customer can cause other people in the organization to do a worse job in their terms (i.e. against their performance metrics). The challenge of seamlessness in customer relationships is often to find a way around barriers created by the organization's own processes and structures to prevent them damaging customer relationships. It should not be so but it so frequently is.

The approach suggested by Figure 4.4 has been turned into a Work-sheet for mapping cross-functional relationship strategies, which is given in Appendix 4.1.

The Worksheet asks us to identify the issue which is at stake in the top box to focus our attention. Then we can identify the depart-ments and subunits around the issue and evaluate each in terms of the importance of the relationship in the context of the current issue, and the quality of the relationship (both on five-point scales to make it easy). This is usually best done on a group basis to get a full picture of all the possible linkages with different units. The results can then be entered on the chart to clearly identify *partners, friends, priorities,* and *lost causes*. The creative thinking comes in asking how to address barriers in the priorities area, either directly or by leveraging relation-ships in the partners and friends groups. The output should be that we can clearly articulate the barriers to changing things that we need to change, and propose ways of overcoming these barriers. Nonetheless, at the extreme one conclusion we reach may be that something cannot be achieved because there is no way to overcome the barriers which exist—but it is better to figure this out early, rather than to find out late when we have committed to the action.

Building the New Agenda

Getting past the lip-service paid to integration, cooperation, and part-nership inside the organization, all focused on customer value, is an important challenge to the emerging strategic sales organization. Working across traditional functional and organizational boundaries has become a priority in many companies. Nonetheless, achieving this seamlessness is often not easy. There are no 'bolt-on', 'one size fits all' solutions.

The imperative of integration also emphasizes that much of the role of the strategic sales organization will be carried out inside the sup-plier company, rather than externally in interacting with customers. There is another side to this—an internal marketing imperative in support of strategic customer management goals.

146

Appendix 4.1

Mapping Cross-functional Relationships

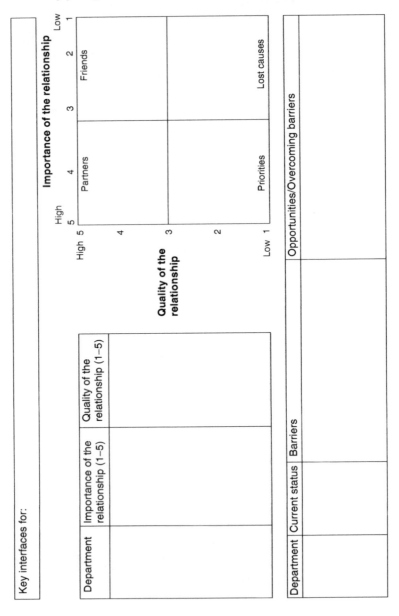

5

Internal Marketing: Selling the Customer to the Company

A strategic approach to the role of sales in managing customer value underlines the importance of positioning and 'selling' the customer value strategy inside the organization. The internal marketplace is company employees and managers (and increasingly partner organizations' employees and managers) whose attitudes, beliefs, and behaviour impact on customers and influence our ability to keep service and relationship promises. For example, we often find that there are differences between internal market and external market criteria of what 'matters'—the priorities of people in the 'back office' or the factory may conflict with those of the external customer.

The risk of undermining the competitive position with a major customer as a result of such internal market factors is too serious to be ignored. One role of the strategic sales organization is likely to be 'selling' the customer to employees and managers, as a basis for understanding customer priorities and the importance of meeting them, as an activity that parallels conventional sales and marketing efforts, as suggested in Figure 5.1. Sales organizations are familiar with the idea that what they are actually selling to customers is the company—its reputation, standing, capabilities, and so on—more than just products. The internal marketing parallel is selling the customer

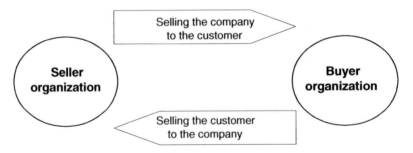

Fig. 5.1 Internal marketing

to the company—to the internal market of employees, managers, and partner organizations.

Clearly, it all depends on exactly how you define what is internal marketing, but research at Northwestern University in the United States has found internal marketing to be one of the top three determinants of a company's financial performance—quite simply, companies with better integration of internal and external market processes report better financial results.[1] Other studies suggest that a lot of organizations are struggling to deliver their value propositions to external customers because of inadequate investment in the internal marketplace and a lack of internal marketing.[2]

However, internal marketing matters at another level too—it defines our capabilities for implementing strategic customer management as a company initiative.

The Issue is Implementing Strategic Customer Management

Generally, the evidence suggests that up to 80 per cent of company change initiatives fail. In fact, the ability to implement may be more

---

[1] Chang, Julie, 'From The Inside Out', *Sales & Marketing Management*, August 2005, p. 8.

[2] 'Survey Reveals "Inadequate" State of Internal Marketing', *Marketing Week*, 3 July 2003, p. 8.

important than the quality of the strategy itself—execution may be more important than good strategic vision.[3] Some would go as far as to say that implementation *is* strategy—on the grounds that without a systematic management approach to the execution of plans and strategies, they simply will not happen, and so remain ideas which never become strategy in any real sense. Others suggest that implementation is *different* to strategy—it is the difficult part.

Like any other radical, change-oriented initiative, strategic customer management is likely to fail without careful attention to making it happen in the internal marketplace of your own company. We can consider the importance of the internal market to successfully implementing strategic customer management in the light of the type of barriers which may be anticipated, and the need to plan around implementation barriers. Internal marketing programmes, at different levels, provide a way of operationalizing this, and provide a further strand to the emerging role of the strategic sales organization.[4]

Why Is the Internal Market Important to Strategic Customer Management?

One reaction of sales and account executives to the idea that they have a growing internal marketing responsibility is mild outrage. Is it not enough that we have to build and maintain productive relationships with aggressive and demanding customers, without worrying about the people inside the organization? The answer is 'no'. Sometimes 'sorry, no', but definitely 'no'. You cannot hope to build an effective strategic sales organization without accepting that a substantial amount of effort will be required to line things up inside the organization, rather than being outside the company with the customer. Already people in roles like global account manager routinely accept

---

[3] Kaplan, Robert S. and David P. Norton, *The Strategy-Focused Organization*, Boston, MA: Harvard Business School Press, 2001.

[4] A more detailed approach to examining implementation and internal marketing can be found in: Piercy, Nigel F., *Market-Led Strategic Change: Transforming the Process of Going to Market*, 4th ed., Oxford: Butterworth-Heinemann, 2009, Chapter 12.

that 90 per cent of their time is spent inside the company trying to get the act together around customer priorities, rather than with the customer—that adds up to four and a half days a week solving problems inside the company and half a day a week actually talking to the customer.

One major implication of a strategic customer management approach is taking responsibility for alignment between supplier processes and customer requirements. This means spending time addressing integration issues (Chapter 4), and also winning the 'hearts and minds' of the people inside the company whose attitudes, beliefs, and behaviours impact on the customer—internal marketing is a way to address this systematically.

Successful change in a company may be in large part dependent on incorporating employees fully into the challenge to change the ways they deal with conflict and learning; maintaining employee involvement; and instilling the disciplines that will help people learn new ways of behaving and sustaining that new behaviour.[5] Managers who fail to get their employees to understand what they are doing and why, and to build their enthusiasm, should not be surprised when change programmes turn into disasters (see Chapter 9 regarding leadership styles).

Also, assuming that people are on the side of strategic change just because they have the title 'manager' may be unwise. Importantly, we are beginning to recognize the managers' everyday decisions can create or destroy a company's strategy—the cumulative impact of resource allocation at any level has more real world effect on strategy than plans developed at headquarters. Joseph Bower, for example, recounts how a company controller was confused by an expenditure request from an important division for a new chimney. Nothing else just a chimney, though a very large chimney. He flew out and discovered that division managers had built an entire new plant using work orders that did not require corporate approval. The chimney was the only thing that could not be broken down into small enough chunks to escape scrutiny. The division was right to want to expand capacity, but it did raise the question of who was actually running the

---

[5] Pascale, Richard, Mark Millman, and Linda Gioja, 'Changing the Way We Change', *Harvard Business Review*, November/December 1997, pp. 127–39.

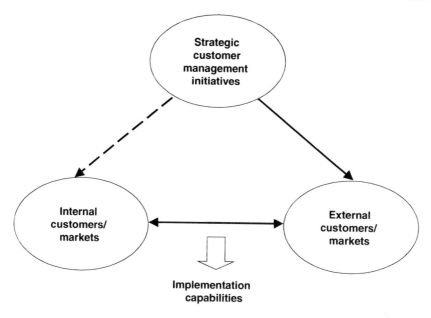

Fig. 5.2 Internal markets and external markets

company.[6] Putting a handle on managers' goals and aspirations that affect their choices looks more and more critical to successful strategic change.

From the comments in Chapter 4 about strategic relationships and the increasing dependence of companies on cross-boundary collaboration, it follows that building and sustaining effective ties with allies is a challenge which strategic customer management will have to confront. The field of strategic alliances and partnerships is full of failed relationships. The reliance on third parties holds political, reputational, and logistical risks.[7] Yet, as we have seen, networked organizations based on collaboration are core to the success of companies like IBM and Proctor & Gamble. While internal marketing is normally framed in terms of winning the support of managers and employees inside the

[6] Bower, Joseph L. and Clark G. Gilbert, 'How Managers' Everyday Decisions Create or Destroy Your Company's Strategy', *Harvard Business Review*, February 2007, pp. 72–9.

[7] Beattie, Alan, 'Unchained Malady: Business Is Becoming Ever More Exposed to Supplier Problems', *Financial Times*, 25 August 2005, p. 13.

company for strategic change, increasingly that internal marketplace will extend to partner organizations, whose buy-in is also needed to make strategy effective.

The internal market is key to the successful implementation of strategic customer management. In the way suggested in Figure 5.2—while an initiative like strategic customer management has a clear external customer marketplace, the ability to implement strategic relationships with customers will be moderated by the links between the external market (customers) and the internal market (employees, managers, partners). Internal marketing is about dealing with implementation issues.

The Great Implementation Barrier: The Parcel and the Wall

One provocative way of opening up the strategic customer management implementation issue with colleagues is the analogy of the parcel and the wall.[8] This analogy suggests that getting things to happen in organizations, getting what you want accepted and resourced in the constraints of a given organization, is a bit like trying to fit a parcel (the strategy) through a hole in the wall (company culture), when the hole is never quite big enough or the right shape for the parcel. We have to balance two factors: the *priority* we place on what it is we are trying to get (and what risks we are prepared to take) and the *acceptability* of our strategy to the company. The model in Figure 5.3 then identifies our options.

Low Risk Strategies

With things that are not essential but are controversial or difficult in the company, we may back off: *quit*—it does not matter that much so a

---

[8] The sad, alcohol-fuelled origins of this model are revealed in: Piercy, Nigel and Peattie, Kenneth J., 'Matching Marketing Strategies to Corporate Culture: The Parcel and the Wall', *Journal of General Management*, Vol. 13 No. 4 1987, pp. 33–44. Piercy, Nigel, 'Diagnosing and Solving Implementation Problems in Strategic Planning', *Journal of General Management*, Vol. 15 No. 1 1989, pp. 19–38.

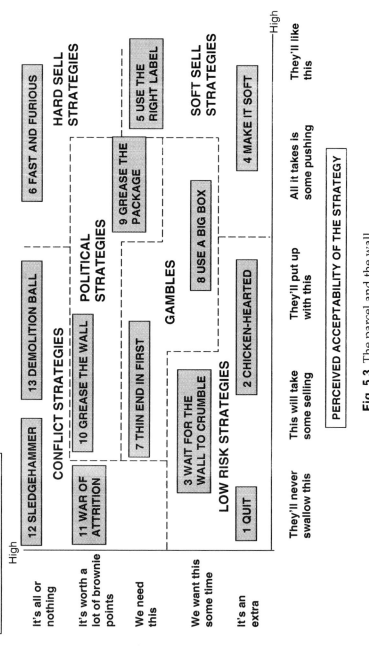

Fig. 5.3 The parcel and the wall

battle is not worth the effort, so walk away: wasting efforts over trivia which you are not going to get anyway makes little sense; *chicken-hearted*—survey the hole in the wall from a distance and trim the parcel until it fits, while the danger is this leads to excessive modification of the strategy and dilutes its effectiveness, it may be all you can get; *wait for the wall to crumble*—if it is not urgent, this is a popular 'Plan B', and many strategies lie in wait for the environment to change—someone leaves, policies change, new priorities are recognized, and then the time is right.

Soft Sell Strategies

If what you want is necessary but pretty much acceptable to the company, then appropriate approaches might be: *make the package soft*—the softer the package, the easier it will fit through the wall. The less opponents have to get hold of the better. It is easier to keep the strategy soft and slippery. One successful sales director had developed an approach to ensuring his plans went through unmolested by insisting on verbal rather than written communications—talking fast and at great length and avoiding commitment to written statements whenever possible; *use the right label*—agree to minor changes, but do not make them. For example, one aerospace company received a 3-page memo rejecting their 180-page business plan and explaining how it should be changed. They responded with total submission but in fact only changed three figures by less than 5 per cent each. Management appeared quite happy with this.

Hard Sell Strategy

This is for essential change items, which are pretty acceptable to the company and is likely to involve: *the fast and furious approach*—getting momentum behind the parcel to get it through the wall—lots of presentations, gaining widespread involvement and ownership, making it seem too good to miss. Leaving insufficient time for anyone to propose an alternative also helps.

Gambles

Where something is important but not very acceptable to the company, then we might try: *thin end in first*—if we know that the parcel will be unacceptably large, then we might unpack it and slide the more acceptable elements through, hoping that when the parcel gets stuck, management will concede it will take less effort to widen the hole in the wall than to change the parcel. Bids for computer hardware needs often seem to neglect to include the costs of software and services until after the equipment has been purchased; *use a big box*—show the wall a very large package, then when the wall communicates it is too big, open the box, take out a smaller package and slip it through the hole. Probably the oldest managerial trick in the world, but effective in manipulating culture while being seen to be constrained and guided by it.

Political Strategies

When something is highly important to our strategy, but not very acceptable, then we might consider: *grease the package*—make the package more politically acceptable without changing it. Often achievable by phrasing the strategy in terms of the latest management 'flavour of the month'. Getting the package associated with a powerful manager also works: 'It isn't common knowledge but the MD is very keen to see this succeed . . .'; *grease the wall*—apply the political grease to the culture rather than the strategy, for example, by gaining the involvement and support of the powerful in the company.

Conflict Strategies

Where something is essential to what we are trying to achieve, yet highly unacceptable to the company in question then outright conflict may be the only way forward (that or give up). Strategies include: *war of attrition*—this involves constantly resubmitting a strategy until eventually it gets accepted. This takes high commitment. It involves bits getting knocked off the parcel and the wall so the strategy gradually becomes more acceptable; *sledgehammer*—this involves putting the parcel down, finding a way of making the hole bigger (use a sledgehammer), and then feeding the package through. This may mean showdowns over trivial issues while the real bone of contention stays out of sight. In one services company when a two-year battle over changing the name of a product was over, the resourcing of the project fell almost automatically into place; *demolition ball*—this involves setting your strategy in stone and using it to smash a big enough hole in the wall. Popular with very confident managers (or those with nothing left to lose). It is likely to reach a situation where the change strategy becomes the central issue in a conflict where no compromise can be reached.

More than anything else, the parcel and the wall is based on observing what people who get things changed seem to do in different circumstances. Some people think the model is silly. Some think it is scurrilous. Few suggest that it not a good representation of organizational realities. We have used the parcel and wall model with many executive groups over a number of years. It rarely fails to generate a debate about what has to change and how, what should be left alone. It seems to be a good way of flushing out implementation barriers and thinking about what to do about them, and choosing priorities. It is not sophisticated but seems to relate quite well to manager experiences in getting things done. It may reveal some useful insights into what it is going to take to get strategic customer management accepted and implemented in the company.

Screening for Implementation Problems, Rather than Wait and See

The traditional approach of going for an initiative like strategic customer management and worrying about implementation later is probably a good route to failure. A systematic analysis carried out when initiatives are being planned and constructed has much to recommend it. Figure 5.4 describes such an approach.

Screen Strategies for Implementation Problems

At the earliest stage possible, screen the changes we are planning for implementation barriers, in terms of the acceptability of each key strategy to the company. In particular, note that the *earlier* this issue is faced, the less wasteful the process will be for two reasons: first, if there is an absolute barrier, and an initiative is not capable of being implemented, it can be abandoned or 'shelved' before it has used up too much

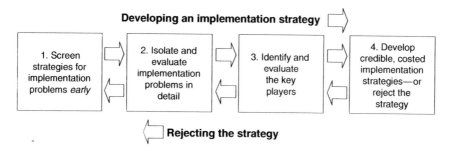

Fig. 5.4 Screening customer strategies for implementation problems

time and effort; however, second, if we identify problem areas early enough we can devote more time to solving them. Implementation barriers may be fundamental cultural mismatches, but often down-to-earth factors like obtaining a budget or head-count—where company policies forbid increased expenditure, or recruitment, or simply expenditure on something like promotion may be seen as 'wasteful' by the corporate culture.

Isolate and Evaluate Priority Implementation Problems

Once we have isolated the changes which, on first sight, are high in priority *and* pose problems in the company, then these can be further analyzed. We can examine the forces surrounding the implementation of these key strategies facing implementation barriers, and try to see the balance between opposing and favourable forces and the likely impact of the various factors identified. It is not unusual, for instance, to find that some of the reasons 'why not' for a change, which are apparently 'insoluble', when tested are not as overpowering as we first thought. While generally the picture which emerges from isolating problems should give us an overview of all those significant factors of different kinds in the company which relate to getting our initiative implemented, and which are most important, we probably will need to refine and reconsider this overview in two ways. First, we can evaluate the key players in our implementation problems. And, second, we can ask what else would have to happen to move the issues, to see if this changes the picture.

Evaluate Key Players in Implementation

First, if our thinking has produced little insight into what is likely to prevent things happening, or what we have to do to make them happen, we may not have got to the heart of the problem—so we may have to be a lot more specific about the people, the departments, the committees, and so on that we have to cope with. We should look for *influential supporters*—they are involved in the critical decisions and are on our side, and need to be kept on-side; *influential opposition*— the key players in the company who are influential and involved, but almost inevitably will oppose our plans, and whose impact must be balanced against our support, and questions asked whether there are ways we could win their support or move them out of the critical decision process; *non-involved supporters*—they are not influential in the decision but support our goals and plans, so the main possibility to consider is what may be done by us or them to increase their influence over the decision; and *non-involved opposition*—they provide unhelpful 'noise' in the system, but since they are not directly influential we may not see these as a major threat.

Develop Implementation Strategies

By going through the implementation issues in this detailed way, we hope to turn apparently intractable, unbeatable barriers into things which may be moved, at least a little. Naturally, in taking this approach we have to accept that some things cannot be overcome—however creative our implementation tactics and strategies may be.

One underlying goal is 'de-mystifying' the barriers to making change work in different situations. Experience suggests that it is very easy to see some things as impossible to implement, not because they fail to make financial sense, but simply because they are innovative, different to how 'we do things here', are against 'company policy', fly in the face of 'organizational myths', and so on. Working on such issues suggests that breaking barriers down into their constituent parts and addressing them at this level frequently leads to the conclusion that strategies may be feasible after all, if we can integrate an appropriate implementation strategy with our plans, and if we are prepared to look into the organizational realities of how things happen in our companies.

It has to be faced that the emerging role of the strategic sales organization is likely to encounter barriers of understanding and resistance from some parts of the company. If the strategic customer management initiative is worth pursuing, then it merits careful analysis of the implementation issues expected on the way.

We can then use an internal marketing framework to put implementation strategy into effect.

Internal Marketing Programmes

Internal marketing focuses on the delivery of corporate promises, both internally and externally.[9] It has the goal of developing a type of marketing effort aimed at the internal marketplace in the company that *parallels* and *matches* the initiatives aimed at the external marketplace of customers and competitors. This model comes from the simple observation that the implementation of external market strategies implies changes of various kinds within organizations—in the allocation of resources, in the culture of 'how we do things here', and even in the organizational structures needed to deliver our market strategies effectively to our customer segments. Such changes may not be welcomed by those most directly affected.

In practical terms, the attraction of internal marketing is that exactly those same techniques of analysis and communication which are used for the external marketplace can be adapted and used to market our plans and strategies to important targets within the company. Indeed, one of the major attractions of talking about 'internal marketing' instead of culture change, implementation, and so on is that we know how to *do* it. The goals of the internal marketing plan are taken directly from the implementation requirements for the external marketing plan and the objectives to be pursued.

Depending on the particular circumstances this process might include *gaining the support of key decision-makers* for the strategic sales organization—and all that it implies in terms of the need to acquire personnel and financial resources, possibly in conflict with established

---

[9] Schultz, Don E., 'Definition of Internal Marketing Remains Elusive', *Marketing News*, 15 January 2006, p. 6.

company 'policies', and to get what we need from other functions like operations and finance departments; *changing the attitudes and behaviour of employees and managers* who are working at the key interfaces with customers and distributors to those required to make plans work effectively; *winning commitment* to make strategic customer management work and to achieve the 'ownership' of the key problem-solving tasks among those units and individuals in the firm whose working support is needed; and ultimately *managing incremental changes in the culture* from 'the way we always do things' to the 'the way we need to do things to be successful' and to make the strategic sales organization effective.

A Structure for Internal Marketing

A structure for an internal marketing programme is summarized in Figure 5.5. The easiest way to make practical progress with *internal marketing*, and to establish what it may achieve, is to use exactly the same structures that we use for planning *externally*. This suggests that we should think in terms of integrating the elements needed for an internal marketing mix or programme, based on our analysis of the

Programme	Contents	Examples
Product	The customer strategy and plan, including the values, attitudes, and behaviours needed to make them work	*For example, the written plan, the new company initiative, customer satisfaction scores*
Price	What we are asking internal customers to 'pay'—other projects abandoned, personal and psychological adjustment to change	*For example, stepping out of their comfort zones for new types of operations important to customers*
Communications	Media and messages to inform and persuade	*For example, reports, plans, presentations, videos, roadshows focused on customer issues*
Distribution	Physical and social venues for delivering the product and communications	*For example, meetings, work-groups, training sessions and workshops, informal meetings, social occasions*

Fig. 5.5 Internal marketing programmes

opportunities and threats in the internal marketplace represented by the company with which we are working.

The structure of an internal marketing programme consists of the *product*—at the simplest level the customer strategy and our plans, as well as the values, attitudes, and behaviours which are needed to make the marketing plan work effectively; the *price*—not *our* costs, but what we are asking our internal customers to 'pay', when they buy-in to the product and the new initiative, such as sacrificing other projects which compete for resources with our plan, but more fundamentally the psychological cost of adopting different key values, and changing the way jobs are done, and asking managers to step outside their 'comfort zones' with new methods of operation; *communications*—the most tangible aspect of the internal marketing programme is the communications media and the messages used to inform and to persuade, and to work on the attitudes of the key personnel in the internal marketplace, including not only written communications but also face-to-face presentations to individuals and groups who are important to the success of the plan; and *distribution*—the distribution channels element of the mix is concerned with the physical and socio-technical venues at which we have to deliver our product and its communications: meetings, committees, training sessions for managers and staff, seminars, workshops, written reports, informal communications, social occasions, and so on.

Interestingly, there is a case that the real internal market distribution channel is lining-up company-wide recruitment, training, evaluation, and reward systems behind marketing strategies, so that the culture of the company becomes the real distribution channel for internal marketing strategies. For example, to support customer commitment, it is increasingly common for companies to involve major customers in staff recruitment and selection decisions; staff promotion and development decisions; staff appraisal, from setting the standards to measuring the performance; staff reward systems, both financial and non-financial; organizational design strategies; and internal communications programmes. This is one route to sustaining interdependent, shared values and shared strategies.[10]

---

[10] Ulrich, Dave, 'Tie the Corporate Knot: Gaining Complete Customer Commitment', *Sloan Management Review*, (Summer) 1989, pp. 19–27.

Levels of Internal Marketing

As well as giving us a model for analyzing internal marketing needs, this structure also provides a way of going deeper into the real workings of the company. For example, the model in Figure 5.6 suggests that when we get to a company we may start by asking about the techniques, the systems, and so on, but behind this the really important questions are 'who *runs* the organization?' and 'who has *influence* in this organization?'

This encourages managers to go beyond the superficial aspects of how their organizations work in planning internal marketing, to distinguish between a level of *surface* analysis, which is primarily about plans, techniques, and systems, and the level of *structure* and *process* analysis. This can have the effect of widening the debate from simply the presentation of the plan to the company to the more difficult and covert issues of power and culture in companies in the way shown.

One attraction of this approach is that managers are often far more comfortable using the term 'internal marketing' to focus attention on the elements of the corporate environment inside the company that need to be changed in order to implement customer strategies and new

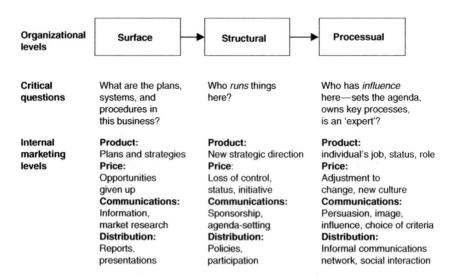

Organizational levels	Surface	Structural	Processual
Critical questions	What are the plans, systems, and procedures in this business?	Who *runs* things here?	Who has *influence* here—sets the agenda, owns key processes, is an 'expert'?
Internal marketing levels	**Product:** Plans and strategies **Price:** Opportunities given up **Communications:** Information, market research **Distribution:** Reports, presentations	**Product:** New strategic direction **Price:** Loss of control, status, initiative **Communications:** Sponsorship, agenda-setting **Distribution:** Policies, participation	**Product:** individual's job, status, role **Price:** Adjustment to change, new culture **Communications:** Persuasion, image, influence, choice of criteria **Distribution:** Informal communications network, social interaction

Fig. 5.6 Levels of internal marketing

initiatives like strategic customer management, and that this terminology provides an acceptable and legitimate framework for unpacking the issues in the company. It may sound tacky, but it seems to work in getting to grips with the processes inside the organization, not just sending out glossy brochures.

Internal and External Customer Satisfaction

One of the issues to which everyone pays attention is customer satisfaction and a whole industry has emerged to measure it. However, an internal marketing perspective highlights another interesting question—if we have internal customers as well as external customers, then what about their satisfaction, and perhaps most particularly the satisfaction of internal customers with external customers? If our internal customers are dissatisfied—and especially if they are dissatisfied with external customers—then what is this likely to do to all our promises of superior value and strong relationships in strategic customer management?

For example, if we think about the outcomes of customer satisfaction (and if we are not concerned with the outcomes we are not really taking customer satisfaction seriously), then consider the framework in Figure 5.7. We would expect that the level of customer satisfaction

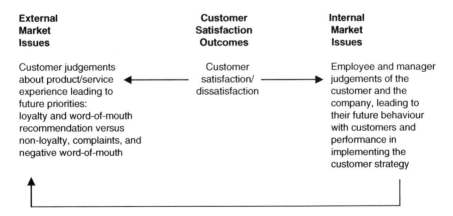

Fig. 5.7 Customer satisfaction outcomes

in the external market should influence future customer choices, particularly in terms of their loyalty and positive word-of-mouth recommendations, or non-loyalty, complaints, and negative word-of-mouth. However, the corollary is that in the internal market, employee and manager judgements of the customer are likely to shape their future behaviours with customers and the level of their performance in implementing customer strategies.

External market issues and internal market issues mirror one another and are directly connected. In other words, external customer satisfaction is both dependent on and a contributor to internal customer satisfaction. The trouble is often these two sides of satisfaction are not managed as the same issue, or even as related issues.

Even more worrying is confusing customer and employee satisfaction—the assumption that if we are terribly, terribly kind to employees, they will be terribly, terribly nice to customers, and we win with both groups. We really do need to question these assumptions. There is hard evidence that the long-held premise that happy staff make happy customers is not true.[11] Undoubtedly, when employee buy-in is focused on what matters to customers, it can be a powerful competitive weapon.[12] But just consider the relationship between internal (employee) and external (customer) satisfaction shown in Figure 5.8.

This suggests that four possible scenarios that result when internal and external customer satisfaction are compared: *synergy*, which is what we hope for, when internal and external customer satisfaction are high, and we see them as sustainable and self-regenerating—this is the 'happy customers and happy employees' situation, assumed by many to be obvious and easily achieved; *coercion* is where we achieve high levels of external customer satisfaction by changing the behaviour of employees through management direction and control systems, which may be very difficult and expensive to sustain; *alienation*, where we have low levels of satisfaction internally and externally, and we are likely to be highly vulnerable to competitive attack in the external

---

[11] Mitchell, Alan, 'In the Pursuit of Happiness', *Financial Times*, 14 June 2007, p. 14.

[12] Rucci, Anthony B., Steven P. Kirn, and Richard T. Quinn, 'The Employee-Customer-Profit Chain At Sears', *Harvard Business Review*, January–February 1998, pp. 83–97.

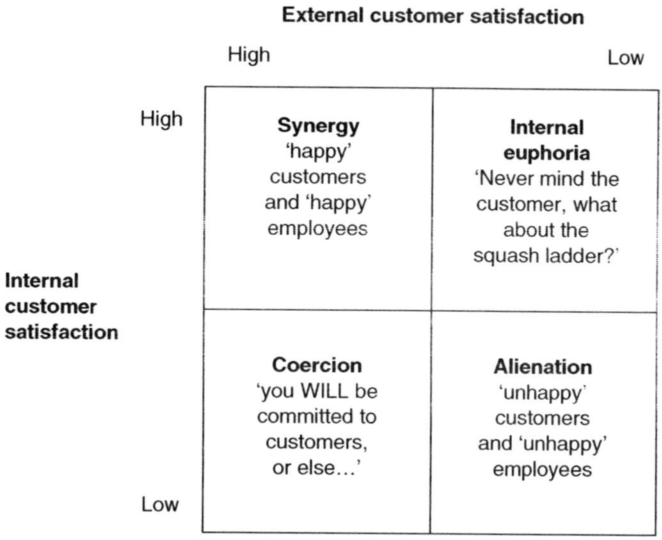

External customer satisfaction

	High	Low
High	**Synergy** 'happy' customers and 'happy' employees	**Internal euphoria** 'Never mind the customer, what about the squash ladder?'
Internal customer satisfaction **Low**	**Coercion** 'you WILL be committed to customers, or else...'	**Alienation** 'unhappy' customers and 'unhappy' employees

Fig. 5.8 Internal and external customer satisfaction

market and low morale and high staff turnover in the internal market; and *internal euphoria*, is where we have high levels of satisfaction in the internal market, but this does not translate into external customer satisfaction—for example, if internal socialization and group cohesiveness actually shut out the paying customer in the external market.

These scenarios are exaggerated, but have provided a useful way of confronting the issues with executives. In these terms, the issues become about balance (between internal and external issues) and focus (of internal characteristics on external success).

Dimensions of Customer Satisfaction

In fact, if selling the customer to the company is a big issue in implementing strategic customer management in your business, you can take it even further.

For example, Figure 5.9 takes the dimensions of customer satisfaction as they have been identified in the classic works in this field.[13] This work suggests that if we are to understand customer

---

[13] For example, see: Berry, L.L. and A. Parasuraman, *Marketing Services: Competing Through Quality*, New York: The Free Press, 1991.

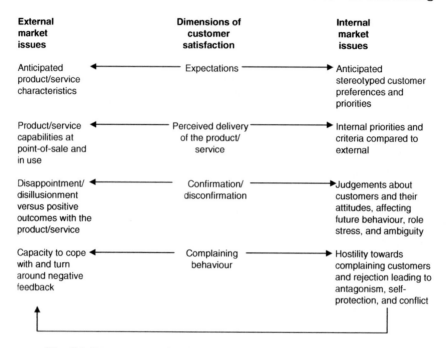

Fig. 5.9 Dimensions of internal and external customer satisfaction

satisfaction, then first we should consider our customers' expectations,[14] how they perceive the delivery of the product or service relative to these expectations, and whether this experience confirms their expectations or not. These factors will shape customer satisfaction and lead to either complaints or word-of-mouth recommendations. This is pretty familiar stuff in the conventional external marketplace.

What is interesting is if we take an internal marketing perspective and look for the mirror-image of external customer satisfaction in the internal market (the right-hand column in Figure 5.9). Here expectations are to do with anticipations by people inside the company of external customer preferences and behaviour, rather than the external customer's view of product/service characteristics. In the internal market, perceived delivery is concerned with differences between

---

[14] Some academics take the view that customers do not have well-formed expectations, so this approach is flawed, but that is just plain picky and unhelpful.

internal and external criteria of what matters—priorities in the 'back office' or the factory compared to those in the external customer marketplace. In the internal market, the confirmation/disconfirmation issue is not about the purchase of the product, but rather the judgements that people inside the company make about the external customer and whether these expectations are met or not. When customers 'disappoint' employees by their adverse reactions or even complaints, then this is likely to impact on future behaviour with external customers, possibly even to the extent of active hostility towards external customers and their 'unreasonable' demands.

When employee satisfaction is measured, it is amazing how often employees who are quite happy with the company, management, the supervisor, and the peer group show high levels of dissatisfaction with the customer. Maybe customers are rude, demanding, aggressive, awkward, ungrateful, disloyal in the eyes of the internal market. This just cannot be ignored, or there is no possibility of living up to external customer expectations and delivering on promises made.

Sometimes, internal/external market divergence comes down to very simple but important differences in perceptions, which can be addressed. For example, in the CIGNA health insurance group, the company had for many years prided itself on its speed in paying out on claims, and saw this as a major competitive strength. Only through a programme of customer visits to the company did the technical insurance specialists find out that their corporate customers placed very little value on speedy payments—what caused them much aggravation was the number of paperwork errors and errors caused by the quest for speed. Once understood, this was easy to address.

In other more worrying situations, the issue is more about attitudes and associated behaviours which undermine the promises made to external customers, and these cases may demand more radical action. Consider, for example, the issue of service quality in external and internal markets.

Internal and External Quality/Service

This reflects the same 'mirror-image' argument. Figure 5.10 lists the factors generally believed to create the perception that external

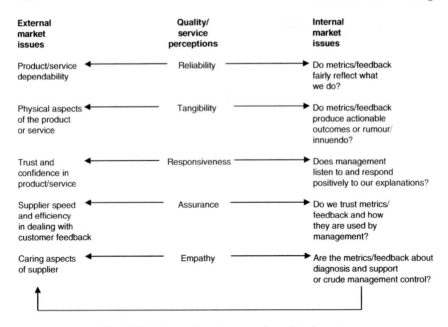

External market issues	Quality/ service perceptions	Internal market issues
Product/service dependability	← Reliability →	Do metrics/feedback fairly reflect what we do?
Physical aspects of the product or service	← Tangibility →	Do metrics/feedback produce actionable outcomes or rumour/ innuendo?
Trust and confidence in product/service	← Responsiveness →	Does management listen to and respond positively to our explanations?
Supplier speed and efficiency in dealing with customer feedback	← Assurance →	Do we trust metrics/ feedback and how they are used by management?
Caring aspects of supplier	← Empathy →	Are the metrics/feedback about diagnosis and support or crude management control?

Fig. 5.10 Internal and external quality/service

customers have of the quality of the service they receive. For external customers these factors are reliability or dependability of the product/ service; tangibility of the service; responsiveness of the supplier in handling customer feedback, assurance about the product or service, and empathy with the supplier. Again, this is familiar territory for generations of people working on service quality.[15]

The same framework can be applied to the internal market. The issue may now be about how management in the company evaluates and responds to feedback from customers on service and quality, and perhaps most particularly in customer satisfaction results. Now we have to ask some different questions: whether customer feedback and satisfaction metrics are believed to be fair to employees (reliability); whether feedback and measurement systems produce actionable conclusions, or just rumour and innuendo about who is doing a good job and who is not (tangibility); whether management listens to, and responds to, the reasons for specific customer feedback

---

[15] For example, see Berry and Parasuraman (1991), op cit.

(responsiveness); whether people trust management's integrity in this area (assurance); and whether customer feedback and satisfaction measurements are used positively or coercively (empathy).

Certainly, discussions with managers and employees about customer satisfaction measurement systems on how they are used as customer feedback in companies identifies some common and potentially incredibly counter-productive characteristics: feedback and satisfaction measurement systems which are little more than popularity polls for the salespeople, where being 'popular' is rewarded and being 'unpopular' is not (apparently regardless of why and how the salesperson has achieved such popularity with the customer . . .); approaches which are wholly negative and encourage only customer complaints and criticism, but do not capture positive feedback or praise for what is good; reporting systems where hard data are only seen by top management, and only 'conclusions' are communicated to employees—often in a negative and critical way; and the blind use of feedback and satisfaction results by management to attempt to coerce employees to change their behaviour in ways apparently desired by customers (or at least that sample of customers who have complained most recently or most loudly).

It is too easy to make assumptions about what is wrong in the internal market because it does not deliver what we need to make strategic relationships with customers effective. You really do need to dig deeper and ask why things are this way, before you leap to conclusions about what needs to be addressed. Examining the different levels of internal market targets and getting to grips with issues of satisfaction and service quality in the internal market is a start. Taking this issue seriously may lead us away from the idea that just doing a few presentations and sending around glossy brochures about customer strategy will change the way people do things. It is likely to be a bit deeper than that. But you probably do not have much choice— it is that or give up on the whole thing.

Indeed, while some executives may see a full-blown internal market analysis and internal marketing programmes as a bit over the top, actually it is not that far removed from what successful sales managers always did. While they would recoil in horror from any terms like 'internal marketing', sales managers who got big things done with external customers were nearly always tightly coupled to key players inside the company, whose efforts were essential to delivering the goods to the customer. Think of the old-style sales director who always had a moth-eaten, bulging Filofax hidden away somewhere. Hidden away inside would be contact numbers for key people in production and the distribution centre, important technical specialists who might be needed to evaluate a customer problem, people in finance and accounting who might be needed to rush through invoices and credit checks, and so on. They did not know it (or care)—but that type of networking or internal marketing is necessary to get things done.

The success of a strategic sales initiative will in many ways depend on the thoroughness and care with which internal market issues are addressed.

Building the New Agenda

A strategic customer management initiative is likely to be a major undertaking for a company. Without careful attention to the implementation of the initiative and alignment of the internal marketplace with the demands of the external marketplace, it simply is not going to happen. Without the commitment and buy-in of managers and employees inside the company, and those in partner organizations, superior value propositions are unlikely to be delivered; relational investments are not going to be matched to customer value and prospects; responsiveness to new market understanding will be elusive. For that reason, part of the agenda for the strategic sales organization focuses first on integration, but then on internal marketing, or implementation.

The next question gets closer to home—how well is the infrastructure of the sales organization itself aligned with the priorities of strategic customer management?

6

Infrastructure: Aligning Sales Process and Structure with Business Strategy

Unhappily, the role of the transforming sales organization is unlikely to be implemented effectively through traditional salesforce structures and processes—they were not set up to do this job. In fact, Benson Shapiro and his colleagues suggested, some time ago, that 'most established sales forces are in deep trouble. They were designed for a much simpler, more pleasant era.... The old sales force must be redesigned to meet the new needs'.[1]

The logic of strategic customer management means that new definitions of the sales task will require substantial shifts in the way that the sales organization is managed. Turbulent and ever more complex and demanding markets mandate constant attention to alignment between sales processes and the goals of market and business strategy.[2]

---

[1] Shapiro, Benson P., Adrian J. Slywotsky, and Stephen X. Doyle, *Strategic Sales Management: A Boardroom Issue*, Note 9-595-018, Cambridge, MA: Harvard Business School, 1998.

[2] Strelsin, Stephen C. and Susan Mlot, 'The Art of Strategic Sales Alignment', *Journal of Business Strategy*, Vol. 13 No. 6 1992, pp. 41–7.

However, the evidence suggests that the move from transactional relationships with customers (selling on the basis of price and product advantages) to value-added relationships is proving extremely challenging for many organizations pursuing this strategic direction.[3] Similarly, the shift from individualistic customer relationships to team-based selling around large customers underlines the urgency of new infrastructural requirements in the sales organization.[4]

Change in the infrastructure supporting the strategic sales organization is likely to span organization structure, performance measurement systems, competency creation systems, and motivation and reward systems—all driven by the definition of the new task and role of the sales operation.[5]

The process of 'reinventing' the salesforce to meet the challenges of new markets and new strategies is likely to require attention to several critical issues: focusing on long-term customer relationships, and also assessing customer value and prioritizing the most attractive prospects; creating sales organization structures that are nimble and adaptable to the needs of different customer groups; gaining greater ownership and commitment from salespeople by removing functional barriers within the organization and leveraging team-based working; shifting sales management from 'command and control' to coaching and facilitation; applying new technologies appropriately; designing salesperson evaluation to incorporate the full range of activities and outcomes relevant to new types of sales and account management jobs.[6]

Our recent study of the antecedents and consequences of sales management strategy reveals several issues which are commonly neglected in leveraging change and superior performance in the salesforce and in aligning sales efforts with strategic direction.[7] It should be apparent

[3] 'Shift to Value-added Selling Is Biggest Challenge in Sales', *American Salesman*, November 2002, p. 13.

[4] Jones, Eli, Andrea Dixon, Lawrence B. Chonko, and Joseph P. Cannon, *Journal of Personal Selling & Sales Management*, Vol. 25 No. 2 2005, pp. 181–98.

[5] Shapiro et al. (1998), op cit.

[6] Cravens, D. W., 'The Changing Role of the Sales Force', *Marketing Management*, (Fall) 1995, pp. 17–32.

[7] Baldauf, Artur, David W. Cravens, and Nigel Piercy, 'Sales Management Control Research—Synthesis and an Agenda for Future Research', *Journal of Personal Selling & Sales Management*, Vol. 25 No. 1 2005, pp. 7–26.

that new business strategies and an evolving role for the sales organization in leading strategic customer management will inevitably require considerable re-evaluation of the management of the sales organization. There are numerous practical challenges in realigning the selection, training, and development of individuals for these new sales roles,[8] as well as the development of sales managers with relevant skills and capabilities for the new challenges.[9]

New Generations of Sales Employees

Not least among the reasons for wanting to examine the infrastructure of new-style sales organizations is the complication that the new generations of people coming into sales and sales-related jobs may be very different from their predecessors. They may be motivated and excited by different things and they may react differently to the incentives they are offered.

It is clear that the effective design of new organizations in sales or elsewhere is, in part, related to the motivation and aspirations of the people who work at different levels in the organization. Booz, Allen, and Hamilton research underlines that for talented people in Western companies today, financial incentives matter far less than non-financial factors—esteem, a challenging and varied job, the chance to work on teams, the opportunity to interact with interesting people. It is increasingly dangerous to assume that people are motivated only by money and to design organizations and processes on that basis. For example, instead, IBM has shifted the emphasis in annual bonus schemes from the performance of the employee's individual unit towards that of the company as a whole. At Toyota, most of a manager's bonus is linked to the performance of the business in the whole of his or her region, and only a small part to individual performance.

[8] Cron, William L, Greg W. Marshall, Jagdip Singh, Rosann L. Spiro, and Harish Sujan, 'Salesperson Selection, Training, and Development: Trends, Implications, and Research Opportunities', *Journal of Personal Selling & Sales Management*, Vol. 25 No. 2 2005, pp. 123–36.
[9] Ingram, Thomas N., Buddy W. LaForge, William B. Locander, Scott B. MacKensie, and Philip M. Podsakoff, 'New Directions in Sales Leadership Research', *Journal of Personal Selling & Sales Management*, Vol. 25 No. 2 2005, pp. 137–54.

The life aspirations of individuals entering professional and management roles are also significant. Designing organizations in which the most talented individuals cannot work productively is a danger with conventional approaches. Think about the issues faced in working with and managing employees from the 'MySpace Generation'. They are the children of the baby-boomers—twenty somethings or Generation Y—and they are already marching into the workplace. The MySpace Generation lives, buys, plays, and socializes online. Social networking websites are a way of life. The MySpace Generation will dominate the staff of our major organizations within a few years. They are ambitious, demanding, and question everything. They are different. They have tattoos and piercings. When it comes to loyalty, the company is the last on the list. They are never far from Lindsay Lohan. They always seem to be at the gym.

To MySpacers the traditional idea of a 'work ethic' does not apply. Home is the only safe place to be (so many continue living with their parents). If they do not like the job, they quit (because the worst that can happen is moving back home). Work/life balance is very important. They want interesting work from the first day, and for people to notice and react to their performance. They are expected to be the most high-maintenance workforce in the history of the world, but also the most high-performing.[10] Many traditional assumptions about what motivates people at work and how they can be managed may be increasingly redundant with the MySpace generation. As Nadira Hira wrote recently in *Fortune* magazine: 'you raised them, now manage them....'

In this chapter we will examine some of the most critical and urgent aspects of realigning the infrastructure of the traditional sales organization with the imperatives of strategic customer management. We will look at the factors underpinning superior salesperson performance in the new environment they face; the shift in the focus of sales management control strategy and the new demands being placed on sales managers; the vexed issue of what we do about the legacy of compensation-based control in most selling situations;

---

[10] Hempel, Jessi, 'The MySpace Generation', *BusinessWeek*, 12/19 December 2005, pp. 63–70; Hira, Nadira A., 'You Raised Them, Now Manage Them', *Fortune*, 28 May 2007, pp. 26–33.

and moves towards team-based selling and the new challenges this creates. To long-term sales specialists these topics may look somewhat familiar and possibly a little predictable. Actually, we are still learning new stuff in all these areas as things unfold, and some of the new realities do not look much like the old theory, so you may still want to read the chapter—we have been surprised how many managers claim they have a handle on the organizational characteristics of their sales organizations, an assertion which does not stand up to closer scrutiny.

Salesperson Performance

The core of everything is how well salespeople perform in delivering our strategies into the customer marketplace. Traditionally we always thought of salesperson performance in terms of outcomes—sales results, and so on. However, now we are more interested in what salespeople do to achieve the sales results. We show this in Figure 6.1, as the distinction between salesperson behaviour performance and salesperson outcome performance.[11]

The logic of Figure 6.1 is that we expect higher salesperson outcome performance (like hitting sales targets and quotas) to lead to higher sales organization effectiveness (meeting organizational goals, beating the competition, and so on). Traditionally, sales manager control strategy focused on outcome performance, and the sales manager

---

[11] The comments in this section and the one that follows are based on the following research sources: Anderson, Erin and Richard L. Oliver, 'Perspectives on Behavior-Based Versus Outcome-Based Salesforce Control Systems', *Journal of Marketing*, Vol. 51 October 1987; pp. 76–88 Cravens, David W., Thomas N. Ingram, Raymond W. LaForge, and Cliff E. Young, 'Behavior-Based and Outcome-Based Salesforce Control Systems', *Journal of Marketing*, Vol. 57 October 1993, pp. 47–59; Babakus, E., David W. Cravens, Ken Grant, Thomas N. Ingram, and Raymond W. LaForge, 'Investigating the Relationships Among Sales Management Control, Sales Territory Design, Salesperson Performance, and Sales Organization Effectiveness', *International Journal of Research in Marketing*, Vol. 13 No. 4 1996, pp. 345–63; Piercy, Nigel F., David W. Cravens, and Neil A. Morgan, 'Relationships Between Sales Management Control, Territory Design, Salesforce Performance and Sales Organization Effectiveness', *British Journal of Management*, Vol. 5 No. 3 1998, pp. 95–111; Baldauf, Cravens, and Piercy (2005), op. cit.

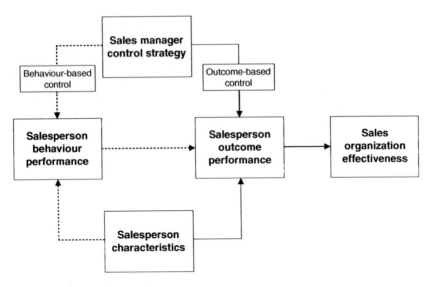

Fig. 6.1 Sales management control strategy

was a 'commander and scorekeeper' figure, chasing sales results and sorting out performance shortfalls among salespeople. (For reasons, which will become apparent in the next section, we label this outcome-based control.) Correspondingly, salespeople with characteristics of task orientation and closing strengths were recruited. However, the shift in focus is from ends to means. We all want sales results (the ends in question). In fact, what has become apparent is that it is what salespeople do in building and sustaining their customer relationships that drives outcome performance—this is what we refer to in the model as salesperson behaviour performance. The logic is that sales manager control efforts should focus on salesperson behaviour performance, as well as the outcome achieved (labelled behaviour-based control).

Indeed, there is a lot of research showing the behaviour and outcome components of salesperson performance to be different and positively related in the sense that behaviour performance drives outcome performance. We briefly summarize below some of the most important findings of research into success characteristics of salespeople and the drivers of superior performance, and how this has changed our view of how they should be managed. These factors underpin the management innovation demanded by a strategic sales organization.

What Do Successful Salespeople Do to Become Successful?

Research suggests that one clear difference between higher and lower effectiveness sales organizations lies in the salesperson attitudes and behaviour. Higher effectiveness is connected with superior salesperson *motivation*. Where salespeople are better motivated in terms of getting a sense of accomplishment from their work, feeling a sense of personal growth and development, where they are stimulated, challenged, imaginative, and creative in their work—then sales organization effectiveness is markedly higher. Having a *customer orientation* among salespeople is also strongly linked to sales organization effectiveness. Where salespeople focus on customer needs, adapt selling approaches to customer requirements, possess good selling skills and product/service knowledge, and base selling strategy on customer needs—then sales organization effectiveness is significantly higher.[12]

Alongside issues of individual motivation and customer orientation, consider the impact of *team orientation*. Where salespeople are willing to accept direction and reviews from the manager and to cooperate as part of a sales team—then sales organization effectiveness is higher. Lastly, *sales support orientation* also distinguishes between higher and lower sales effectiveness. Where salespeople spend time in sales call planning, in non-selling activities, and in sales support activities—then again sales organization effectiveness is higher. These characteristics describe the functioning of a coordinated sales unit, rather than 'lone wolf' salespeople, each pursuing their own objectives rather than those of the organization.

These factors are much 'softer' than traditional approaches to sales management, which emphasize compensation and sales expense and productivity measurement as the basis for direction and control. As characteristics of salespeople that relate to the effectiveness of the sales organization these factors offer useful benchmarks. However they lead

[12] For example, see: Baldauf, Cravens, and Piercy (2005), op. cit.

us next to consider whether salespeople with these characteristics also
display high performance.

The Drivers of Salesforce Performance

Research findings regarding salesforce performance generally relate
to two areas: outcome performance (e.g. sales results) and behaviour
performance (as shown in Figure 6.1). These factors uncover highly
important hidden differences between higher and lower effectiveness
sales organizations, which are hidden in the internal processes of the
company, rather than openly displayed in their sales productivity measurements.

First, consider the difference between outcome performance, or
achieving goals, in higher and lower effectiveness organizations. The
higher effectiveness salesforces are those where salespeople obtain a
high market share as well as high sales revenue, and beat sales targets
and objectives, but also emphasize sales of high margin products and
sales to major accounts and new product/service sales. The differences
here are substantial and important. These issues also provide good
benchmarks for executives to appraise the results of their own sales
units and to position them against the higher effectiveness groups in
our research.

However, while high performance in outcomes can be linked to
selling activities, the differences found between the higher and lower
effectiveness sales organizations concerning *sales presentation* and *technical knowledge* performance are quite small. The really major differences lie in the performance of non-selling activities. In the areas of
performance we have identified as salesperson adaptiveness, teamwork, sales planning, and sales support, we see major and highly significant differences between the higher and lower effectiveness sales
organizations.

The issue of salesperson *adaptiveness* in selling suggests that the
higher effectiveness sales organizations are those where salespeople
are flexible and experiment with the selling approaches they use, and
adapt and vary their selling styles between different customers and
different selling situations. It is worth executives considering whether
the capacity for adaptiveness of this kind is included in salesperson
appraisal and development in their organizations and how their sales
units would compare to the best on these benchmarks.

Turning to the question of *teamwork*, in the higher effectiveness salesforces salespeople are rated highly in successful team selling and in building working relationships with other employees to close sales and to solve customer problems and meet service requirements. This raises the important issues for executives concerning whether these activities are fostered and developed in their own sales organizations, and how they compare with the higher effectiveness sales operations in our research.

In a similar way, the more effective salesforces in our studies were significantly ahead of the rest in *sales planning* activities. Where salespeople were rated highly in the performance on planning sales calls, customer sales strategies, and account coverage, as well as daily activities, then the effectiveness of the sales organization is higher. These are important practical benchmarks for the development and appraisal of salespeople in activities and behaviour which relate significantly to effectiveness.

Lastly, and perhaps even more significant, the higher effectiveness sales organizations are those where salespeople perform well in *sales support* activities of various kinds. Where salespeople are rated highly in providing after-sales service, checking on product delivery, handling customer complaints, following-up on customer product use and troubleshooting on customer application problems, as well as identifying new product/service ideas from customer experience—then the effectiveness of the sales organization is higher. This provides further benchmarks for appraising sales performance leverage and the challenge to executives is again to compare their own sales units with the most effective salesforces in our research.

The dominant conclusion from our own research studies and those of our colleagues is that the sales organizations which are consistently outstripping their competition and beating their own objectives are those where salespeople display superior performance in adaptiveness, teamwork, sales planning, and sales support. It is on these 'softer' factors that the gap between the higher and lower effectiveness salesforces really opens up. The more effective organizations do score better in the important selling performance areas of sales presentation and technical knowledge but these differences are far less significant. These findings raise important questions about whether sales training and salesperson appraisal in our companies are focusing on the factors that really drive effectiveness.

Behaviour Performance and Behaviour Control

In short, salesperson behaviour performance consists of the behaviours employed by salespeople in meeting their job responsibilities. Evaluating behaviour performance is important because salespeople have more control over their activities and strategies than the outcomes of these actions. The activities may be directly linked to generating sales (e.g. technical knowledge and sales presentation) or less directly related to immediate sales goals (e.g. sales support). Traditionally salesperson performance assessment emphasized sales results (outcomes). Outcomes are important to sales managers, but studies suggest that managers are concerned with team and customer relationship-building activities of salespeople, as well as short-term sales results.[13] Research evidence also suggests when senior sales managers consider sales force performance factors, they place greater emphasis on behaviour-based factors rather than outcome-based factors.[14]

The important issue then becomes what can you do to build and support higher levels of salesperson behaviour performance? In fact, there is a considerable amount of research evidence supporting the proposition that sales manager control strategy is related to higher levels of salesperson behaviour performance[15]—we look at behaviour-based manager control strategy in the next section of this chapter.

[13] Corcoran, K. J., L. K. Petersen, D. B. Baitch, and M. F. Barret, *High Performance Sales Organizations: Creating Competitive Advantage in the Global Marketplace*, Chicago, IL: Irwin, 1995.

[14] Morris, M. H., D. L. Davis, J. W. Allen, R. A. Avila, and J. Chapman, 'Assessing the Relationships Between Performance Measures, Managerial Practices, and Satisfaction When Evaluating the Salesforce', *Journal of Personal Selling & Sales Management*, Vol. 11 (Summer) 1991, pp. 25–35.

[15] For example, see: Cravens, Ingram, LaForge and Young (1993), op cit.; Oliver, Richard L. and Erin Anderson, 'An Empirical Test of the Consequences of Behavior- and Outcome-Based Sales Control Systems', *Journal of Marketing*, Vol. 58 October 1994, pp. 53–67. Babakus, Cravens, Grant, Ingram, and LaForge (1996), op cit.; Baldauf, Artur, David W. Cravens, and Nigel F. Piercy, 'Examining Business Strategy, Sales Management, and Salesperson Antecedents of Sales Organization Effectiveness', *Journal of Personal Selling & Sales Management*, Vol. 21 No. 2 2001, pp. 109–22; Baldauf, Artur, David W. Cravens, and Nigel F. Piercy, 'Examining the Consequences of Sales Management Control Strategies in European Field Sales Organizations', *International Marketing Review*, Vol. 18 No. 5 2001, pp. 474–508.

Sales Management Control Strategy

'Control strategy' sounds a little sinister to some—it really only means the way in which managers manage, the methods they use to achieve results, and the emphasis they have in guiding the efforts of their sales-people towards achieving company goals. We emphasize the importance of the sales supervisory role in implementing strategic change, then look at the conventional wisdom about managing salespeople, and then consider some of the challenges in matching the theory to practice in developing the strategic sales organization.

The Pivotal Role of the Sales Manager

A first point we would like to emphasize is that one of the things we have learned is that the role of the first line of supervision in the sales organization—the team leader, the field sales manager, the branch manager—is one of the most critical in getting things to happen (or not). Yet this role is frequently largely ignored and sales supervisors are treated just like senior salespeople. The first-line manager is the pivot. This is the place where your strategic initiatives will be turned into reality with salespeople, or they will be discarded. There is value in looking carefully at the way in which supervisory management operates in the sales organization, and getting buy-in to change at this level.

If the people who are in day-to-day supervisory contact with real, live salespeople do not buy-in to what you want to change, or simply do not understand because no one bothered to explain it, then you have only yourself to blame if your strategic initiative gets stuck at this level and does not impact on what salespeople do in managing customer relationships.

Controlling Behaviour or Outcomes?

Generally speaking, the purpose of management control in organizations is to direct and influence the attitudes and behaviours of participants to achieve the organization's objectives.[16] The classic

---

[16] Anderson and Oliver (1987), op cit.

work by Anderson and Oliver defines a sales force control system as 'an organization's set of procedures for monitoring, directing, evaluating, and compensating its employees'.[17] They suggest a continuum ranging from behaviour- to outcome-based control. Behaviour control is described in terms of (1) specific sales management activities and (2) the extent to which managers perform the activities.

In particular, behaviour-based sales management control strategy is characterized by 'high levels of supervisor monitoring, direction and intervention in activities, and subjective and more complex methods of evaluating performance, typically centered on the salesperson's job inputs'.[18] Where companies adopt behaviour-based control systems, salespeople are likely to be compensated by a relatively high proportion of fixed salary compared to incentive pay. On the other hand, under outcome-based control systems, the salesperson's incentive pay (commission or bonus) accounts for a much larger proportion of total compensation, and managers' monitoring, directing, evaluating, and rewarding activities are limited. Behaviour-based control has been shown to be an antecedent to several favourable salesperson attitudes and behaviours.[19]

So, turning back to the available research studies, another highly important question to address is what do field sales managers *do* in the most effective sales organizations to achieve the superior salesperson behaviour and sales organization results they obtain?

In a number of research studies, sales managers have been asked questions about their work activities. It is not the only way to do it, but a frequently used grouping of manager work activities is into monitoring, directing, evaluating, and rewarding activities. The comparisons between more and less effective sales organizations show dramatic differences in the extent to which the sales manager performs these activities in the most effective sales organizations, compared to the lower effectiveness group. What we see very clearly in the more

---

[17] Anderson and Oliver (1987), op cit., p. 76.

[18] Oliver, Richard L. and Erin Anderson, 'An Empirical Test of the Consequences of Behavior- and Outcome-Based Sales Control Systems', *Journal of Marketing*, Vol. 58 October 1994, pp. 53–67.

[19] Cravens, Ingram, LaForge, and Young (1993), op cit.; Oliver and Anderson (1994), op cit.

effective sales organizations is the sales manager functioning as a coach rather than scorekeeper or commander.

Sales manager *monitoring* activities distinguish the most effective sales organizations. Importantly, this is not simply about spending time in the field with salespeople. Monitoring in the effective sales organizations is far more about observing selling performance and reviewing call reports with salespeople and making joint calls with them, as well as watching travel costs and expenses, and the credit terms given to customers. These monitoring activities help the sales manager to more effectively coach and develop the sales team. These factors provide some insightful benchmarks for considering how our own sales managers monitor salespeople, and how they compare with the most effective sales organizations in the research studies.

Even more dramatic are differences in the form of sales manager *directing* in the most effective sales organizations. In the effective sales organizations, sales managers place great emphasis on helping salespeople to develop their potential, in actively participating in on-the-job training, in coaching sessions and discussions of performance evaluations with salespeople, as well as providing rewards for good results. Direction in the most effective sales organizations is very different to the 'command and control' approach popular in many of the traditional approaches to sales manager training and development. These are notable benchmarks for examining how our sales managers direct salespeople, and how this compares to the really effective sales organizations.

There are also important differences in how sales managers *evaluate* salespeople in the more effective sales organizations. The distinctive differences between high and low effectiveness sales organization are in the emphasis on evaluating the professional development of salespeople and the quality of their sales presentations, as well as appraising their sales results, sales calls, and profit contribution. The balance between these approaches to management evaluation of salespeople contains important insights into the working of the most effective sales organizations. While managers in both the more and less effective sales organizations perform these evaluation activities, the former do so to a greater extent.

Other important characteristics of the most effective sales organizations are found by examining how sales managers approach the *rewarding* of salespeople. The big difference in the more effective sales organizations centres on the efforts made by sales managers to provide performance feedback and to compensate salespeople on the basis of the quality of their sales activities, using more non-financial incentives but still linking rewards to achievements. Less dramatically, sales managers in the more effective sales organizations use incentive compensation, linked to sales results, and reward salespeople for the quantity of sales activities, but the differences here are smaller. These factors provide a useful framework for examining how a company's salesperson reward mechanisms operate, and how they are perceived to work by salespeople and sales managers.

The activities of field sales managers in the most effective sales organizations are characterized by two important differences: in the more effective sales organizations, field sales managers are more active in all areas of behaviour control studied, rather than falling back on traditional compensation controls to manage their salespeople; and the balance of their activities in monitoring, directing, evaluating, and rewarding salespeople is quite different. They place more emphasis on observing sales performance and reviewing call reports, they emphasize coaching and helping salespeople develop their potential, they evaluate sales results but also their salespeople's professional development, and they provide more performance feedback and emphasize the quality of sales activities as well as simply the quantity of activities.

It is these sales management activities which distinguish the most effective sales organizations. It is also the extent to which these activities are performed which underpins the superior salesperson performance and sales results achieved in the most effective sales organizations. We suggest that these issues provide a powerful set of benchmarks to compare a company's sales management practices with those in the most effective sales organizations. The findings also have major implications for recruiting, training, and developing sales managers to achieve high effectiveness—the orientation and skills of a coach are different from those of a command and control manager.

This is quite a significant shift in thinking about managing salespeople, with which many organizations are still struggling. Remember the change in control logic illustrated in Figure 6.1. We are all interested in overall sales organization effectiveness (achieving goals, beating the competitor, and so on). This remains the case under different control regimes. The traditional route to effectiveness stressed salesperson outcome performance (meeting sales targets, keeping to budget, share of customer wallet, and so on). Accordingly, recruitment and training of salespeople emphasizes outcome-related characteristics at the extreme, the 'lone-wolf road warrior' who closes deals. The sales manager control role is commander and scorekeeper—to allocate work, chase targets, and penalize shortfalls in outcome performance. We exaggerate, but not much. A considerable emphasis is placed on financial incentives to direct salespeople—commission, bonus, and so on. These are the relationships shown in solid lines in Figure 6.1.

However, logic suggests that if it is what salespeople do and how well they do it when they work with customers (behaviour performance) drives outcome performance and sales organization effectiveness, then focusing management control attention on enhancing salesperson behaviour performance kind of makes sense, as does recruiting and developing people to enhance these skills. These links are shown as the dotted lines in Figure 6.1.

Is It Really 'Either/Or'?

It is tempting to see behaviour-based and outcome-based approaches to managing salespeople as alternatives—at either end of a continuum of control strategies. In fact, the commonest approach is a hybrid, where you have elements of both outcome- and behaviour control. Sales results (outcomes) always matter, and a manager who forgets about them will not last long. While managing the salesperson behaviours that drives the sales results is an important point of focus, for most of us it cannot be the only point of focus. The hybrid approach combines some outcome-based control (e.g. sales commission) with behaviour-based control (e.g. coaching and training). The question then becomes the balance between the two approaches, and the risk that one will undermine the other. We will consider this particular problem shortly.

So Now You Want Sales Managers to be Everyone's Best Friend?

There is a danger that some people may interpret behaviour-based control strategy as the soft option—the revival of 1960s happy-clappy management approaches based on the notion that happy employees work harder and do a better job and make customers happier. Not so. Behaviour-based control is a direct management intervention in how people do their jobs, how they are rewarded (and what for), and the priorities in their work activities. Generally speaking, it is not less control, it is more control.

From a salesperson perspective, if you are paying me largely by volume-based commission (and it is nearly always volume-based, one way or another), then I will bring you transactions, because that is what you are paying me for. How I generate those transactions is my business. If you want 'relationships', customer service, problem-solving, and all that stuff—tough, it is not what you are paying me for. Only by reducing the amount of variable compensation driven by transactions and sales volume can you buy the right to closely direct the salesperson's activities into the areas that you want.

You can rely on the fact that some salespeople and some sales managers will hate this change. In some important ways you are reducing the individual's freedom and discretion in how they do their work, as well as introducing more uncertainty and ambiguity into the sales job. In some cases this will not make you popular. It is also true that some salespeople and sales managers will not successfully make this transition.

But Do You Know What Sales Managers Do?

The move towards coaching and facilitation in sales management and away from commission and bonus as the primary ways of controlling salespeople is widely supported. Interestingly, there are a couple of useful things that emerge from testing how much we know about what sales managers in the company actually do when they work with salespeople.

How Much Coaching and Facilitation?

Often you find that companies pay much lip-service to the role of their managers as coaches who closely manage their salespeoples' activities in support of customer relationship-building strategies. This is fine. Or at least it is fine until you start looking at reality. One metric says it all. That metric is sales manager selling time (the percentage of the working week that the sales manager spends selling to his or her own accounts). Frankly, if line sales managers are spending 80–90 per cent of their time selling (which is not uncommon), then they are not doing a lot of coaching, facilitation, or 'leading the team'. They are, in effect, senior salespeople selling to major accounts, with a bit of admininstra-tion thrown in to justify the 'manager' title. They are not in a position to play a major role in leading strategic change initiatives or leading sales teams in new ways of working. In these situations, companies appear to think they have implemented behaviour-based sales man-agement control strategies, when they really have not. They should not expect to see the benefits of behaviour-based control as we have described them above, because they do not really have behaviour-based control in place.

The Matter of Interpretation

A further issue in knowing what sales managers actually do relates to how they interpret company mandates for different approaches to managing sales teams. We have said this role is pivotal—well, this can work for you or against you. Consider the model in Figure 6.2. It compares the company-wide sales control system decided by senior people at the centre (outcome-based or behaviour-based) with the line manager's style and approach. Where you have company-wide

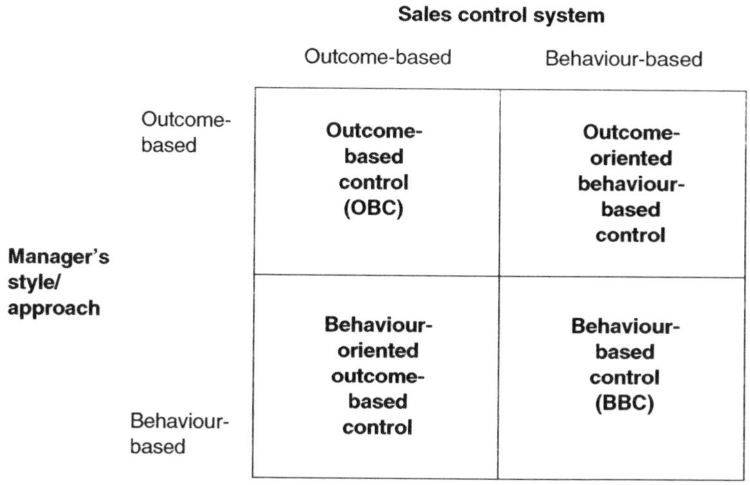

| | | **Sales control system** | |
		Outcome-based	Behaviour-based
Manager's style/ approach	Outcome-based	**Outcome-based control (OBC)**	**Outcome-oriented behaviour-based control**
	Behaviour-based	**Behaviour-oriented outcome-based control**	**Behaviour-based control (BBC)**

Fig. 6.2 Do we really know what our sales managers do?

outcome-based control and this is how the manager operates, then this is what you have got—outcome-based control, probably dominated by financial incentives. Similarly, if the company-wide system is behaviour-based control and this is how sales managers manage their teams, then this is what you have got (though do check the sales manager selling time percentage to know how much of it you have got).

What is more interesting is where there is a mismatch between company-wide control strategy and manager style or approach. This you usually uncover by talking to salespeople. When company financial incentives are high and linked to sales targets (outcome-based control), yet salespeople tell you that the manager is pushing them into non-sales visits and careful planning of customer strategy, and to take a longer-term view of the customer relationship (because that is how you earn next year's commission and bonus), then you have a kind of hybrid 'behaviour-oriented outcome-based control'. Conversely, if a company thinks its sales managers are coaches and facilitators focused on the quality of selling and customer relationships (behaviour-based control), yet what salespeople say is that the only behaviour the manager wants is sales results and beating quotas, then what you have is a potentially confusing 'outcome-oriented behaviour-based control'.

These control hybrids may work, at least in the short term. However, you really need to look at the reality of what is happening in a company between sales managers and salespeople before you accept assurances that control strategy is clear and transparent.

A good question to pursue is why successful sales managers may adopt their own approaches to controlling salespeople, even if they conflict with company-wide control strategy. It is depressingly frequent that we have to conclude that smart front-line managers may actually be right. This leads to two related issues: matching control with the selling situation and matching control with what your sales managers are capable of implementing.

Matching Control with Selling Skills and Performance

One caveat to the general prescription of behaviour-based control is that it may depend a bit on what is the sales task faced and

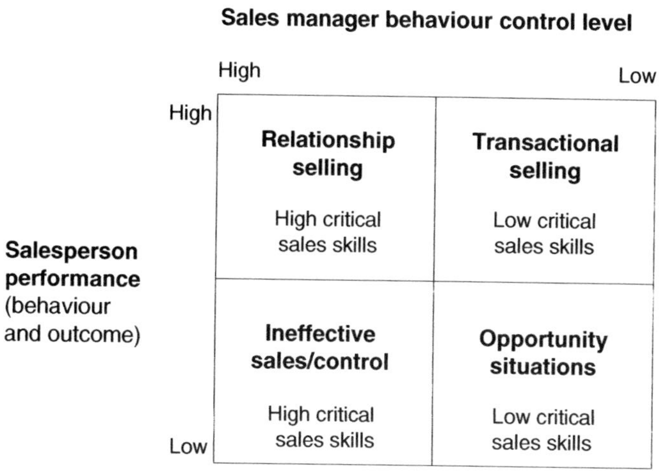

Sales manager behaviour control level

	High	Low
High	**Relationship selling** High critical sales skills	**Transactional selling** Low critical sales skills
Low	**Ineffective sales/control** High critical sales skills	**Opportunity situations** Low critical sales skills

Salesperson performance (behaviour and outcome)

Fig. 6.3 Sales manager control and salesperson performance combinations (adapted from Piercy, Cravens, and Lane 2007)

consequently what are the most important selling skills. In a recent research study, we matched the sales manager control approach with the critical sales skills in the selling situation faced and the salesperson performance level (behaviour and outcome performance). Selling situations vary from the transactional to the collaborative, and are likely to require different selling skills from salespeople. For these purposes, critical sales skills were measured as the selling and non-selling capabilities required in different selling situations. In this study, we got the picture shown in Figure 6.3.[20]

The combinations of management control type and salesperson performance level show a number of quite different results or different selling situations:

• *Relationship selling*—the managers in this group had the highest level of behaviour control and the highest levels of salesperson performance. These managers assigned the highest importance to critical sales skills. This follows since we would expect that high levels of management control will

[20] Piercy, Nigel F., David W. Cravens, and Nikala Lane, 'Enhancing Salespeople's Effectiveness: When Is More Sales Management Control Better Sales Management Control?', *Marketing Management*, September/October 2007, pp. 18–25.

be essential in selling situations which require high levels of critical sales skills.

- *Ineffective sales/control*—the level of behaviour control being used by managers was lower than the first group (relationship selling), but substantially higher than the transactional and opportunity groups. However, salesperson behaviour and outcome performance was significantly lower than for the relationship or transactional groups. This group had a high score for critical sales skills importance, but salesperson performance was surprisingly low. Possibly managers in this group have overestimated the importance of critical sales skills, or it may simply be that sales manager behaviour control is being implemented less effectively than in the relationship selling group.

- *Transactional selling*—The level of behaviour control reported by managers in this group was considerably lower than in the first two groups (relationship selling and ineffective selling). However, the importance of critical sales skills is also much lower. Apparently, these managers believed that in their selling environment, efforts to develop higher levels of selling and relationship-building skills were less important. Interestingly, salesperson performance was relatively high in this group—most notably it was higher than that in the ineffective sales/control group with its higher level of behaviour control level. The association of lower levels of behaviour control and lower selling skills importance with higher salesperson performance points to companies involved in transactional selling situations.

- *Opportunity situations*—the managers in this group indicated the lowest levels of sales manager behaviour control, and the lowest salesperson performance in the study. The importance of critical sales skills is higher than in the transactional selling cases, but still relatively low. The selling situation might call for a somewhat higher level of manager behaviour control to enable managers to work more closely with salespeople to improve their performance. The companies in this group appear to have an opportunity to improve selling results by increasing the level of management control.

Opportunities for Improvement

In the same model (Figure 6.3) there appear to be ways to achieve higher sales unit effectiveness. This is particularly true for the ineffective sales/control and opportunity situations groups. These findings suggest that variations in the importance of critical sales skills call for different sales management control approaches. The relationship selling and transactional selling groups indicate management control initiatives that appear to match the selling situations faced. The ineffective sales/control and opportunity situations display possible imbalance between control and other factors.

The other important difference between the more effective and less effective control/performance combinations was sales manager control competencies—not just how much behaviour control managers undertake, but how well they do it.

Matching Control and Manager Competencies

Very little consideration has been given to manager competencies in behaviour control approaches. The closest is the view taken of sales management competencies in a more general sense. For example, in their textbook Cron and DeCarlo place considerable emphasis on six core sales management competencies, defining sales management competencies as 'sets of knowledge, skills, behaviors, and attitudes that a person needs to be effective in a wide range of industries and various types of organizations'.[21] Their sales management competency model includes coaching competency (providing feedback, role modelling, building trust) and team-building competency (designing teams, creating a supportive environment, managing team dynamics appropriately). These competencies are similar to behaviour-based control dimensions such as monitoring, directing, and evaluating. Similarly, Spiro, Stanton, and Rich[22] in their book emphasize the team leadership role of the sales manager and the skill-set appropriate to this role.

Several studies examine the new competencies considered to be needed for the effective management of strategic account relationships.[23] However, only one research study specifically addresses sales

---

[21] Cron, W. L. and T. E. DeCarlo, *Dalrymple's Sales Management*, 9th ed., Hoboken, NJ: Wiley, 2006, p. 12.

[22] Spiro, R. L., W. J. Stanton, and G. A. Rich, *Management of a Sales Force*, 11th ed., Burr Ridge, IL: McGraw-Hill/Irwin, 2003.

[23] For example, see: Harvey, M. G., M. M. Novicevic, T. Hench, and M. Myers 'Global Account Management: A Supply-Side Managerial View', *Industrial Marketing Management*, Vol. 32 No. 7 2003, pp. 563–85.

management competencies.[24] This work was undertaken by MOHR Development with the Strategic Account Management Association (SAMA), using SAMA members as respondents. The study suggests that sales management effectiveness will be differentiated by a new emergent set of competencies. Among the highest rated of these competencies are 'coaching strategically' and 'diagnosing performance', which are similar to the behaviour control activities of directing and evaluating.

However, no one really seems to have got to grips with the question of whether sales managers have the competencies required to successfully implement behaviour-based control strategies, that is, how well the sales manager performs the control activities of monitoring, directing, evaluating, and rewarding salespeople assigned to the manager's sales unit.

The level of control is not the same as the quality of control. For example, one important activity which forms part of monitoring control activities is for the manager to make joint sales calls with the salesperson. However, the manager skills required to make an effective joint sales call are quite different from those required to successfully sell to the customer. The ineffective joint sales call is probably when the manager simply takes over and runs the visit because she or he believes they can do better than the salesperson. The result is likely to be undermining the salesperson's confidence and standing in the customer's eyes. Similarly, providing regular feedback is an important element of rewarding control activities. Yet the skills and abilities required to provide insightful and positive feedback to a salesperson, to achieve positive impact on the salesperson's behaviours and results, are unlikely to have been acquired through experience in selling.

Indeed, this should be put in the context of research findings suggesting that the training of sales managers is neglected in many companies, and many sales managers frequently receive no formal development for the sales management role, particularly regarding the managerial aspect of the job.[25] It seems many companies continue to

[24] Rosenbaum, B. L., 'Identifying Sales Management Competencies for 21st Century Success', *Velocity*, Q1 2000, pp. 37–42.

[25] For example, see: Anderson, R. E., R. Mehta, and J. Strong (1997), 'An Empirical Investigation of Sales Management Training Programs for Sales Managers', *Journal of Personal Selling & Sales Management*, Vol. 17 No. 3 1997, pp. 53–66; Dubinsky, A. J.,

assume that a newly promoted 'top salesperson' ought to be able to pass on selling skills to salespeople, thus making a successful transition from salesperson to sales manager. This reasoning underestimates the skills and roles involved in managing rather than selling.

In fact, the second major finding in our research study described in Figure 6.3 was that sales manager control competencies (how well they perform monitoring, directing, evaluating, and rewarding control activities) were significantly different between the groups, and tell us more than sales manager control levels alone. In particular, if we compare the relationship selling group with the ineffective sales/control group, while both groups display high levels of control, manager control competencies are much lower in the ineffective sales/control group.

Manager control competencies are highly relevant because they indicate how well control activities are being performed. Even when control activities are at appropriate levels for the selling situation, manager control competencies may require attention. Sales manager control competencies offer a logical explanation for why behaviour control achieves variable success in improving salesperson performance, and merit far greater attention than they usually receive.

If we are serious about adopting a sales management behaviour control strategy, to be aligned with our priorities for customer relationship-building and value delivery, then we need to give attention to more than just how much control managers use. We need to examine closely the following:

- The real selling situations that exist in the company's customer and competitive environment, the different relational investments required for different customers, and the ways they are changing and developing.

- The critical relationships between management control level and competencies, critical sales skills and salesperson behaviour and outcome performance.

- Pursuing sales manager and salesperson recruiting and career development initiatives to (1) appoint highly and appropriately qualified managers in field sales unit positions, (2) improve manager competencies, and (3) match salespeoples' capabilities with the organization's selling situations.

R. Mehta, and R. E. Anderson, 'Satisfaction with Sales Manager Training: Design and Implementation Issues', *European Journal of Marketing*, Vol. 35 2001, pp. 27–50.

• Identifying and meeting the sales manager training and development needs to address the skills needed in this vital and changing role.

The Figure 6.3 model provides a framework for analysis and action. The process involves (1) positioning your own sales units relative to the sales manager and performance groups and comparing with existing and planned sales strategies to identify the performance and effectiveness implications; (2) examining the needed levels of sales manager control and competencies—moving from 'what is' to 'what should be' by asking if the manager control level is too high, too low, or about right for the selling situation, and recognizing that manager control competencies may be a major hurdle that has to be addressed; and (3) adjusting control level and improving control competencies—identifying training and development needs for sales managers, reallocating managers' responsibilities to achieve the best use of their skills and capabilities, possibly finding alternative ways of accomplishing the control activity needed.

Overall, the superior salesperson behaviours needed to implement strategic customer management are linked to the pivotal sales manager role. However, assuming that shifting from traditional outcome-based (commission) to behaviour-based control (intensive monitoring, directing, evaluating, and rewarding activities by the sales manager) is straightforward is a mistake. In fact even assuming that you know how salespeople are really managed without bothering to find out may also be a serious error. What is required is a detailed comparison of sales strategy with what is needed in terms of critical sales skills, salesperson behaviour and outcome performance, sales manager control level and competencies. If this is something important to the achievement of a strategic sales organization, then it has to be taken seriously.

However, this still leaves the issue of the legacy of compensation control system (outcome-based control) that most companies face.

Compensation Control

Everybody in the world seems to believe in compensation control in the sales area. Managers feel comfortable it means unseen salespeople in the field will still be working—no results means no money. It provides a market mechanism, linking selling costs to sales volume. Salespeople and sales managers generally seem to quite like the excitement of financial incentives too. Any challenge to the role of commission and bonus in motivating salespeople is hugely controversial in most companies. The only trouble is when we find ourselves incentivizing things that we do not want, that destroy the value in the customer.

The Trade-off Between Outcome and Behaviour Performance

One of the big concerns if we rely on outcome-based control (compensation, commission, bonus) alone, then we will get outcomes like sales volume but not the salesperson behaviours that build and sustain long-term customer relationships. Consider the scenario in Figure 6.4.

This suggests that at very low levels, compensation control makes little difference to behaviour performance, because it is low anyway. Then at higher levels of compensation control (more of the take-home

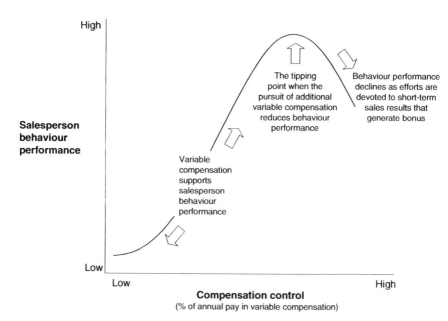

Fig. 6.4 The dangerous trade-off

pay is variable), it is reasonable to expect that behaviour performance is likely to increase as salespeople leverage their customer relationships and service commitments to achieve the outcomes that drive their financial compensation.

However, the worry is that at some stage you reach a level of compensation control that there is a tipping point. This is the point when salesperson behaviour performance reaches a plateau and then may decline. The reason is that we have reached the point where the financial stakes are so high for the salesperson that supportive behaviours towards customers are replaced by a drive for volume and revenue to generate personal income for the salesperson. The concern is that we reach a point when the salesperson gets out of bed on Monday morning and faces a choice: do I spend the morning making non-sales calls to keep established customer relationships warm, or do I go after some quick deals wherever I can get them because that puts food on the table (and possibly a Porsche in the garage)? We may reach a stage where it costs the salesperson money (i.e. commission they forgo) to do the things we say we want in supportive, relationship-building behaviour with customers.

This is the classic unintended consequence of poorly designed control systems and underlines 'the folly of rewarding A, when what you actually want is B'.

For example, in the UK, PCWorld announced in 2006 it was scrapping sales commission for its retail staff to encourage them to give good advice to customers, rather than pressure them into buying.[26] Similarly, as far back as 1989, leading US electronics retailer Best Buy stopped paying sales commission, a move made in the company's very successful shift of focus from product to customer.

However, there is one 'get out of jail free' card. The Figure 6.4 scenario applies mostly to situations where we rely wholly or primarily on compensation control. There is some evidence that in many situations you can actually have high compensation control together with high behaviour performance. The defining characteristic is higher levels of behaviour control activities by sales managers. If you have a behaviour-based sales management control strategy

---

[26] Poulter, Sean, 'Computer Stores Is Ending Hard-Sell', *Daily Mail*, 24 March 2006, p. 43.

in place, it looks like you can also have high compensation control as well without undermining salesperson performance—high overall control (behaviour-based and compensation-based) seems to matter more than the specific type of control. This underlines the importance of the line sales manager, and his or her approach to managing sales-people. What is dangerous is relying primarily on compensation-based control.

Where Does that Leave Us with Compensation Control?

If we are not careful, tampering with financial incentives systems can leave us with seriously annoyed salespeople and very grumpy sales supervisors. Messing with the way in which people are rewarded and the esteem that comes from being seen as a big-hitter is risky. The debate about whether we should reward salespeople and managers with variable compensation is hugely controversial, and there are no really clear-cut guidelines for what to do.

Nonetheless, there is a large body of research evidence that higher levels of variable compensation have little or no impact on perfor-mance, or any of the other results in which we might be interested (salesperson motivation, commitment to the company, and so on). Worse, higher compensation control may have negative influences on things like salesperson citizenship behaviour, behaviours with cus-tomers, team-work, and so on, which are also things we say we want.

Overall, it looks like the reasonable conclusion is that if commission and bonus systems are in place, if people like them, if they are the norm in your industry, if management believes in them as a 'market mechanism', then as long as you do not believe they provide you with control, you should probably leave them alone.

One interesting idea to solve the dilemma of whether to pay bonus or just fixed salary is to let the salespeople and managers concerned choose for themselves. US company Skyline Construction Inc. and a European bank are forerunners in compensation systems that allow managers to choose whether to put some of their salary at risk in exchange for the chance of a higher bonus (that if achieved will make them better off). Early signs are that in these companies the vast majority of managers offered the deal chose lower salaries and higher potential bonuses.[27] This may be an interesting precedent to consider in resolving the compensation control dilemma in the sales organization.

However, the critical point is that if you want to change anything important, you probably cannot rely on compensation systems to achieve it for you. You need something else with more leverage, and that brings us straight back to the role of first-line sales managers and behaviour-based control strategies.

Team-based Selling

It is not much news to anyone that the use of teams in managing buyer–seller relationships has become the norm in many situations. Particularly with strategic customers, many sellers have devoted more dedicated resources like formal and informal (ad hoc) selling teams to managing buyer relationships. Over time, it has become the norm for strategic accounts to be served by some sort of team of supplier personnel, and the use of teams—large or small, permanence or temporary—and this is increasingly the norm for sales strategy with accounts of all sizes.[28]

Working in teams extends beyond groups within the sales function to include working with cross-functional teams and even to working with partner organizations to deliver customer value.

For example, Johnson Controls in the United States is the market leader in the automotive seating, interiors, and batteries market, with an enviable record of sales growth and enhanced dividends over a long period. Teamwork underpins this superior performance. Executives from sales, marketing, and other functions meet frequently, collaborate, train together, make joint sales calls, and

[27] Tuna, Cari, 'Salary or Bonus? Employee Picks', *Wall Street Journal*, 7 July 2008, p. 30.
[28] Jones, Eli, Andrea L. Dixon, Lawrence B. Chonko, and Joseph P. Cannon, 'Key Accounts and Team Selling: A Review, Framework, and Research Agenda', *Journal of Personal Selling & Sales Management*, Vol. 25 No. 2 2005, pp. 181–98.

share information. Sales strategy to win the Ford F Series truck business involved a team of five—three from sales and two from marketing. Customer visits often involve sales, marketing, engineering, and design personnel together. Johnson's teamwork philosophy means salespeople are paid end-of-year bonus not commission, with other functions similarly paid bonus on company performance. Their approach has led to successful partnering inside the company (and with external partners to develop complete solutions to customer problems).

While there are many attractions in the use of teams in managing important customer relationships, there are few questions we might consider before assuming this is easy to achieve.

Teams?

If your sales and customer strategy relies on 'teams', are you sure you have got teams? If you look at how people define 'teams', then you find statements like 'a team is a group of two or more people who must interact cooperatively and adaptively in pursuit of shared, valued objectives' and 'teams are sets of interdependent individuals bound by a common aim'.[29] Cooperation, adaptiveness, interdependence, common aims?

If those are the defining characteristics of a team, then it does suggest that simply putting people into groups on the basis of their jobs may produce work groups rather than teams, and fail to achieve the benefits of genuine teamwork. The assumption that we can unilaterally mandate people to behave as a team seems a little optimistic. You probably have to work a little harder than that to build an effective team and a culture that supports teamwork.

You really do have to recognize that simply writing names down on a sheet of paper does not create a team, just a list. Indeed, it is almost a career-damaging insult these days, but some people do not have natural aptitudes for team working—in the popular management cliché they are not 'good team players' —which is not helped by the usual lack of provision of skills training in group-based working.

---

[29] Glassop, Linda I., 'The Organizational Benefit of Teams', *Human Relations*, February 2002, pp. 225–35.

Teams Don't Always Work

The issue is how well we design teams and how well we support them. If we want participation to work we should design teams for a purpose. In fact, we know quite a lot about the roles people can play in teams, and broadly what adds to and what detracts from the effectiveness of a team.

What we can try to do is to focus on the different contributions we want from different team members, and what we want a team leader to do. We need to recognize not just *task roles* (expertise to get the job done, to provide the purpose) but also *maintenance roles* (keeping the group cohesive, to provide the basis of cooperation). The *task roles* we need may include *the initiator*—starts things off, possibly the team leader; *the clarifier*—interprets and gets things specific; the *information provider*—gives expertise, research, or knowledge; *the questioner*—confronts the basic issues for the group; and *the summarizer*—pulls things together for the group. On the other hand, *maintenance roles* may include *the supporter*—gives emotional support to contributors; *the joker*—provides humour, light relief, release of tension; the *experience sharer*—uses personal feelings, experiences to open things up; and the *process observer*—stands back and helps free-up blockages in progress. We need to recognize the importance of both types of role and we can look at our planning teams in this light.

Identifying these roles suggests the analytical framework in Figure 6.5. This identifies the scenarios of *effective team*—a good balance of task roles to get the work done, and maintenance roles to keep the group together; *ineffective team*—dominated by maintenance roles—everyone has a wonderful time but they do not get the job done; *non-cohesive team*—dominated by task expertise, but with no social fabric to hold the group together as a working unit; and *no team* at all—just a group of people with no relevant task roles and little cohesion, which is likely to produce no results and turn people off.

The classic research of R. Meredith Belbin[30] tells us more about the characteristics of unsuccessful teams. It is not that they have poor morale or lack of conflict, but unsuccessful teams lack 'clever' people;

[30] Belbin, R. Meredith, *Management Teams: Why They Succeed Or Fail*, 2nd ed., Oxford: Butterworth-Heinemann, 2003; Belbin, R. Meredith, *Belbin: Beyond The Team*, Oxford: Butterworth-Heinemann, 2000.

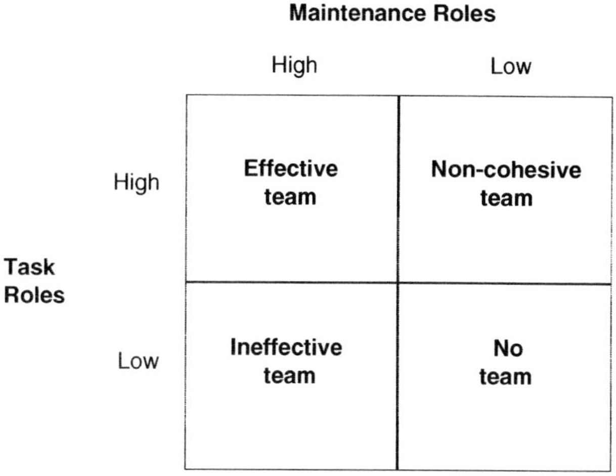

Maintenance Roles

	High	Low
High	Effective team	Non-cohesive team
Low	Ineffective team	No team

Task Roles

Fig. 6.5 Balancing roles in team design

parallel the shortcomings of the corporate culture from which they are drawn; have ineffective combinations of roles; have team-role clashes, overlaps or voids; and allocate manpower to roles badly. The Belbin work suggests that successful teams have the following characteristics: (a) team members can make two types of contribution: technical or professional expertise, *and* by taking a team-role; (b) each team needs a balance of functional roles and team roles, the ideal mix depending on the team's goals and tasks; (c) team effectiveness is greater when members recognize and adjust to the relative strengths in the group both in technical expertise and in ability to engage in specific team roles; (d) personal qualities fit members for some team-roles more than others; and (e) a team can use its technical abilities to the best only when it has the needed range of team roles to enhance efficient team work.

However, this still leaves the question of how we can support and manage teams to achieve results.

Managing Customer Relationships Through Teams

If teams matter in implementing strategic customer management, then attention is needed to the factors which underpin and sustain team success. This is likely to involve developing a supportive culture and organizational climate; adopting appropriate team-based compensation, rewards, and training; managing relationships between the team and the company; as well as designing teams effectively to achieve specific tasks.[31] These are not trivial issues. The benefits of team-based sales strategies may not be achieved easily in some situations in some companies. If they are to be achieved then there are some fundamental issues to be confronted. Nothing is for nothing. The development of effective team-based working is essential to strategic customer management.

A Structured Approach to Transformation

In some company situations the strategic sales organization imperatives we propose will be a matter of refinement and adjustment rather than revolution. In other situations the change implied will be more profound.

Experience suggests that in approaching large-scale strategic change initiatives, careful thought should be given on who to involve, the level at which decisions should be made, and the timing of the initiative's different phases. For example, an initial planning framework is suggested in Figure 6.6.

The suggestion is that we should be looking for involvement in sales force design at senior and middle management levels and addressing both strategic and operational issues. The focus should be on realignment of the business strategy and the changes in the company's routes to market. Strategy realignment can then be mapped onto how the infrastructure of the salesforce needs to be changed and developed to meet the needs emerging from change in business strategy. Only then should we be at the stage of implementing change in salesforce structure and processes—when we can see what changes are needed to develop the sales organization of the future that is capable of delivering against strategic priorities.

Some executives protest that this structure cannot work because strategy changes too fast and is too unclear to allow them to plan and

---

[31] For example, see Jones et al. (1996), op cit.

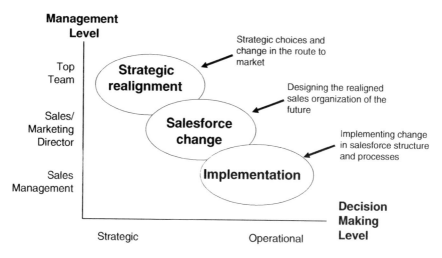

Fig. 6.6 Structuring the transformation

implement salesforce change around strategy. If so, you are probably not identifying what is really business strategy and what is not—if this is the problem, try going back to Chapter 2 and our examination of what it takes to put a handle on strategy.

What does seem to be a disaster scenario is if we start the initiative at the implementation level by imposing new mandates, structures, and processes on the salesforce, which are not closely tied to an overall redesign approach to a new type of sales organization closely aligned to business strategy. That way lies a lot of unproductive expenditure and time-wasting, and probably a lot of unhappy salespeople and sales managers (and quite possibly alienated customers too when they meet a dispirited and confused sales operation). There has to be a clear logic and rationale for change into which key players are prepared to buy.

Building the Agenda

There are no 'quick-fixes' in the essential realignment of the infrastruc-ture of the sales organization with new and evolving business strategies. High on the agenda are issues concerned with the drivers of superior salesperson performance and the type and level of performance needed by different customer targets. One of the major drivers is the sales management control system and the shift away from compensation- or outcome-based control to behaviour-based control approaches. Part of the change is likely to require examination of team-based approaches to selling and the management of customer relationships. In every case, scratching the surface of these issues reveals that if you want to do more than pay lip-service then you need to get into some of the realities of performance measurement and management practices—otherwise you have little chance of changing anything much that matters. Certainly, the evidence is that a logical and structured approach to transformation has advantages.

At this stage we have opened up the closest imperatives for the strategic sales organization (Figure 1.3): *involvement*—putting sales back into the strategy debate; *intelligence*—using market-based learning to better inform strategy and to develop new sources of competitive advantage; *integration*—getting the company's act together around customer value; *internal marketing*—selling the customer to the company; and *infrastructure*—aligning sales processes and structure with business strategy. This provides an agenda for the strategic sales organization to develop and for strategy to move towards a strategic customer management perspective. It is a demanding agenda to address.

Yet, there is more to add to the agenda for change. We now turn our attention to some broader shaping influences on the strategic sales organization: *inspiration*—meeting the challenge of leadership; *influence*—the power to change things; *integrity*—the requirements for higher standards in corporate responsibility and ethical behaviour demanded by customers; and *international*—looking beyond national boundaries.

Part III

Meeting Broader
Challenges Yet

7
Inspiration: Filling the Leadership Gap

Part II of this book was concerned with the most immediate issues to be managed in the process of strategizing the sales organization and developing a strategic customer management model—to improve how companies make decisions about customers and develop sustainable and profitable relationships with the right ones. What we have looked at so far has really been about the routes to the strategic sales organization—getting into the strategy debate, building new, aligned sales processes, and so on. However, there are some broader issues to factor into our thinking as well. If you are serious about strategic sales, then these issues come with the territory. Part III opens up these issues. We have identified them as inspiration, influence, integrity, and international—but they are linked by the concept of leadership.

The rationale for Part III is as follows. One clear implication of a strategic sales organization is that the enhanced role brings with it a responsibility for the executives involved to undertake leadership roles which extend way beyond the traditional confines of the salesforce. That leadership will need to provide inspiration, not just feedback and supervision. It will need to be exercised at several levels both within and outside the company. It may be one of the most important challenges that we face in making the strategic sales organization initiative effective.

Of course, no word in management has been more used and abused than 'leadership'. Nonetheless, we do observe a worrying leadership gap surrounding how companies manage the front-end of their operations where they meet the market. This gap has several important dimensions to consider. The first is concerned with meeting the needs for leadership within the sales and account organization. But there are equally important leadership needs more broadly in the company and in external relationships of different kinds, where leadership gaps are often apparent. In the environment we have described so far in this book, that leadership will need to be inspirational and transformational. This is the focus of the current chapter.

However, there is more to filling the leadership gap than providing inspiring vision and role models. Leadership also means exerting influence over how important things are evaluated and significant actions are taken. The next chapter examines the topic of influence, as the power to change things.

Leadership also demands integrity, and there is nowhere more exposed to ethical traps and the exposure of unacceptable behaviours than the part of the organization that meets customers. The mandate for integrity in leadership includes developing and sustaining challenging ethical standards in external relationships, but also confronting the role of corporate social responsibility initiatives in shaping customer perceptions and the type of value we deliver to them. The public scrutiny of our values and behaviours has never been so intense, and the penalties for being found wanting have never been so high. We examine this area of leadership in Chapter 9.

It is impossible to avoid the need for an international perspective in the strategic sales organization. There is pretty much no such thing as a 'domestic business' any more. Thanks to the Internet and aggressive globalization in most business sectors, we are now all competing in a global marketplace. Key issues relate to how we deal with the global customer buying for international operations and looking for global deals. Other questions to consider are concerned with managing global sales operations as they develop—do market and country differences mean that we have to change the way we manage sales organizations as they globalize, or is the world actually becoming 'flat'? These questions probably include some of the most important issues that will be facing strategic sales organizations for some time to come. We examine international issues in Chapter 10.

The Leadership Priority

There is growing evidence that leadership questions are given more critical importance in many organizations, operating in the market environments they now face, than ever before. When Sam Palmisano took over as CEO of IBM in 2002, he built a flatter organization with fewer bureaucratic levels, and allocated $100 million to teach his 30,000 managers to lead, not control their staff. (Interestingly, he also asked the board to cut his 2003 bonus and set it aside as a pool of money to be shared by about 20 top executives—worth around $5 million—based on their performance as a team.) He now works with three top teams, each focused on a different aspect of the business and employing the best brains from throughout the company.[1]

Indeed, for more than 20 years many of the world's top companies have been 'academy companies' offering intensive leadership training to their executives, because their best young employees are hungry for leadership development. Prime examples are General Electric, Proctor & Gamble, and Nokia. The 'academy company' logic is that competitors can copy every advantage you have got, except one. So, the best companies have realized that their real business is building leaders.[2]

However, less positively, a recent Roffey Park management agenda study reports that while the overwhelming majority of board directors (82%) rated the leadership enjoyed by their organization as good or excellent, only half of middle managers (52%) felt they could take such an optimistic view of leadership in their businesses. Even bigger gaps opened up regarding the related issues of morale and the values of the organization.[3] It looks like the leadership issue may still need some work in a lot of companies. Leadership issues are likely to be among the more critical in developing a strategic sales organization.

We consider first, leadership within the strategic sales organization—how can senior and middle-ranking executives in the sales organization implement the leadership and followership

---

[1] This illustration is based on: Ante, Spencer E., 'The New Blue', *BusinessWeek*, 17 March 2003, pp. 44–50; Ante, Spencer E., 'Beyond Blue', *BusinessWeek*, 18 April 2005, pp. 36–42.

[2] Colvin, Geoff, 'Leader Machines', *Fortune*, 1 October 2007, pp. 60–72.

[3] Reported in: Stern, Stefan, 'The Lofty View from Davros Could Just Be a Mirage', *Financial Times*, 29 January 2008, p. 14.

characteristics relevant to the strategic sales initiative; second, leadership within the company and the 'top team' responsibilities that come with higher profile—achieving cross-functional and high-level influence to support the goals of strategic customer management; third, leadership in external relationships—playing a key role in the tangled web of relationships common in linking suppliers, collaborators, and customer value; and then lastly leadership in the broader professional business community—winning a seat at the management 'top table' to influence opinion, public policy, and the professional futures of sales and account management.

Leadership in the Strategic Sales Organization

When we talked about the infrastructure for the strategic sales organization (Chapter 6) we looked at the move from traditional control models based on sales outcomes (revenue, gross margin, market share) towards behaviour-based control (based on the inputs in the form of salesperson behaviours with customers that drive the outcomes we want). We made the point then that this amounted to a major shift in the role of the front-line sales manager—from 'commander and scorekeeper' to 'coach and facilitator'. In fact, what we described then can be taken further, on the grounds that what we want is the shift in sales management from supervision (often part-time as the manager still sells to his or her own accounts) to leadership (working much more closely with salespeople to improve the quality of what they do in building and sustaining effective customer relationships).

The issue of leadership in the sales organization is complicated by several factors which make sales management quite a lot different to management roles elsewhere in the company. The fact is that sales organizations face ever-increasing demands for coping with complexity, managing collaboration, and meeting accountability requirements.[4] For example, increasing *complexity* is caused by the bundling of products and services, the infusion of technology, shorter product

---

[4] Ingram, Thomas N., Raymond W. LaForge, William B. Locander, Scott B. MacKensie, and Philip M. Podsakoff, 'New Directions in Sales Leadership Research', *Journal of Personal Selling & Sales Management*, Vol. 25 No. 2 2005, pp. 137–54.

life cycles, and more adaptations to customize products to customer needs, which crosses with more complicated competitive landscapes with new types of competition developing. *Collaboration* with customers and other units in the sales organization and elsewhere in the company is increasingly important for success—cross-functional teams are a specific example of new ways of working jointly with others to meet customer requirements. The requirement for *accountability* regarding efficiency, effectiveness, and ethical and legal compliance has never been so high.

It is in this context that we consider here the related issues of: salespeople as leaders; leadership as 'getting things done'—sometimes working around the systems and structures not just through them; the characteristics of management as leadership; and the comparison of transactional and transformational leadership models, in the sales organization.

Salespeople as Leaders

Sometimes it is easy to confuse formal responsibilities and rank in the organizational hierarchy with leadership. There is also a growing requirement to consider the need for more leadership activities at all levels in the sales organization, including at the salesperson level.[5] With growing task complexity and ever higher job demands, the leadership characteristics of salespeople becomes a higher priority for the sales organization. For example, one interesting view is that whenever a team comes together to solve a problem or exploit an opportunity, companies hamstring the group right from the start by putting someone in charge. The alternative is shared leadership, passing to whoever has the most expertise for the immediate task in hand and then on to others. Research suggests that when teams share leadership, their companies usually see big benefits.[6] Of course, shared leadership does not work in all situations, particularly when the company's culture is one of strong central authority. Nonetheless, the idea of fluidity in the leadership process is appealing in meeting complex situations and involving salespeople in working with managers to solve problems.

[5] Ingram, et al. (2005), op cit.
[6] Pearce, Craig L., 'Follow the Leaders', *Wall Street Journal*, 7 July 2008, p. R6.

Leadership as Getting Things Done

Nonetheless, however well-developed and clever are our strategic initiatives and change programmes, one critical resource we should absolutely not ignore is the ability of our managers in the sales organization to get things done—their execution skills. Quite simply, however much we talk about strategic initiatives, in reality, the way the change process is managed at the interpersonal level is likely to be one critical determinant of success.

In fact, the point is that in many cases it is true that managers' personal skills of leadership and action may have to *substitute* for having the right structures and administrative policies—because important things often change faster than companies can respond with their formal systems. One way of looking at managerial execution skills was laid down by Tom Bonoma as four sets of skills, as follows.[7]

Interacting skills refers to how a manager behaves and influences the behaviour of those around him or her, and includes leadership by example and setting the standards by providing a role model, as well as bargaining and negotiating and using power to get the right things to happen. In most organizations, the managers who have superior interacting skills are well-known for their bias for action and getting things done. *Allocating skills* are about how a manager sets the agenda for others by budgeting time, money, and people around the highest priorities to achieve implementation, even if this is at the expense of 'fair play' and administrative 'neatness'. In some cases this may even involve 'cheating' the system to get things done, and reward those who perform—even if this is not formally approved behaviour.

Monitoring skills refers to how the manager develops and uses feedback mechanisms that focus on the critical issues for success, rather than just the information provided by the company's information systems. This may involve face-to-face discussions, participation in key tasks, and coaching, more than score-keeping and awarding penalties. *Organizing skills*—in the sense not of designing formal organizational arrangements, but of networking and arranging and fixing things to achieve the right kind of action.

---

[7] Bonoma, Thomas V., *The Marketing Edge: Making Strategies Work*, New York: Free Press, 1985.

The importance of these issues is that manager leadership capabilities in execution represent a hidden but vital resource for implementing change. This is a resource we need to consider when we look at the sales organization and ask questions like: what are we really good at doing here, and who do we need on our side to make the strategic sales initiative happen?

However, leadership as getting things done is about coping with more than the need for execution skills. At a deeper and more worrying level, a company may have learned routines for implementing change, which are flawed and ineffective—but, in spite of the flaws we continue with the routine. This is what Chris Argyris calls 'designed error'.[8] The problem is that we not only have to find out what is wrong with the management process but also why we continued unaware that it was wrong, or why when we knew it was wrong we still did nothing about it, that is, the defensive routines that people have, to protect themselves from the discomfort and disruption of having to change. The real barrier to change is usually not gaps in skills, or even recalcitrant attitudes and change-resisting behaviour from line managers and operatives. The real barrier is those defensive routines and the 'designed error' that they protect from challenge. If we are to get to grips with changing the way things are done, leaders must also confront these issues.

Important to the process of change is the leadership style which managers adopt in the sales organization and how they approach things.

Managers and Leadership

One observation is that often managers just 'don't get it' when they are first put into a role where they have to lead others. They may be misled by the mythology surrounding how managers are 'supposed' to behave in leading others. Linda Hill exposes the gap between myth and reality about leadership in the following terms[9]:

[8] Argyris, Chris, *Strategy, Change and Defensive Routines*, New York: Harper and Row, 1985.
[9] Hill, Linda A., 'Becoming the Boss', *Harvard Business Review*, January 2007, pp. 48–56.

	The myths...	The realities...
The role of the manager is about	*Authority*—The freedom to implement one's own ideas	*Interdependency*—We depend on each other to get things done
The source of power	*Formal authority*—Being at the top of the ladder	*Everything else*—People are wary, and you have to earn the right to lead
The desired outcome	*Control*—Getting compliance from subordinates	*Commitment*—Getting compliance is not the same as getting peoples' commitment
Managerial focus	*Managing one-on-one*—Building strong relationships with individual employees	*Leading the team*—Creating a situation where the group can live up to its potential
The key challenge	*Make the operation run smoothly*—Keep everything in working order	*Make changes that allow the team to perform better*—Responsible for initiating changes that enhance group performance

Traditional 'command and control' approaches to leadership are looking increasingly shaky as ways of getting things done and living up to peoples' expectations of their leaders. Recall we mentioned earlier the joys of working with new cohorts of people in sales and account management roles who have the woeful characteristics of the MySpace Generation. Participative management is widely advocated. Besides, we live in an era of rising educational participation and democratization of decision-making processes. Incidents like the Iraq War and government sleaze outbreaks have led many people to mistrust the traditional institutions of authority. If you are a parent, contrast parental authority now with when you were a child—when was the last time you got your child to do something just on the basis of your parental authority?[10]

The pressure is for managers to show quite different approaches to leadership to those of the past. This is as true in the sales organization

---

[10] Pfeffer, Jeffrey, *Managing With Power: Politics and Influence in Organizations*, Boston, MA: Harvard Business School Press, 1994.

as elsewhere, though it may have taken longer for the message to reach some places.

Leadership Style

A lot has been written about the manager's leadership style, and much applies within the sales organization. Importantly, our thinking about leadership is increasingly moving 'beyond myths and heroes to leading that liberates', reflecting the fact that many people are 'disillusioned by their encounters with leaders and leadership: with idealised heroic performances, impoverished theories and oversimplified templates'.[11] The fashion for leaders who 'are aggressive, results-driven achievers who insist on top performance from themselves and others' appears to be on the wane, while the world looks to managers to be more consultative and inclusive.[12] Interestingly, Ludeman and Erlandson characterize the former as 'alpha male syndrome', while the latter is more like the way women manage. The theme that there is high demand for the less dominating leadership style women might display more often than men is also reflected by Linda Coughlin.[13] Interestingly, our research among sales managers also underlines the high effectiveness of female sales managers in implementing behaviour-based control and coaching strategies, compared to their male counterparts.[14]

Nor is the aggressive overachiever the leadership model of choice any more, because overachievers 'command and coerce rather than coach and collaborate, thus stifling subordinates'—overachievers are liable to be so determined to get results that they cut corners, fail

---

[11] Sinclair, Amanda, *Leadership for the Disillusioned: Moving Beyond Myths and Heroes to Leading that Liberates*, Sydney: Allen and Unwin, 2007.

[12] Ludeman, Kate and Eddie Erlandson, *Alpha Male Syndrome*, Boston, MA: Harvard Business School Press, 2006.

[13] Coughlin, Linda, Ellen Wingard, and Keith Hollihan (eds.), *Enlightened Power: How Women Are Transforming the Practice of Leadership*, San Francisco: Jossey-Bass, 2005.

[14] For example, see: Piercy, Nigel F., Cravens, David W and Nikala Lane, 'Sales Manager Behavior Control Strategy and Its Consequences: The Impact of Manager Gender Differences', *Journal of Personal Selling & Sales Management*, Vol. 23 2003, pp. 221–37; Lane Nikala and Nigel F Piercy, 'The Ethics of Discrimination: Organizational Mindsets and Female Employment Disadvantage', *Journal of Business Ethics*, Vol. 44 2003, pp. 313–25; Piercy, Nigel F., David W. Cravens, and Nikala Lane, '*The New Gender Agenda in Sales Management*', *Business Horizons*, July/August 2003, pp. 39–46.

to communicate their plans, and ride rough shod over anyone who opposes them.[15]

We are told that leaders must: have a *less dominating* management style and become a generator of solutions[16]; be *versatile* but avoid being 'lop-sided' (the 'heroic' leader who is too forceful and too strategic, the 'field general' who is too forceful and too operational, the 'presidential leader' who is too strategic and too enabling, or the 'one of the troops' leaders who is too operational and too enabling),[17] be *facilitative* (creating an organization that is participative, responsive, and essentially self-managing)[18]; *gain willing followers*—showing strong values, with aspiration and action to build upon the common good[19]; make *great judgement calls* that are not just rational and analytical but also emotional and full of human drama[20]; and be *vigilant*, with a heightened state of awareness to avoid narrow vision—characterized by curiosity, alertness, and a willingness to act on incomplete information.[21]

Quite where we find such paragons of leadership virtue is less than clear, or how we match these new concepts of leadership to the priorities we face in strategizing the sales organization. Nonetheless, the challenge in the strategic sales initiative for many of us is abandoning outdated stereotypes about what good leadership looks like and what good leaders look like, and thinking carefully about the types of leadership style and leadership we want to see at all levels of the sales organization, to achieve the things that we want and need. We consider some leadership style models.

[15] Spreier, Scott W., Mary H. Fontaine, and Ruth L. Malloy, 'Leadership Run Amok: the Destructive Potential of Overachievers', *Harvard Business Review*, June 2006, pp. 72–82.

[16] McCrimmon, Mitch, 'How to Tame the Alpha Male Leader', *Ivey Business Journal Online*, Vol. 72 No. 2 March/April 2008.

[17] Kaplan, Bob and Rob Kaiser, *The Versatile Leader: make the Most of Your Strengths—Without Overdoing It*, San Francisco: Pfeiffer, 2006.

[18] Bens, Ingrid, *Facilitating to Lead: Leadership Strategies for a Networked World*, San Francisco: Jossey-Bass, 2006.

[19] Macoby, Michael, *The Leaders We Need and What Makes Us Follow*, Boston, MA: Harvard Business School Press, 2007.

[20] Tichy, Noel M. and Warren G. Bennis, 'Making Judgment Calls: The Ultimate Act of Leadership', *Harvard Business Review*, October 2007, pp. 94–102.

[21] Day, George S. and Paul J. H. Schoemaker, 'Are You A "Vigilant Leader"', *MIT Sloan Management Review*, Spring 2008, pp. 43–51.

The Manager as Promoter Versus Trustee

Our colleagues in *The Sales Educators* in the United States talk compellingly about the role of the sales manager as fostering the entrepreneurial spirit in a company.[22] They make an interesting distinction between the manager as promoter and the manager as trustee.

The *promoter* manager is higher on entrepreneurial characteristics, and is opportunity-driven—looking to capitalize on bold new opportunities, even if they require resources not currently available. The promoter moves quickly, to exploit new opportunities, often without the complete commitment of those higher in the organization. The promoter experiments with different approaches and invests incrementally in new paths that produce results. The promoter will 'beg, borrow or steal' resources from wherever they can be found. The promoter prefers flatter structures, open channels of communication, and decentralized decision-making. The promoter sees employees as the ultimate source of value creation in the company.

The *trustee* manager is stronger in terms of administrative competence—concerned with managing existing resources (budgets, salespeople, logistics, and so on) as efficiently as possible. The trustee moves slowly on new opportunities, wanting a guarantee of results before acting. The trustee exhaustively analyses a new course of action and then makes a complete resource commitment. The trustee is more conservative and is uncomfortable with borrowing, sharing, or temporarily using resources. The trustee seeks to control all the required resources, and often views resources as a reflection of status and influence. The trustee is more comfortable with a highly structured organization and a 'command and control' approach—she or he believes in hierarchy. The trustee views employees in terms of their competence at the specific sales tasks that must be performed.

The trouble is that effective sales organizations need promoters *and* trustees—while leadership demands more than administrative competence, highly entrepreneurial managers often fail because they lack the necessary administrative and political capabilities to make change stick. Sometimes, the same manager needs to display promoter and trustee characteristics—both recognizing and chasing innovation

---

[22] The Sales Educators, *Strategic Sales Leadership: BREAKthrough Thinking for BREAKthrough Results*, Mason, OH: Thomson/South-Western, 2006.

opportunities, but also with strong administrative skills. That provides a problem because most people tend to be more comfortable with one style or the other.

Certainly, the way in which the competitive landscape is becoming more turbulent and is being disrupted by new competitors and business models underlines the need for promoters to move fast to exploit opportunities. Against this, you have to balance the need for people who are good at actually running the business. There does not appear any simple 'quick-fix' for this dilemma. It is nonetheless an extremely important element of how you design and staff the infrastructure of the strategic sales organization.

A related issue is concerned with transformational and transactional approaches to leadership in the sales organization.

Transformational and Transactional Leadership

The issue of transformational leadership has been around for a long time, though only relatively recently considered in the sales organization.[23] The theory suggests a continuum of approaches to how we lead.

Laissez-faire leadership is the complete avoidance of leading. This is the manager who is 'relatively inattentive, indifferent, frequently absent and uninfluential'.[24] Unsurprisingly, relatively few organizational authorities (none) actually recommend this as an approach to leading.[25]

Transactional leadership is based on the exchange of something of value between the leader and the follower. For example, the leader gives people something they want (a bonus) in exchange for something the leader wants (sales results). Transactional leadership is characterized by 'payment-by-results' systems, and 'management by

[23] Humphreys, John H., 'Transformational Leader Behavior, Proximity and Successful Services Marketing', *Journal of Services Marketing*, Vol. 16 No. 6 2002, pp. 487–502; MacKensie, S. B., P. M. Podsakoff and G. A. Rich, 'Transformational and Transactional Leadership and Sales Performance', *Journal of the Academy of Marketing Science*, Vol. 29 No. 2 2002, pp. 115–34.
[24] Dubinsky, A. J., F. J. Yammarino, M. A. Jolson, and W. D. Spangler, 'Transformational Leadership: An Initial Investigation in Sales Management', *Journal of Personal Selling & Sales Management*, Vol. 15 No. 2 1995, pp. 17–29.
[25] Strangely, the laissez-faire manager may be coming into fashion—in very rapidly changing situations with highly skilled and motivated employees, there is something attractive about a manager who stays out of the way and resists the temptation to interfere in what other people are doing—see Salespeople as Leaders, p. 213.

exception'. Transactional leadership is the traditional approach in business and has been linked positively in the past with follower attitudes and performance.

Transformational leadership is less based on simple exchange. Transformational leaders operate out of deeply held personal value systems—those values cannot be negotiated or exchanged between individuals. Transformational leaders unite their followers and change their goals and beliefs. The theory associates transformational leadership with several dimensions: *charisma*—providing vision, instilling pride among the group, and gaining respect and trust; *inspirational motivation*—communicating high expectations, expressing important purposes in simple ways; *intellectual stimulation*—promoting intelligence, rationality, logic, and careful problem-solving; and *individual consideration*—paying close attention to individual differences among followers.

Research suggests that transformational leadership behaviours by sales managers, compared to transactional leadership behaviours, are positively associated with salesperson performance and organizational citizenship behaviours (being a 'good soldier' and contributing to the team).[26] Interestingly, transformational leadership has a lot in common with what we described earlier a behaviour-based sales management control strategies (Chapter 6), though it is a broader idea.

All of which is well and good because we all know how high the esteem is among managers for organizational theorists and their soft-skills ideas. The trouble is that there is growing evidence that the characteristics of transformational leadership (or at least some of them) may be vitally important in the strategic sales organization we have been describing.

Followership

Another interesting perspective is that there is actually no point in looking at leadership without considering followership. The argument is that while the importance of leadership is well known, we are only just beginning to understand the real importance of 'followership'.[27]

---

[26] MacKensie et al. (2002), op cit.

[27] Riggio, Ronald E., Ira Chaleff, and Jean Lipman Blumen (eds.), *The Art of Followership: How Great Followers Create Great Leaders and Organizations*, San Francisco: Jossey-Bass, 2008.

Based on the observation that large companies are increasingly dependent on how well they understand low-ranking employees and make them effective, Barbara Kellerman suggests followers are becoming more important and leaders less so.[28]

As the Internet flattens traditional lines of command, it empowers grassroots employees in organizations. Increasingly, low-ranking employees drive organizational change. In the United States, Best Buy's retail channel vice president applies this to her own company, and the success of its local store sales initiatives: 'Look at why big companies die. They implode upon themselves. They create all these systems and processes—and the end up with a very small percentage of people who are supposed to solve complex problems, while the other 98% of people just execute. You cannot come up with enough ideas that way to keep growing.'[29]

In fact, Kellerman divides followers into five categories based on how much they care about the organization, and advises each group should be managed differently: *bystanders*—observe, but do not participate, happy with the status quo; *participants*—somewhat engaged and can support or oppose leaders; *activists*—eager, energetic and engaged, but can support or oppose leaders; *diehards*—highly dedicated, their cause is all-consuming; and *isolates*—detached, do not care what their leaders think.[30] Focusing on followership as well as leadership underlines our goal in aligning employees with strategies, but also highlights the challenges in doing this effectively. Tellingly, Kellerman notes 'Bad leaders...cannot possibly do what they do without bad followers. They depend on them absolutely.'

The revitalization or transformation of a company may be in large part dependent on incorporating employees fully in the challenge to change the ways they deal with conflict and learning; leading differently to maintain employee involvement; and instilling the disciplines that will help people learn new ways of behaving and sustain that new

---

[28] Kellerman, Barbara, *Followership*, Boston, MA: Harvard Business School Press, 2008.

[29] Quoted in: Anders, George, 'How to Empower Passionate Employees', *Wall Street Journal*, 24/26 December 2007, p. 27. Quoted in: Anders, George, 'How to Empower Passionate Employees', *Wall Street Journal*, 24/26 December 2007, p. 27.

[30] Kellerman (2008), op cit.

behaviour.[31] Managers who fail to get their employees to understand what they are doing and why, and to build their enthusiasm, should not be surprised when change programmes turn into disasters. This applies as much to the strategic sales initiative as any other.

Designed Balance in Leadership Styles

The point is that while leadership is about more than sales managers' formal job responsibilities and taps into how they engage people, you need to think about balance in the context of both the company and the job that has to be done. The danger is veering from one perspective to the other in response to short-term events, and confusing everyone about what you expect from them.

It is all well and good encouraging managers to be 'promoters', but someone has to take care of the 'trustee' role of actually running the day-to-day business. It is great to go after the 'hearts and minds' with transformational leadership, but only if you still get the results that you need to pay the bills (as in transactional leadership).

Leadership issues require us to think hard about what we need to achieve in the strategic sales initiative. Then we can talk sensibly about the right balance of leadership and followership styles that we want to cultivate in a particular situation. The trouble is this is not a 'one size fits all' issue, it requires careful thought and analysis because it is very important to success.

A Leadership Role in the Company

Thinking about leadership in the strategic sales organization is important. However, thinking about the role of senior sales and account management executives in playing a leadership role more broadly in their companies is also important. Participation in company-wide activities is one of the responsibilities that comes with playing a more strategic role. Senior sales executives will be increasingly responsible

---

[31] Pascale, Richard, Mark Millman, and Linda Gioja, 'Changing The Way We Change', *Harvard Business Review*, November/December 1997, pp. 127–39.

not just for communicating company strategy to the sales organization but also for working as leaders in the company, collaborating with other functions, becoming an integral part of the senior executive team, and funnelling customer-related insights to the rest of the senior management team.[32]

However, our observation is that conventionally sales executives are more distant from internal company issues than are executives from other departments and functions—this is, probably highly unfair to sales executives we have not observed, who may be closely engaged with the key internal processes of their companies. Nonetheless, it seems that often the external-focus of the sales organization in building customer relationships, the likelihood that sales personnel spend a lot of their working time away from the company in the field, intense pressures to meet customer requirements in fiercely competitive markets, and the role of sales executives as the customer's champion in the company, has led to a degree of detachment from the company.

However, as the traditional sales organization adopts a more strategic role in aligning business strategy with the marketplace and driving innovation and value creation, then the critical question becomes: how well do senior sales executive live up to their responsibilities as managers by their engagement with the organization and participation in its activities, outside the sales function? It is likely that this question should be revisited on a frequent basis in the process of strategizing the sales organization.

For example, the fierce competitive battle between Boeing and Airbus is very publicly led by sales leaders. Airbus dealmaker John J. Leahy struck fear into the hearts of Boeing executives, as the 'supersalesman' pulled off last-minute deals to put Airbus ahead of Boeing in the mid-2000s. Nonetheless, Leahy met his match in his counterpart at Boeing, Larry S. Dickenson, who won successive Asia-Pacific deals to boost Boeing's bottom-line for decades to come and restored Boeing's market position in commercial aircraft. Both men are part of an exclusive international club of 'über-salesmen', who battle over deals worth billions of dollars which are big enough to affect the balance of trade between countries. They do not just have to win over airline

---

[32] Colletti, Jerome A. and Mary S. Fiss, 'The Ultimately Accountable Job: Leading Today's Sales Organization', *Harvard Business Review*, July–August 2006, pp. 124–31.

executives (the customer) but also politicians, and they construct complex offers that cut across internal departments and functions. While this is an extreme example, it illustrates the potential for breaking free from functional boundaries to become a business leader in the broader sense.[33]

Probably there is nowhere leadership issues are more important than for senior sales executives to play a role in the 'top team'. While the stereotype of the 'lone leader' issuing wide edicts from an isolated position still persists, the reality seems to be that the top teams in companies are actually rather more important than the leader on the hill. The 'cult of personality' in top management still fascinates us all, and most of us like the stories of legendary business heroes. However, for several reasons the management groups surrounding senior executives may be a more important focus in understanding leadership processes in businesses.

Indeed, recent research commissioned by the consultancy Cognosis shows that the effective development and execution of strategy has more to do with what senior managers succeed in conveying to the rest of the organization, than what top leaders say and do alone. The research found that leadership teams were four times as important as leaders in the process of developing strategy. Richard Brown of Cognosis concludes that 'Leaders have only an indirect influence on creating a more strategically effective culture' and that the leader's job is to 'catalyse and orchestrate his or her top team', in order that the top team can influence the rest of the company. The evidence seems to be that top teams matter rather more than top bosses.[34]

For example, Lee Scott, CEO of Wal-Mart, explained to the *Financial Times* that 'I don't run the company...as CEO if you have to get up every morning and tell them what to do, then you've got the wrong people in the jobs.'[35] However, there is no universal way in which bosses work with their top teams. Of course, one flaw in the top team argument is when a company ends up with one-dimensional teams

---

[33] This illustration is based on: Holmes, Stanley, 'Boeing's Jet Propellant', *Business-Week*, 26 December 2005, p. 40.

[34] This paragraph is adapted from: Stern, Stefan, 'At Last, Some Good News for Leaders: You are Not Alone', *Financial Times*, 3 June 2008, p. 16.

[35] Quoted in: Stern (2008), op cit.

of executives hired in the boss' image—staffed by people who have got where they are by trying to be as much like the boss as possible. The challenge is to develop top teams with a mix of qualities that are relevant to new and emerging problems, to create a more convincing and inspiring approach to business. 'Executive cloning' is not generally a good way to create top teams who will actually challenge the leadership to innovate.

But you know what our next question is, don't you? What role do the leaders of the strategic sales organization play in top teams, what role should they play, and how do they get there? The answer largely comes down to what we have to contribute to the important strategic decisions the company faces. However, in part it also reflects the need to build a base of influence within the company, which we discuss in the next chapter.

Leadership in External Relationships

We talked earlier about the challenge for the strategic sales organization of integrating processes around customer value—working across functional and organizational boundaries to achieve this. In fact, the point is worth underlining in terms of the leadership challenge of managing a complex set of internal and external relationships, all linked by their focus on customer value.

Proctor & Gamble, for example, has transformed itself from an inward-facing organization to an outward-facing one—the target is for 50 per cent of innovation to come from outside the company. The move to a new way of doing business was driven by A. G. Lafley's turnaround strategy for the company, and his vision.[36]

Nonetheless, considerable complexity comes from the different types of collaborative and partnership-based relationships that surround customer value delivery, and often the ambiguity surrounding these relationships. Increasingly often the old clarity of seeing external organizations as either customer or competitor, as supplier or partner, have gone.

[36] Newing, Rod, 'From Inward to Outward', *Financial Times*, 27 June 2007, p. 14.

It is often difficult to sort out the type of relationships we have with different parties. For example, Company X produces specialty pharmaceutical chemicals for the healthcare industry. X was approached by a customer asking them to manufacture a new material for clinical diagnostic purposes, which had actually been developed by the customer's own R&D Department. However, Company X had the production facilities for the new compound, but did not have access to the raw materials needed or the packaging plant required. The customer agreed to supply the raw materials from another source, and arranged for Company X to lease packaging line time at Company Y (Company Y also supplies the customer but is the major competitor of Company X). Company X supplies the new material to the customer in bulk for re-packaging and in specialized packaging for laboratory use. The customer packages the bulk material itself. Company X and the customer both sell the bulk material and the packaged material to other healthcare companies, including Company Y.[37] This arrangement has proved profitable for all concerned, but it is far from a straightforward set of relationships.

Quite evidently, we may have to look at customer, competitor, and collaborator relationships when it is the same company we are talking about in each relationship. In turn this poses problems—if we attack a competitor with a new product, which is also a customer for existing products, do we undermine the original business, for example? If we form a partnership with a company, how does it affect relationships we have with other companies?

Neil Rackham and colleagues from Huthwaite suggest that the critical success factors in partnering—with suppliers, customers, and others—are *impact*—the capacity of the relationship to add value and deliver tangible results; *intimacy*—close, sharing relationships and mutual trust; and *vision*—a compelling picture of what the relationship can achieve and how it is going to get there. The challenge is managing results, the move forward from transactional relationships and providing vision as the guidance system for partnering.[38] Their framework

[37] This is a real situation, but the companies concerned prefer not to have their names published.
[38] Rackham, Neil, Lawrence Friedman, and Richard Ruff, *Getting Partnership Right: How Market Leaders Are Creating Long-Term Competitive Advantage*, Burr Ridge, IL: McGraw Hill, 1996.

describes the parameters for leadership in external relationships and the need for a 'culture of collaboration'.

Interestingly, the requirements or enablers for a 'culture of collaboration' have been identified by Lynda Gratton as *leadership role modelling*—employees are unlikely to behave collaboratively and to value collaboration if senior managers do not buy in to this way of working; *people practices*—the selection and development of people looks for collaborative attitudes and abilities; *individual reward structures*— are a barrier to collaboration; and *informal networks*—collaboration is enhanced if it is reflected in informal ways, such as shared social activities, communities of practice or social enterprise activities.[39] Gratton's conclusions underline the leadership demands of new collaborative ways of working.

As tangled webs of interlocked yet ambiguous relationships become more common in a networked world, the challenge of leadership in external relationships (and linking key internal processes to those relationships) becomes a major priority. One important contribution of a strategic sales organization is in providing a shared leadership role in managing these networks alongside executives from other parts of the business.

Leadership in the Professional Community

Although it may seem a strange observation to make here, we also suggest that there is a compelling case to be made that as the sales organization becomes a more strategic force inside companies, there is a growing need for attention to the professional status or voice of the sales organization and its managers as part of the broader community of professions which influences policymakers, public opinion, the communications media, the education sector, and so on.

It may be cynical, but it seems broadly true to say that the sales profession in the UK has never achieved a professional presence of any substance. Of course, there are providers of academic credentials related to sales and account management skills, and professional

[39] Gratton, Lynda, 'Building Bridges for Success', *Financial Times*, 29 June 2007, pp. 2–3.

institutions that organize local meetings for practitioners to socialize, and the like. Although it has a larger infrastructure, much the same applies to the marketing profession—its professional institutions have never got much beyond generating income from certificates and diplomas and training courses, in order to provide a strong and coherent voice for the professionals it represents. Indeed, 'marketing' has almost become a term of abuse in popular usage.

The lack of a public voice may seem inconsequential. In fact, it may help explain the difficulties that many organizations face in recruiting the brightest and the best to work in sales and account management positions. The status of such positions and the career prospects seem dubious to many graduates and MBAs, compared to other areas of work. Lack of voice may also undermine efforts to have the responsibility for managing buyer–seller relationships taken seriously as a professional activity by other professionals, for example, in engineering, finance, accountancy, and so on. How often has it happened that the views of those in this position have been ignored because they are just 'salespeople' with no real business or technical perspective?

If the strategic sales organization is developed along the lines we are proposing here, then it probably brings with it a leadership responsibility for participating in external professional initiatives to gain greater standing and credibility for its members, and to achieve a louder and more effective voice in the management forums that represent business to the wider social and government communities.

It is impossible to predict what types of forum can or will emerge. However, the ones that matter will probably do more useful things than grub around to make money from 'professional qualifications' and short training courses for executives. Worse would be simply creating another 'talking shop' that never achieves more than a lot of hot air. The forum that matters will be one that represents the most senior figures from the profession, that sponsors and disseminates research on important questions, that is consulted by government policymakers and the media on relevant issues, and that provides a forum for networking and communication by those who lead their organizations in strategic customer management roles.

What does also seem both unavoidable and challenging is a mandate for strategic sales and account personnel and business schools to show more vision in projecting this profession to the wider audience, and participating in the influential debates of the day. This is about winning a place at the top table where the management agenda is formed.

Building the Agenda

In this chapter we have tried to put a handle on the importance of inspiring leadership in making the strategic sales organization a force for value innovation and creation in the company. This encompasses not just changing leadership priorities within the sales organization but also broader issues concerning the leadership challenges for senior sales executives working alongside colleagues from other units at a company level, in managing external relationship networks, and in the professional community that surrounds businesses.

The strategic sales organization demands more commitment from executives than simply changing formal job responsibilities. The strategic sales initiative mandates accepting leadership responsibilities. Re-thinking leader priorities within the sales organization is a start. However, the responsibility extends beyond this to a strategic sales role in the general management processes of the business, in complex external relationships with collaborators and suppliers, and in representing the strategic customer management role to the professional community outside the company.

However, in many ways and at all these levels, effective leadership is judged by the influence exerted over things that matter. In the next chapter we turn to the issue of influence as the power to change things.

8

Influence: The Power to Change Things

Inspiring leadership is important. But leadership has to turn into influence if things are going to be changed. The Roman politician Cato the younger made an incisive comment which even now is still relevant to this debate. He said: 'When Cicero spoke, people marvelled. When Caesar spoke, people marched.'[1] The secret to changing things, in this sense, is not making speeches—speech alone is just rhetoric—'It is speech that makes people march. Good judgment without action is worthless.'[2]

In fact, one of the biggest problems our colleagues in marketing departments have faced in recent years is not so much that they have nothing worth saying, but that they are being ignored when they say it. One potentially disastrous outcome of the low esteem in which many functional specialists appear to hold marketing (and probably the rest of us 'hucksters' at the front of the organization) is that they stop *listening*. For example, research suggests that when marketers try to share insights and information with other departments, they are frequently ignored or misunderstood—so, often

---

[1] Quoted in Tichy, Noel M., and Warren G. Bennis, *Judgment: How Winning Leaders Make Great Calls*, New York, Portfolio Books, 2007.
[2] Tichy and Bennis (2007), op cit.

the fight now is actually to get the customer's voice heard in the company.[3]

Part of the problem is insufficient or weak efforts at communicating with other departments. This is why we see integration (Chapter 4) and internal marketing (Chapter 5) as so key to strategizing sales in companies. However, there is more to it than that. For example, in studying the integration of marketing and R&D, research findings suggest that it is inter-functional rivalry and political pressures that severely reduce R&D's use of information supplied by marketing and sales personnel.[4] It seems it is not just that they do not like us—they will not believe what we say either. That is pretty serious.

This speaks to declining influence and credibility in contributing to the important debates and decisions within the business. It fundamentally undermines the ability to change things, even though there may be a desperate need for them to be changed. In the absence of formal authority and perhaps weak credibility in some companies, those looking to the strategic sales organization as a force for important change will rely on rebuilding influence within the organization to achieve these goals.

This chapter looks at influence in organizations as developing the power to change things that matter. Let us consider first why influence matters, and the shift in emphasis in modern thinking from formal authority ('hot power') to influence and persuasion ('cool power'). Then we can examine the landscape of power and influence inside a company, that will likely be a powerful determinant of how the strategic sales initiative succeeds or fails, and the strategic influence and change that appear to work in organizations. In some ways this is an unfamiliar agenda for those whose careers may quite reasonably have been built by creating and sustaining customer relationships in the external marketplace. Our view is that achieving the type of change we have described in strategizing the sales organization will depend in part on the success of executives in engaging with the rest of the

---

[3] Cited in Fazio Maruca, Regina, 'Getting Marketing's Voice Heard', *Harvard Business Review*, January–February 1998, pp. 10–11.

[4] Maltz, Elliot, William E. Souder, and Ajith Kumar, 'Influencing R&D/Marketing Integration and the Use of Market Information by R&D Managers', *Journal of Business Research*, Vol. 52 No. 1 2001, pp. 69–82.

organization and confronting the realities of how it makes important decisions.

Why Influence Matters

Influence is linked to leadership and formal authority. But the power to change things may not be so simple. Consider two senior sales executives interviewed in our research.

John Smith[5] is a sales director in an engineering company. He spends a great deal of his time on the road, making joint calls with his salespeople, and dealing with his own major accounts. The role involves a considerable amount of foreign travel. He is seen by his salespeople as tough but reasonable—he comes down hard on transgressions and performance shortfalls, but treats his people fairly. His sales operation is highly successful in meeting the company's sales and growth targets, and it operates on a tightly managed budget. When he is in the UK and needs time to catch up on the paperwork, he frequently works from home. Because he lives some distance from the company's head office, his social life is quite separate from his business life. His travel and geographic location make him a fairly anonymous individual within the head office of the business. This said, his senior position in the company and his excellent technical qualifications in engineering make him a figure of respect. When he gets to the office, his first question to everyone he meets (including his long-suffering secretary) is along the lines of 'Hi! What's new? What's happening? Any gossip?'. When at the office, he normally skips lunch to fit in more work time. He seems on reasonably good terms with most of his colleagues, including the Managing Director, but most contacts he has with them are at the level of formal meetings. He has little interest, or involvement, in the activities of the other departments. He fights fiercely and effectively to protect his sales department's 'turf', but beyond this he leaves everyone else to 'do their own thing'. Notwithstanding his advanced credentials in engineering, he defers to

---

[5] We would not dare to use their real names.

his colleagues on all matters of a technical nature. Business planning comes out of the Managing Director's office and John plays no role in this other than providing sales forecasts and adjusting them to fit with strategic decisions.

Jack Jones is also a sales director, though his company's products are data storage and other resources for information technology systems. He is responsible for a small direct salesforce and a chain of third-party resellers. His salespeople deal direct with end-users, while he manages key account reseller relationships himself. While the business is not straightforward—there are emerging conflicts between the direct sales operation and the intermediaries, and there are major changes in the competitive landscape which need to be confronted—it has grown at a phenomenal rate in recent years, which is reflected in very attractive profitability and share prices. Jack estimates he spends around two days a week with the resellers and three days a week in the office—he only works from home at weekends. Much of his social life revolves around the company—he is one of the few senior executives who participate in the company's sports and social events. He is well known to people in most of the departments of the company, partly because he is active in seeking technical and support expertise from other departments to support the salesforce. He is on first-name terms with other department executives and the Chief Executive and frequently participates in lunches and other social contacts with this group. In addition to his sales department responsibilities, Jack is frequently consulted by other departments on matters as diverse as employee job grading schemes, training programmes, and process improvement programmes. He participates in several cross-functional teams focused on technical strategy and relating the technology to customer needs. He plays an important role in liaison with the company's owners in the United States, briefing them on market changes and trading conditions alongside the Chief Executive of the UK company. His secretary tends to ask him: 'Hi! What's new? What's happening? Any gossip?'.

Both are extremely successful senior sales executives with comparable job responsibilities and organizational 'rank'. One has substantial influence across the business in which he works, the other does not. One has power inside the business, the other does not. One is part of managing change in the business, the other is not. One has *'hot power'*, the other has *'cool power'*.

Hot Power versus Cool Power

The term 'power' is often misunderstood and frequently seen as something bad or underhand. In the simplest terms, power is 'the ability to obtain the outcomes one wants'.[6] But power in organizations has always been associated with formal job responsibilities, the control of resources, and the ability to reward or sanction peoples' behaviour.

As Robert Malott, the then CEO of FMC, said, speaking for many of his peers: 'Leadership is demonstrated when the ability to inflict pain is confirmed.'[7] Comments like these refer to what is becoming recognized as 'hot power'. Hot power was always fundamental to business. When Rockefeller ran Standard Oil he destroyed his competitors by underpricing them and getting railroads to refuse to carry their product. That is the use of 'hot power'.

On the other hand, Apple has a small market share in computers that by traditional standards is meaningless. Apple-founder Steve Jobs has never had any market power—no big distribution network, no huge factories. But Jobs has ideas. The iPod was not even a new product—just a better designed version of an existing product. The power was in the idea of iTunes, the iPod, and a new business model. The iPhone is a similar breakthrough idea (essentially a mobile computing platform to replace the PC), for which the network operators have competed for the right to sell. They wanted Jobs' power to attract customers with his superior ideas. 'Cool power' beats 'hot power'. In modern markets, a big idea is worth more than a big market share.[8]

The parallel shift inside organizations is from the use of 'hot power' to 'cool power' by successful managers to get things done effectively. Geoff Colvin, writing in *Fortune* magazine, notes that in the 1980s when Fortune used to run articles on America's 10 toughest bosses, they were masters of hot power—they intimidated, humiliated, and threatened. But now other factors have robbed managers of traditional

---

[6] Nye, Joseph, quoted in Colvin, Geoff, 'Power: A Cooling Trend', *Fortune*, 10 December 2007, pp. 37–51.

[7] Malott, Robert, quoted in Colvin, Geoff, 'Power: A Cooling Trend', *Fortune*, 10 December 2007, pp. 37–51.

[8] Colvin, Geoff, 'Power: A Cooling Trend', *Fortune*, 10 December 2007, pp. 37–51.

hot power—companies have been humbled by scandals, shareholders wield more power than CEOs, and executives have shorter tenures, so it is easier for employees to wait them out rather than comply with unpopular orders.[9]

Increasingly, the only way for managers to be effective is to get employees and colleagues on their side. One executive head-hunter from Spencer Stuart says the kind of leader he is asked to find these days uses a new approach: 'Rather than telling the troops, it's a question of asking probing questions that force the team to think and come up with the right answers. It's subtle and more acceptable than dictating.'[10] Hot power or 'soft power' is about the ability to get what you want by attracting others to your cause—it is about bringing people to share our values and help us pursue common goals.[11]

Cool power is about strategies of influence and persuasion in organizations rather than traditional 'command and control' approaches to managing. Cool power is about attraction rather than coercion.

Understanding Power and Influence in Organizations

Being given formal responsibility for doing something, along with the necessary resources, is one way of getting things done in organizations.[12] Formal power is, however, limited in several respects: people may not accept your authority and push back, and some of the people whose cooperation you need are likely to be outside the formal chain of command in which you are located. Changing social norms (e.g. about democracy and participation) and greater cross-functional and cross-border dependencies have made formal authority less effective than it once was. An alternative perspective emphasizes getting things done by developing a shared vision or culture. This is slower and may be difficult to achieve if the 'vision' you are pursuing is far removed from the one your colleagues currently share. Developing a common vision is increasingly challenging in

---

Colvin (2007), op cit.   [10] Leff, Tom quoted in Colvin (2007), op cit.
[11] Nye (2007), op cit.   [12] This section is based on Pfeffer (1994), op cit.

organizations which are more and more heterogeneous—in terms of race and ethnicity, gender, language, age-groups, and even culture.

Jeffrey Pfeffer underlines the possible importance to effective implementation of new strategies of achieving change without having or using formal authority, and without relying on a strong and shared organizational culture. He points to the simple fact that in many problematic situations, people get things done by working through the 'unofficial' processes of power and influence. From this perspective, he suggests that the process of changing things in organizations can consist of the following stages:

1. Deciding your goals and what you are trying to achieve.
2. Diagnosing the patterns of dependence and interdependence in the organization—which individuals or groups are influential and important in achieving the goals?
3. What are their points of view likely to be—how will they feel about what we are trying to achieve?
4. What are their power bases in the organization? Which of them are the most influential in the decisions that impact on achieving our goals?
5. What are your bases of power and influence? What bases of power can you develop to gain more control over the situation?
6. Which strategies for exercising power seem most appropriate and are likely to be most effective in this situation?
7. Based on the points above, choose a course of action to get things done.

At the practical level, some people find it insightful to do a simple force-field analysis, using the type of structure shown in Figure 8.1. This just asks us to compare where we are now on the issue that matters—the current situation—and where we want to be—the target situation. Then we identify all the forces helping us move in the direction we want to go, such as top management support, external pressures, and resources available. Finally, we have to tease out the forces acting against us, for example, management opposition, lack of resources, and resistance to change. The balancing of the forces for and against implementation provide insights into the way forward and where we need to exert influence and how.[13]

[13] For a more detailed coverage of implementation issues, see Piercy, Nigel F., *Market-Led Strategic Change: Transforming the Process of Going to Market*, Oxford: Elsevier/Butterworth-Heinemann, 2009.

Fig. 8.1 Force-field analysis

Very often, force-field analysis turns out to be much more about people and the politics of the organization than about resources, systems,
and technical capabilities. One analysis which focuses on this issue
is shown in Figure 8.2. Again it is an approach which some people
have found useful in putting a handle on what it will take to change
things.

**Influence of the key player
over this issue**

	High	Low
Supports		
	Influential supporters	**Non-involved supporters**
Attitude of the key player to this issue		
	Influential opposition	**Non-involved opposition**
Opposes		

Fig. 8.2 Key player matrix

The analysis focuses on evaluating the key players who are significant to the successful implementation of the changes we have in mind. First, if our thinking has produced little insight into what is likely to prevent things happening, or what we have to do to make them happen, we may not have got to the heart of the problem—so we may have to be a lot more specific about the people, the departments, the committees, and so on, that we have to cope with. Broadly the categories into which our key players will fall are as shown in Figure 8.2. Their characteristics and the opportunities we face are described below.

Some people we will see as *influential supporters*. With these key players the goal is to utilize and reinforce this source of support for what we are trying to achieve. We will be concerned to ensure that these key players stay on our side, and remain involved in the decision with which we are concerned. On the other hand, the *influential opposition* consists of the key players who are influential and involved in the important decisions, but almost inevitably will oppose our plans. First, we have to consider whether their influence is great enough to outweigh our supporters (or vice versa). If it is, we may want to consider whether there are strategies we can employ to win their support— perhaps by doing 'deals' on things important to them, or by negotiating, or by 'selling' our ideas to them. Alternatively, we may want to consider what may be done to reduce the influence of intractable opponents. We may consider how these key players might be eased out of the decision-making unit—by the action of a senior player who is on our side, or perhaps more surreptitiously by removing them from the circulation list, or influencing the agenda for the decision-making unit.

On the other side of the model, we identify *non-involved supporters*. With these key actors, who are not influential in the decision but who support our goals and plans, the main possibility to consider is what may be done by us or them to increase their influence—the reverse of the tactics above for influential opposition.

The *non-involved opposition* are the parties providing unhelpful 'noise' in the system, but since they are not directly influential we may not see these as a major threat. However, if it seems likely that their influence will increase or they provide support for the influential opposition, then we may need to allow for this extra problem and consider the appropriate stance to take.

This is a very crude analysis, but it can be effective in starting to put our minds around the processes of influence that surround decisions about important strategic issues. However, central to adopting approaches of these kinds is understanding the sources of influence in organizations and how to mobilize them to achieve change.

Sources of Influence

While people in organizations are influenced by context (how problems and opportunities are understood and presented to them), organizations are social settings in which we are influenced by what our colleagues are doing and saying, how we feel about those colleagues, and the emotions created in social settings. Interpersonal influence shapes outcomes in organizations. While we can develop a reasoned, rational business case for the strategic sales role, we need to think about how other people will feel about this, and how they can be influenced.

Jeffrey Pfeffer takes a fairly brutal view and describes interpersonal influence as involving three things: what people say and do, or the effect of social proof; what people do to get us to like them and feel good about what they are doing; and the emotions that are created in social settings.[14]

Social Proof and Social Influence

When faced with uncertainty and ambiguity, most of us cope by asking for the opinions of associates through informal social communications. Often, these shared views come to influence our own view of the situation. In this sense, beliefs and judgements are socially constructed. Moreover, complying with, or publicly confirming, the views of others gains us acceptance—we engage in an exchange where we trade conformity for social acceptance. Also, sharing views with others becomes a foundation for interpersonal attraction, because consensus and shared views emphasize similarities.

---

[14] This section is based on Pfeffer (1994), op cit.

The principle of social proof suggests it is invaluable for change agents to have allies and supporters to provide evidence of social consensus around a particular issue. The influential manage the informational environment so the necessity of what they are doing appears to be taken for granted by everyone in the organization. This is often achieved by simple repetition of ideas and messages, as well as pointing out others who agree with you.

To be effective, we may need to support the strategic sales initiative with shared 'social proof' that builds consensus around the importance of what we are trying to achieve.

Liking and Ingratiation

In examining the psychology of influence, Robert Cialdini notes that 'Few of us would be surprised to learn that, as a rule, we most prefer to say yes to requests of people we know and like'—he calls liking 'the friendly thief'.[15] Who we like rests on a lot of factors, including social similarity—we tend to like people more if they resemble us; physical attractiveness—attractive people are more liked and more likeable; compliments and flattery—we like people who like us and who express positive sentiments towards us; contact and cooperation—we tend to like people we know well particularly if we have worked with them on a shared task; association with positive things—we like people who bring us good news and dislike those who bring us bad news.

The implication of the liking principle brings us back to the question of management style. Many managers in the past were successful by being aloof and intimidating and exercising formal power through the hierarchy. Changing social norms and values suggest that there are fewer opportunities for classical, tough, numbers-oriented managers. Pfeffer concludes: 'The liking principle suggests that managers who are warmer, more humorous, and less intimidating will, all other things being equal, have an easier time exercising influence.' Without such influence, it is likely that the strategic sales initiative is going nowhere.

[15] Cialdini, Robert S., *Influence: The Psychology of Persuasion*, New York: Harper-Collins, 2007.

Influence through Emotions

Some interpersonal influence strategies rely on the emotional aspect of social life. The behaviour of others is in part dependent on the emotions we display. Pfeffer tells us that

Getting along in organizations often involves being able to transact business, in a pleasant and effective manner, with people whom you don't like and possibly don't respect, but whose cooperation you need to get things done. The emotions and feelings you display are important, and we all learn from our childhood on to 'be polite', and to 'not let our feelings show', and perhaps, even to use emotional displays intentionally to influence others to behave as we want them to.

To Pfeffer's list, Robert Cialdini adds the following additional insights into how influence works.[16]

Reciprocation: The Old Give and Take . . . and Take

The rule of reciprocity means we are obligated to the future repayment of favours, gifts, invitations, and so on, even if those favours were not requested in the first place. The rule of reciprocity and the sense of obligation it creates are pervasive in human culture. The rule has great strength, often producing a 'yes' response to a request that, except for an existing feeling of indebtedness, would definitely have been refused. In the company's underground economy, favours are the currency by which goodwill and cooperation is gained—even though some 'favours' are just people doing the jobs they are supposed to do.[17]

Commitment and Consistency: The Hobgoblins of the Mind

Cialdini tells us that people have an almost obsessive desire to be, and to appear, consistent with what they have already done. Once a person has made a choice or taken a stand, he or she will encounter personal and interpersonal pressures to behave consistently with that

---

[16] Cialdini, Robert (2007), op cit.

[17] Sandberg, Jared, 'Doing a Favour, Asking for One', *Wall Street Journal*, 18 December 2007, p. 27.

commitment. These pressures cause us to behave in ways which justify our earlier decision.

Authority: Directed Deference

People have a deep-seated sense of duty to authority. They react in their behaviour and compliance to symbols of authority as well as real formal authority.

Scarcity: The Rule of the Few

Most salespeople will concur with the scarcity principle—that opportunities seem more valuable to us when their availability is limited. Often people seem to be more motivated by the thought of losing something than by the thought of gaining something of equal value.

Cialdini's case is that those who exert influence over others often do so because, knowingly or not, they trade favours to leverage social obligations, appeal to people's needs for consistency, represent real or symbolic authority, and appeal to people's fear of missing out on something. Influence-exerting behaviours of this kind may be extremely relevant to the strategic sales initiative and an important part of our preparation.

In fact, some of the insights above will actually be familiar to people who have been on selling training courses. There is much in common with techniques of persuasion traditionally provided as sales training, and patterns of influence within organizations. The point we are making in this quick review is that getting things done and building effective change in companies may take a lot more than just making a rational case for change and sitting back. Changing things takes more effort than that, unless you are incredibly lucky. The responsibility of leadership brings with it the need to find ways to exert influence over important issues.

Strategies of Influence and Change

Leading management thinker Gary Hamel jokes: 'Trying to get an organization to innovate is like trying to teach a dog to walk on its hind legs. If you get its full attention and hold a biscuit in front of its nose, it might take a few steps. But as soon as you turn your back, it goes down on all fours.'[18] Hamel argues that 'management monotony' undermines innovation by its obsession with budgeting and 'best practice', while management innovation—changing decision-making, organizational structure, and how time is used—leads to the most durable competitive advantage.[19] However, the fact is that most managers work in organizations that give no incentive to explore new ways of doing things. For the strategic sales initiative to work, we need to think carefully about how we can exert influence as a route to successful change.

John Kotter of Harvard Business School is one of the world's leading experts on organizational change. His outstanding research on how people successfully change things in organizations leads him to conclude: 'the core of the matter is always about changing the behavior of people, and behavior change happens in highly successful situations mostly by speaking to people's feelings. . . . People change what they do less because they are given *analysis* that shifts their *thinking* than because they are *shown* a truth that influences their *feelings*.'[20]

Kotter's research leads him to identify eight steps for successful large-scale change in organizations: (*a*) *increase urgency*—when people start telling each other they need to get moving and change things; (*b*) *build the guiding team*—forming a group powerful enough to guide a big change and getting them working together; (*c*) *get the vision right*—the group develops the right vision and strategy for the change effort; (*d*) *communicate for buy-in*—getting people to buy-in to the change and to start to change what they do; (*e*) *empower action*—the stage when more people feel able to act on the vision and do so; (*f*) *create short-term wins*—momentum builds as people try to fulfil the vision, while fewer and fewer resist the change; (*g*) *do not let up*—people make wave after wave of changes until the vision is fulfilled; and (*h*) *make change stick*—getting new and winning behaviours

---

[18] Quoted in Stern, Stefan, 'Corporate Doers and Thinkers Miss a Chance to Experiment', *Financial Times*, 25 January 2006, p. 15.

[19] Hamel, Gary with Bill Breen, *The Future of Management*, Boston, MA: Harvard Business School Press, 2007.

[20] Kotter, John P., and Dan S. Cohen, *The Heart of Change: Real-Life Stories of How People Change Their Organizations*, Boston, MA: Harvard Business School Press, 2002.

to continue, despite the pull of tradition, change of personnel, and so on.[21]

However, importantly the Kotter research provides several insights into what you need to think about and do within each of the steps. Rarely is the core method of change about giving people analysis, so that data and analysis change how they think and new thoughts influence behaviour. Instead, the researchers find that the core approach to achieving change is far more frequently characterized as (*a*) *help people see*—creating compelling, eye-catching, dramatic situations to help others visualize problems and solving problems; as a result (*b*) *seeing something new hits the emotions*—the visualizations provide useful ideas that hit people at a deeper level than surface thinking, reducing emotions that block change and enhancing those that support it; so that (*c*) *emotionally charged ideas*—change peoples' behaviour or reinforce changed behaviour.[22]

These frameworks provide a powerful mechanism for addressing the type of organizational change and upheaval we have been describing in building the strategic sales organization. Major organizational change is about people and emotions, not just plans. Achieving change requires a strategy of influence that goes beyond rational facts and figures and leads the 'hearts and minds' in the direction we need. This is a key part of the strategic sales proposition, although it is an unfamiliar one to many in sales and account management positions at present.

Building the Agenda

Perhaps the single key message in this chapter is that those who want to champion change and to see it happen may have to focus more on the real inner workings of the organization and how it frames, shapes, and makes decisions, as well as carrying forward the strategic sales message. Transformation and revolution in something as important as how a company understands its market and how it designs and delivers effective customer relationships is unlikely to happen if it is

---

[21] Kotter and Cohen (2002), op cit.   [22] Kotter and Cohen (2002), op cit.

opposed and resisted by the influential and powerful in the company. Rational analysis and the business case for what we are proposing will take you so far. But the questions then become: who runs things here (for real), who consistently gets things their own way, who sets and shapes the agenda that is addressed by senior decision-makers? Without understanding the internal political landscape in the company, we are likely to struggle with gaining support and commitment for the strategic sales organization. This is the reason why we consider influence as one of the leadership forces driving the strategic sales initiative.

9

Integrity: The Challenge of Corporate Responsibility and Ethics That Matter to Customers

For the strategic sales organization to fill leadership commitments and exert influence in a company also brings the responsibility for championing integrity—both in dealing with external customers and partner organizations and in working with others in the company. This responsibility brings not only some limitations on what actions can be taken, but more importantly is also a source of competitive strength in the marketplace.

Certainly, the level of scrutiny of the ethical standards and corporate social responsibility initiatives undertaken by companies has never been so searching. The attention of pressure groups and the media coverage given to company behaviour is unprecedented, and frequently hostile. The importance is that damage to corporate reputation, however it is brought about, reduces the ability to compete and can undermine the value of a company.

Historically, it has been easiest for critics and observers to focus on the selling behaviour of suppliers and much attention has been give to the 'front-end' ethical standards of salespeople and sales management. This continues to be the case. However, the debate has moved on to a much broader ground concerning corporate social responsibility—initiatives to show 'green' or environmental improvements, protecting the working conditions of employees at different stages of the supply chain, reducing the use of scarce resources in the value chain, and so on. This debate has reached a level of maturity now such that it has a substantial impact on buyer–seller relationships and the competitive position of selling organizations. That is the reason why the integrity issue has to feature high on the agenda of any strategic customer management initiative.

It has been clear for a while that peoples' judgements of a company's moral standards and corporate responsibility influence whether they want to work for you, whether they want to invest in you, whether they want to supply you, even whether they want to sell for you—but now it is about whether customers want to (or are able to) buy from you.

Many of the most visible and high-profile issues of ethics and morality happen at the buyer–seller interface where there is really no place to hide. The test of whether corporate social responsibility initiatives actually enhance customer value happens there too. This underlines the topicality and significance of issues of integrity to the strategic sales organization.

One problem, of course, is that whatever you do to improve ethical standards or to undertake corporate responsibility initiatives, you will be wrong, at least to some people. One person's legitimate sales promotion payments (e.g. BAE selling aircraft to Saudi) are another person's illegal bribery and corruption (e.g. the Serious Fraud Office and the US government's Department of Justice[1]). One person's highly cherished investment in alternative energy sources for running retail stores (e.g. M&S) is another person's misappropriation of shareholder funds for an unmandated management ego-trip (e.g. some M&S shareholders[2]). We are dealing with issues where there is rarely an absolute right and wrong. Cynics would say that all you end up doing is trying to please those who can hurt you most—BAE does not want to lose its priceless franchise with the US government, and M&S does not want

---

[1] Michaels, Daniel, 'BAE Corruption Probes Aren't Likely to End Soon', *Wall Street Journal*, 20 May 2008, pp. 1 and 31.

[2] Rigby, Elizabeth, 'M&S Chief Faces a Gruelling AGM', *Financial Times*, 5/6 July 2008, p. 16.

to be left behind in the 'environmental arms race' to win favour with the green consumer. Optimists would say that nothing is ever perfect and if the end-result is something better than we had before then that is probably OK.

But things can get complicated. In 2001, bankers at HSBC found themselves dropped by a group of medical charities as a direct result of giving in to pressure from animal rights activists (by refusing to handle shares in the animal testing company Huntingdon Life Sciences)—or 'caving into extremists' as the Association of Medical Research Charities put it as it moved its £16 billion to another bank. You will struggle to please all the people all the time.[3]

The one thing that is sure is that issues of integrity in seller behaviour and the development of corporate social responsibility initiatives that make business as well as social sense is a high priority for business leaders. Not least among the reasons is the evidence that when major customers are actually asked what they want from sellers, then honesty and integrity top the list.[4]

We will look at the issue of corporate reputation and why it has become more significant as a competitive resource. We can then identify some of the moral challenges facing sellers—both familiar and emerging dilemmas. Finally, we will look at corporate social responsibility, particularly as it is affecting buyer–seller relationships and competitive positioning.

Corporate Reputation

Apart from any ideas of right and wrong, ethical issues and corporate social responsibility initiatives are at the front of management thinking because they impact on corporate reputation. Corporate reputation seems to matter quite a lot for a number of reasons.[5]

---

[3] English, Simon, 'Charities Drop Bank for Bowing to Activists', *Daily Telegraph*, 24 April 2001, p. 8.

[4] Galea, Christina, 'What Customers Really Want', *Sales & Marketing Management*, May 2006, pp. 11–12.

[5] An interesting review of corporate reputation issues can be found in Arthur W. Page Society, *The Authentic Enterprise*, New York: Arthur W. Page Society, 2007 (www.awpagesociety.com).

'Public Relations' or Corporate Reputation?

Conventionally, public relations has been concerned with the trivia of press releases and sponsorship deals and the like, to gain 'publicity'. Corporate reputation, on the other hand, has become an increasingly strategic issue impacting on the ability of companies to compete effectively.

Corporate reputation is not just about being known in the marketplace, but what you are known for—what your name stands for. Sometimes being well known may be a positive disadvantage. A recent survey suggested that the top four brands in the UK, by awareness in their sectors, were also the most hated (out of interest, they were Tesco, British Airways, Manchester United, and The Sun).[6] The days of 'all publicity is good publicity' have long since disappeared.

Recent estimates have examined what difference corporate reputation really makes to the value of a company. Communications Consulting Worldwide predicts what would happen to the stock price of several major corporations if they could switch corporate reputations with a peer which has a better reputation, so: if Wal-Mart had the reputation of Target, its stock would rise 4.9 per cent (boosting market value by $9.7 billion); if Coca-Cola had the reputation of Pepsi, its stock would rise 3.3 per cent (worth $4 billion); if Colgate had the reputation of Procter & Gamble, its stock would rise 6.2 per cent (increasing market value by $2 billion).[7] This just got a lot more serious than arranging boxes at Wimbledon for favoured customers and the rest of the 'PR' trivia.

Managing risk to corporate reputation has acquired a high priority in many companies because of the impact of reputation on market value and the ability to compete. Reputational risk is already subject to systematic management attention in major companies.[8] The damage to companies like BP (plant safety issues), Siemens, Volkswagen, and Samsung (bribery and corruption allegations), Mattell (safety issues in children's toys), Next and Asda (using 'slave

[6] Fenton, Ben, 'The Top Four Brands Are also the Most Hated', *Financial Times*, 13 May 2008, p. 20.

[7] Engardio, Pete and Michael Arndt, 'What Price Reputation?', *BusinessWeek*, 9/16 July 2007, pp. 70–9.

[8] Eccles, Robert G., Scott C. Newquist, and Roland Scatz, 'Reputation and Its Risks', *Harvard Business Review*, February 2007, pp. 104–14.

labour' in overseas factories) is massive and warrants a strategic response.

Indeed, it was not great news for US pharmaceutical company Merck when its infamous 'Dodgeball' sales training package became public knowledge (it prepared salespeople to duck and dodge doctors' questions about the pain drug Vioxx's links to heart and stroke risks). It was even more unfortunate that 'Dodgeball' was revealed in the context of lawsuits by plaintiffs claiming injury or death caused by Vioxx (the plaintiffs won).[9]

However, conventional marketing approaches in this area have tended to be 'mere "messaging", nifty marketing, and PR'.[10] In fact, while companies used to control their identities and the content of messages about themselves, now information about a company is 'created, exchanged, and modified by a vast, distributed ecosystem of employees, customers, partners, communities and interest groups'.[11] While at one time managers used to control channels of communications, 'Today, channels are exploding in number, easy to use, freely available and, as a result, now "belong" to everyone'.[12] Generally, it seems that traditional approaches to managing corporate reputation have not provided the analytical power and capabilities to anticipate potential problems and develop mechanisms to deal with them.

In fact, companies may have to take an increasingly aggressive stance in protecting corporate reputations that goes way beyond simple PR. When an organization finds itself in the position of being 'the accused', opponents care less about whether you are guilty and mostly about beating you. It may be the strategic response to reputation attack is never to admit guilt and to meet each accusation with a counterattack. While PR is essentially a conciliatory engagement with attackers, a strategic response may be more aggressive. The rule seems to be that when you have done wrong is the time to be repentant and conciliatory (traditional PR), but when you have been wronged the response should be a vigorous defence.[13]

---

[9] Bowe, Christopher, 'Steer Clear of Flippancy—Or Pay the Price', *Financial Times*, 6 September 2005, p. 14.

[10] Stern, Stefan, 'Wanted: Chief Attention Officers Who Can See Round Corners', *Financial Times*, 1 February 2008, p. 14.

[11] Stern (2008), op cit.   [12] Stern (2008), op. cit.

[13] Dezenhall, Eric and John Weber, *Damage Control: Why Everything You Know about Crisis Management Is Wrong*, New York: Portfolio, 2007.

Certainly, a major point of concern is that companies often seem uncertain how to repair damaged reputations—it may take a careful analysis of what is causing reputational damage, which constituencies are affected (customers, investors, employees), and what needs to be fixed. Responses to reputational damage vary from charm offensives to more rigorous counter-attacks.[14] For example, 2008 saw BAE Systems, Britain's largest defence contractor, launching a large-scale advertising campaign and roadshow based on the theme 'Real Pride, Real Advantage' to 'reinvigorate' its image among key stakeholders. This move may be connected to an array of bribery investigations linked to BAE across the world and the negative press associated with it.[15]

The point is that corporate reputation as a company resource or liability represents a cross-functional challenge for companies, which goes way beyond the traditional remit of 'PR' and marketing communications.

Corporate Reputation Is about Customers

At the end of the day, the strength or weakness of an organization's corporate reputation matters because it impacts on customer perceptions of how attractive it is to do business with that company. Obviously, it also has an impact on investors, the City, the ability to recruit talent, and the commentary of analysts and the media. But most of all, corporate reputation is about the ability to compete.

At the extreme, a poor corporate reputation—regarding your handling of suppliers and customers, your honesty and fairness in deals, your behaviour towards the environment, the working standards for employees in your value chain, and so on—can actually make you toxic. Customers may reject you because they do not want to be contaminated by association, and to face the criticisms of their own customers and shareholders—why would they take this risk if they can avoid it by buying elsewhere?

[14] McGovern, Gail and Youngme Moon, 'Companies and the Customers That Hate Them', *Harvard Business Review*, June 2007, pp. 78–84.
[15] Pfeffer, Sylvia, 'BAE Systems Launches Ad Blitz', *Financial Times*, 31 January 2008, p. 18.

On the other hand, a strong corporate reputation may make you more attractive than your competitors to some customers because they benefit by being associated with you. Your corporate reputation adds to the value of the relationship. It provides the customer with an assurance as to your good standing and that it is safe to deal with you without risking their own reputation.

A Strategic Sales Perspective

Our focus is therefore on the impact of corporate reputation on buyer–seller relationships, rather than more generally on investors, employees, and other stakeholders. This focus appears frequently missing from the way that people look at business ethics and corporate social responsibility initiatives. This gap provides an important opportunity for executives managing the interface with customers—the strategic sales organization. The opportunity extends way beyond the traditional marketing perspective on 'publicity' or 'PR'.

Two specific points of attack on this issue are the ethical standards shown by the company in its dealings with others, and the corporate responsibility shown in initiatives designed to meet social needs and priorities.

Ethics and Customer Value

Ethical issues have long been associated with the relationship between the seller (or salesperson) and the buyer.[16] Where the company meets its customer is a very public place in which to be found wanting in ethical standards.

An old story is that about 30 years ago, a priest liked to attend the Friday lunch meetings of the Sales Executives of New York, where he preached about honesty in business. Once when he was asked why he had made the sales club his flock, his reply was 'What sales executives have to do puts them, among all businesspeople, at the

[16] This section is based on Piercy, Nigel F. and Nikala Lane, 'Ethical and Moral Dilemmas Associated with Strategic Relationships between Business-to-Business Buyers and Sellers', *Journal of Business Ethics*, Vol. 72 2007, pp. 87–102.

greatest risk of losing their souls.'[17] Well, now it looks like you stand to lose your soul and to have everyone know about the loss. Faustian pacts appear to be off the agenda.

It is no news that salespeople have been frequent targets for criticism regarding ethical standards—they are exposed to more ethical pressures than people in other jobs; they work in relatively unsupervised settings; they typically face demanding sales revenue targets; and many are largely 'paid by results'. For example, a survey of sales managers by *Sales & Marketing Management* revealed that 49 per cent of managers said their salespeople had lied on a sales call, 34 per cent said their salespeople made unrealistic promises to customers, and 22 per cent reported that their salespeople had sold products their customers did not need—notwithstanding recognition that a salesperson's ethical behaviour plays a critical role in forming and sustaining long-term customer relationships.[18]

Familiar Ethical Dilemmas

In the past, ethics concerns in marketing and sales were focused on issues like misleading buyers and misrepresentation as a form of dishonesty, and the avoidance of such situations. The issue of bribery also poses problems, particularly for those operating in international markets. Nonetheless, while these issues are familiar, the evidence is we continue to get them wrong. The problem is that the profile is now much higher and the intensity of the scrutiny of our ethical standard is infinitely more rigorous than it used to be.

Even though the penalties have escalated in significance, and we know what the ethical traps in the marketplace are—we still keep falling into the same old traps.

For example, in 2008 medical products giant Smith & Nephew was belatedly ruing its £460 million purchase of the Swiss company Plus Orthopaedics, as it became aware of widespread unacceptable sales

---

[17] Quotation from Arthur Bragg, cited in Wotruba, Thomas R., 'A Comprehensive Framework for the Analysis of Ethical Behavior, with a Focus on Sales Organizations', *Journal of Personal Selling & Sales Management*, Vol. 10 (Spring) 1990, pp. 29–42.

[18] Román, Sergio and José Luis Munuera, 'Determinants and Consequences of Ethical Behaviour: An Empirical Study of Salespeople', *European Journal of Marketing*, Vol. 39 No. 5/6 2005, pp. 473–95.

practices.[19] About 30 per cent of the sales that Plus brought to S&N had to be abandoned, amid claims of improper payments to hospital doctors for using devices made by Plus. S&N itself had earlier paid $30 million in the United States to settle a Department of Justice investigation into payments made to surgeons using their products. All companies in the industry in the United States must now monitor payments to show that nobody is being bribed.

In the UK consumer sector, 2008 found gas and electricity supplier Npower accused of serious mis-selling by its door-step sales teams.[20] Investigative journalists had found Npower salespeople lying to householders to persuade them to change utilities to Npower; denying to consumers that they were salespeople; claiming they were from the 'electricity board'; lying about standing charges and prices charged by the company; and obtaining signatures on contracts by telling consumers they were only sending for more information and not actually changing suppliers by signing. The salespeople apparently considered what they were doing to be 'wrong' but not 'very wrong'. Npower's response started with denial, moved to admitting the need for staff 'retraining', and in the face of an imminent Ofgem enquiry sacking sales staff.

Following the arrest in the United States of one of its sales executives suspected of rigging contracts for oil industry customers, tyremaker Bridgestone admitted in 2008 that there was evidence of inappropriate payments by its sales managers in the global marine equipment business.[21] The payments were thought to have been made to foreign government officers. In making the admission, Bridgestone's CEO quite rightly observed: 'I expect the impact on our brand will be quite large. . . .' The company has chosen to quit the marine hoses market, where inappropriate payments had been uncovered, losing

---

[19] This illustration is based on Laurance, Ben, 'Deal That Left Medical Firm in Casualty', *Sunday Times*, 4 May 2008, pp. 3–7.

[20] This illustration is based on Foggo, Daniel and Claire Newell, 'Inside the Cheating World of Npower's Rogue Sales Teams', *Sunday Times*, 6 April 2008, Section 1, pp. 4–5; Swinford, Steven and Jasmine Gardner, 'Lying Sales Reps Reined in after Undercover Exposé', *Sunday Times*, 13 April 2008, pp. 1–7; Foggo, Daniel and Claire Newell, 'Energy Firm Sacks Staff as Probe into Mis-Selling Begins', *Sunday Times*, 27 April 2008, pp. 1–5.

[21] This illustration is based on Soble, Jonathan, 'Tyremaker to Broaden Price-Fix Inquiry', *Financial Times*, 13 February 2008, p. 30.

$41–$55 million in annual sales. The company remains accused of price-fixing in other product-markets—possibly going back to 1999.

A survey by insurers Sheilas's Wheels found that one in five of the women they surveyed admitted pulling out of a car deal because of offensive, sexist comments made by a sales*man*, the patronizing behaviour of sales*man*, or the off-putting 'macho' showroom environment.[22] About 44 per cent of the women surveyed admitted walking out of a car showroom because of the intimidating atmosphere. Don't these people know that women buy a lot of cars—and choose most of the rest? They are messing around with around £1 billon in sales here, and really should learn to remove sexism from their sales operations.

There are many more examples that could be cited. Is it surprising that even our own salespeople get embarrassed about working for some of us when we let things like this happen?[23] Is it surprising that we have difficulty in attracting many of the best university graduates to careers in sales?

None of the behaviours described are particularly original. They may reflect poor management, weak control, or simply the belief that this is how the world works and you probably will not get caught. Whatever the cause, demonstrably unethical sales practices are likely to cost you dear when they are exposed. The chances they will be exposed have never been higher. The cost when they are exposed has never been higher. It seems that even in the twenty-first century, integrity may remain a critical challenge for the strategic sales organization.

New Types of Ethical Dilemma

But the domain of ethics is not static. New situations and new business models bring new challenges, which may take some time to be recognized and given priority. Perhaps most worrying is the 'conflicted consumer'—customers who buy your product, even though they would rather not, because they have ethical concerns about your company and are poised to switch as soon as a viable alternative

[22] This illustration is based on 'Showroom Sexists Cost Car Firms £1Bn a Year', *Daily Mail*, 6 September 2007, p. 38.
[23] Anders, George, 'Companies Seem Uncertain How to Restore Tarnished Reputations', *Wall Street Journal*, 9 January 2008, p. 6.

emerges.[24] The moral dimension of business has greatly expanded, and along with it the ethical issues surrounding important decisions. That broadening of interest has extended ethical dilemmas to the way in which a company treats its employees and the demands it places upon them; standards in the way in which supplier relationships are conducted, and the dangers of treating some unfairly by favouring others; the requirements for fair and proper behaviour in the conduct of relationships with partners in strategic alliances and networks; relationships with competitors and whether they are managed with integrity; as well as concerns about customer relationships. Behaviour that is regarded as uncompetitive, in particular, can attract substantial penalties.

The Way We Treat Our People

Our reputation for treating our own people fairly and justly is important for several reasons. It is not just a question of wanting to be seen as a decent company that takes responsibilities towards employees seriously; failure to do so may make us very unattractive to some customers—they may not want to buy from us because our moral and ethical standards might tarnish their own corporate reputation.

For example, US data storage leader EMC has long prided itself on its hard-driving salesforce.[25] It says it hires salespeople with 'the passion to walk through walls', who will fit 'a culture of doing whatever it takes'. Training for salespeople includes walking across hot coals and breaking boards with karate chops. Less impressive were claims by Tami Ramien and Debra Fletcher, former EMC salespeople, that gender discrimination cost them their jobs, and that one had been subjected to 'profanity-laced and gender-based tirades' when she worked for the company. She was allegedly told on one occasion that she was not qualified to fill a position on the Motorola Inc. account because she would not 'smoke, drink, swear, hunt, fish and tolerate strip clubs'. Yet worse, a succession of former salespeople described in interviews what they said were 'locker-room antics, company-paid

---

[24] Fraser, Karen, 'Conflicted Consumers', *Harvard Business Review*, February 2007, pp. 35–6.

[25] This illustration uses facts and quotations taken from Bulkeley, William M., 'Tech and Testosterone: A Data-Storage Titan Confronts Bias Claims', *Wall Street Journal*, 12 September 2007, p. A.1.

visits to strip clubs, demeaning remarks or retaliation against women who complained about the atmosphere'. The company denies the allegations but a series of lawsuits are in progress. Whatever the eventual outcome of the legal cases, EMC has been damaged by the claims, particularly regarding its relationships with major customers whose names have been included in the allegations. It also does not help when the whole thing is played out on prominent pages of the *Wall Street Journal*.

Closer to home, the Bank of Scotland was found to have an interesting motivational tool of forcing bank staff who failed to meet sales targets to keep a cabbage on the desk—naturally, in full view of colleagues and customers, which was kind of the point. When challenged on this technique, the bank apologized and said it was unacceptable. It appears then to have switched from cabbages to cauliflowers, which makes all the difference.[26]

On the other hand, when it is reported that you make your sales staff stand up when they take phone calls to ensure they stay alert and responsive to sales leads, apparently a policy from the top at Bloombergs in London in 2003, then you just look silly.[27]

Supplier Relationship Standards

It cuts both ways. The integrity we display in our relationships with our suppliers at earlier stages of the value chain are likely to be one of the things that customers use to judge us.

For example, it was not Starbucks moment of greatest glory when it became involved in a very public dispute with the Ethiopian government over trademarks.[28] Starbucks is actually a very ethically minded company. Nonetheless, it found itself in the position of being accused of 'neo-colonialism' and unfairly using the power of a multinational company to crush the ambitions of one of the poorest countries in the world to trademark some of its most famous coffees. As Douglas Holt at Oxford University's Said Business School remarked at the time, the

[26] Culley, Maureen, 'Bankers Who Failed the Cauliflower Test', *Daily Mail*, 17 August 2005, p. 23.

[27] Garahan, Matthew, 'Strand Up for the Company, Bloomberg Sales Staff Told', *Financial Times*, 23 May 2003, p. 10.

[28] This illustration is adapted from Rushe, Dominic, 'Starbucks Stirs Up a Storm in a Coffee Cup', *Sunday Times*, 4 March 2007, pp. 3–7.

company was 'playing Russian roulette' with its brand. Interestingly, Starbucks stands accused of losing touch with its core values, and founder Howard Schultz has returned to the business with the aim of reinstating them.

Favouritism in the Customer Portfolio

Recall the discussion in Chapter 2 about strategic account management (SAM) approaches to relationships with dominant customers. There is an increasingly widely held view that SAM has an important ethical dimension which has been largely ignored to date, and which may rein in more enthusiastic attempts at partnering with major customers—the relationship is founded on the good of the few at the expense of the many. Actually, by definition, SAM is a policy that favours the few (strategic accounts) at the expense of the many (smaller accounts and other organizational stakeholders). If this were not so, then what would be the attraction of this type of relationship for the customer?

For example, it is likely that strategic accounts will demand and receive lower prices and more advantageous terms of trade than other customers. The effect is likely to be twofold: smaller accounts receive poorer value, negatively influencing their performance, and if they compete with your strategic accounts in the end-use market, their competitiveness is undermined and their survival may be threatened. Importantly, smaller accounts pay more, usually not because they are more expensive to serve, but because they lack the power to demand and get lower prices. In a very real sense, SAM means that smaller accounts are providing a cross-subsidy to larger accounts. This underlines the moral question of whether it is right and fair to treat smaller accounts in this way. (Incidentally, at some point it may become a legal issue as well because policies of cross-subsidy are unlawful in some countries.)

Even if price differences for strategic accounts are not an issue, one other defining characteristic of SAM is information sharing between the partners. This may include information relating to costs and prices, new product plans, and other strategic developments. Suppliers share information with major customers because it offers those customers a competitive advantage. The same logic then applies and the question becomes whether it is right and fair to disadvantage smaller customers by excluding them from access to proprietary information, simply because they are too small to demand it.

In an interesting training session on strategic account management, we talked with executives from buyer and seller organizations on how their collaborative strategies worked. They stressed the importance of trust and the sharing of proprietary information. When pressed, the executives reluctantly admitted that their own organizations and their chief executives did not know how much information had been shared, which was just as well because they were unlikely to have formally approved. So, the question arises that in the strategic account manager, we have created an organizational role in which the individual must choose whether or not to breach organizational policies by disclosing confidential information to his or her counterpart in the partner organization. Have we, in fact created an incentive for unethical behaviour by the way the role has been designed? If so, we should hardly be surprised if unethical practices follow.

It begins to look like the strategic account management approach to doing business may be flawed not simply because of the business weaknesses we highlighted in Chapter 2, but also because of the ethical dilemmas which are fast emerging.

Partnerships

Some similar issues arise in how people judge us to behave in our relationships with partners in strategic alliances and networks. Critical issues here are whether customers trust us not to exploit our knowledge about them and not to share their secrets with third parties in alliances; whether we are known to be the sort of company which will not pursue opportunistic behaviour at their expense—for example, working in a network or alliance to develop products that compete with the customer.

Competitor Relationships

How nicely we play with the other children tells observers a lot about our values and ethics.

Some people take it to extremes. A question raised in the *Sunday Times* recently was 'What kind of man travels half way round the world to sabotage the biggest deal of your career, publicly humiliates your mother, and then threatens you with legal action? For supporters of Anil Ambani, the second richest man in India, the answer is "your older brother".'[29] Any thoughts that the feud between these brothers ended when the Reliance family business was divided between them were somewhat optimistic. In another robust approach to competing, in Russia companies are paying government officials to raid the offices of business rivals and subject them to criminal investigation—BP is looking at its executives being denied visas to remain in the country because it has fallen out with its Russian partners at joint venture TNK-BP.

And some people are just rude. One of the most important companies to emerge from the software industry is VMware, which produces virtualization software allowing companies to run tasks simultaneously on a single server by fooling each application into thinking it has sole use of the machine. Larry Ellison decided, wholly characteristically, that VMware needed a slap. He claimed VMware would be crushed, and that the base level of software was so simple his cat could write it. VMware's then CEO, Diane Greene, responded in the *Financial Times*: 'If his very smart cat could write it, my very smart tortoise could write his database.' These guys are not going to be friends.[30] It is not for nothing that Mr Ellison is known as one of the fiercest competitors in the technology business, with a reputation as a crafty opportunist who exploits rivals' weaknesses.[31]

Blood feuds between competitors where the main motivator is revenge and spite may be good for customers, in the sense of driving price down, as in the case of the war between Intel and AMD in computer chips.[32] However, generally 'the power of retribution, spite, and loathing in the world of business' is unattractive and sends undesirable signals.[33]

The point is that the standards of your behaviour in relationships with your competitors say a great deal about your company, and say it pretty publicly.

[29] Nelson, Dean, 'Warring $85bn Brothers Battle On', *Sunday Times*, 29 June 2008, Section 3, p. 1.

[30] Waters, Richard, 'VMware Undaunted by Rival's Catty Comments', *Financial Times*, 19/20 January 2008, p. 19.

[31] Ricadela, Aaron, 'Oracle vs. SAP: Sound or Fury?', *BusinessWeek*, 9 April 2007, p. 38.

[32] Kirkpatrick, David, 'The Joy of Blood Feuds', *Fortune*, 19 March 2007, p. 27.

[33] McGregor, Jena, 'Sweet Revenge', *BusinessWeek*, 22 January 2007, pp. 64–70.

As business relationships become more complex, the chances for failing to meet the ethical standards that people expect of us increase. Predicting which will be the most intense moral dilemmas will not be easy, but we have to try.

Providing Managers with a Simple Ethical Framework

It is interesting to note that ethics training for staff has seen considerable growth in recent years, as companies have become aware of the penalties for being perceived as weak in ethical standards—survey evidence suggests that 7 out of 10 large UK companies now offer staff some ethics training. However, it is frequently the case that senior executives do not participate in that training. This is kind of missing the point that ethical standards are part of the leadership process in a business, not just gaining 'tick-box' compliance by employees to ethical codes.[34]

More positively, well-known work in the field of practical business ethics[35] suggests that developing an ethical culture around important corporate issues might be approached more effectively by senior managers routinely asking probing questions about the nature and consequences of decisions being made, than by formalized and complex ethical guidelines that tend to reduce business ethics to a 'box ticking' exercise. For example, in evaluating the ethical issues surrounding strategic account management, these questions might take the following form:

- Who are all the people affected by this issue—employees, managers, shareholders, competitors, other third parties, and the wider community and environment?
- Does our position on this issue actually or potentially cause harm to any of those affected, beyond the acceptable effects of fair competition?
- Has our behaviour been deceptive? Would you regard it that way if you were in the position of any of the other stakeholders?

[34] Maitland, Alison, 'No Excuse for Absense from Lessons in Right and Wrong', *Financial Times*, 7 March 2008, p. 18.

[35] Persaud, Avinash and John Plender, *All You Need to Know About Ethics and Finance: Finding a Moral Compass in Business Today*, Longtail Publishing, 2006; Plender, John and Avinash Persaud, 'Good Ethics Means More than Ticking Boxes', *Financial Times*, 23 August 2005, p. 10.

• Are there disguised conflicts of interest between the parties directly involved and those affected by the issue?

• If everyone behaved in the way we are behaving, what would happen? If harm would result from everyone treating customer, third parties, shareholders, and others as we are doing, should we refrain from continuing this behaviour?[36]

There are also advantages in incorporating such questions in the training and development of executives, and addressing them in personal appraisals. It has also been suggested that the issues get taken more seriously if as well as codes of ethics and explicit ethical policies to impact on practice, one major impact can be achieved by asking executives to consider ethics as a determinant of business success—asking ethics questions becomes more significant if they are seen to address issues which are truly important to executives.[37]

The Consequences of Ethical Shortfalls

At the extreme, of course, you get sent down. If ethical standards decline to the extent that laws and regulations are broken, then you risk legal penalties, some of which may be severe. Less severe, but not pleasant, is being held responsible for ethical shortcomings and being asked to take the blame and move on to alternative employment opportunities.

Corporate Social Responsibility and Buyer–Seller Relationships

Some companies have long been involved in corporate philanthropy (charitable donations), mission statements aspiring to superior corporate citizenship, and codes of conduct to guide decision-makers in ethical behaviour. But things just got a lot more serious. In March 2007, Microsoft dropped one of its UK suppliers because that supplier did

---

[36] Adapted from Plender and Persaud (2005), op cit.
[37] For example, see; Singhapakdi, A., 'Perceived Importance of Ethics and Ethical Decisions in Marketing', *Journal of Business Research*, Vol. 45 1999, pp. 89–99.

not conform to Microsoft's employment diversity standards. British supermarkets spent much of the same year in an 'environmental arms race' attempting to out-green each other. Environmental issues have become increasingly decisive in customer decision-making—the 'green consumer' is alive and well and populating many markets. The scope of corporate social responsibility (CSR) has gone way beyond just meeting society's new standards, to become an essential part of how we compete.[38] It is no small matter when companies like Wal-Mart and Unilever look to the Rainforest Alliance to certify the coffee and tea they sell.[39]

There is a growing business case surrounding ethical initiatives based on the belief that projects with environmental and social goals do not just improve corporate reputation, but also foster innovation, cut costs, and open up new markets. For example, Unilever's research into water saving in clothes washing in emerging country markets led directly to its Pureit product (a portable water purifier) that is looking at huge markets in rural India and China.[40]

What Is CSR about?

CSR has been defined by a European Commission Green Paper as 'a concept whereby companies integrate social and environmental concerns in their business operations and in the interactions with stakeholders on a voluntary basis'.[41] The Green Paper identifies four factors underpinning growing attention by executives to CSR issues: the new concerns and expectations of consumers, public authorities, and investors, in the context of globalization and industrial change; social criteria influencing investment decisions of individuals and institutions; increased concern about the damage caused to the physical environment by economic and business activity; and the new transparency

[38] See Hooley, Graham, Nigel F. Piercy, and Brigitte Nicoulaud, *Marketing Strategy and Competitive Positioning*, 4th ed., Harlow: FT/Prentice-Hall, 2008, Chapter 18.

[39] Skapinker, Michael, 'Why Companies and Campaigners Collaborate', *Financial Times*, 8 July 2008, p. 15.

[40] Skapinker, Michael, 'Virtue's Reward? Companies Make a Business Case for Ethical Initiatives', *Financial Times*, 28 April 2008, p. 9.

[41] Commission of the European Communities, *Green Paper: Promoting a European Framework for Corporate Social Responsibility*, COM, July 2001, p. 6.

of business activities created by new media and new information communications technologies.

But CSR attracts a mixed press among businesspeople. Some argue that it is not the role of business to become involved in social issues—the goal of management is to deliver value to shareholders, and for them to disburse earnings as they wish. This line suggests that if society requires certain behaviours from business (or that business should desist in certain actions), then it is up to law-makers to produce appropriate regulation to enforce society's wishes, and for society to pick up the bill through higher prices. In this view, corporate philanthropy—voluntarily funding 'good works' like charities and the arts—is tolerated within limits as a contribution to reputation as a 'good corporate citizen'.[42]

A more extreme perspective suggests incompatibility between business and social aims. They point to the 'little green lies' that suggested that it was possible to make a company environmentally friendly while still being cost-effective and profitable, when really it is not.[43] They point to the unintended consequences of CSR initiatives—such as the planting of trees in Uganda to off-set greenhouse gas emissions in Europe, which seemed a great idea, but actually entailed the eviction of Uganda farmers from their land—some at gunpoint—to make room for a forest.[44] They argue that in any case, customers have different concerns in different countries and hence different perceptions of what constitutes good corporate responsibility—in China the hallmark of a social responsible company is safe, high-quality products, while in South Africa what matters most is a company's contribution to social needs like healthcare and education.[45]

The contrasting view suggests that since business is part of society it has an obligation to pursue social initiatives that are to the benefit of the communities they populate—at the very least to minimize and repair damage to the environment created by value chain operations, and possibly much more. However, this view has developed into a

---

[42] Grow, Brian, 'The Debate Over Doing Good', *BusinessWeek*, 5/12 September 2005, pp. 78–80.

[43] Elgin, Ben, 'Little Green Lies', *BusinessWeek*, 29 October 2007, pp. 45–52.

[44] Faris, Stephen, 'The Other Side of Carbon Trading', *Fortune*, 3 September 2007, pp. 67–74.

[45] Maitland, Alison, 'A Responsible Balancing Act', *Financial Times*, 1 June 2005, p. 11.

case that social initiatives are not simply a way of making good damage done, but of developing new kinds of competitive strength based on innovative business models. The issue then becomes the ways in which CSR impacts on the value offering made to customers.

A powerful piece of advocacy by Porter and Kramer from Harvard Business School offers the prospect that 'If...corporations were to analyze their prospects for social responsibility using the same frameworks that guide their core business choices, they would discover that CSR can be much more than a cost, a constraint, or a charitable deed—it can be a source of opportunity, innovation, and competitive advantage.'[46]

Others refer to the 'sustainability sweet spot' where shareholders' and society's interests overlap—such as Unilever's Project Shakti in India, training 13,000 women to distribute its products to rural customers, providing increased family incomes but also expanding Unilever market penetration. In these terms, sustainability is about conducting business in such a way that it benefits customers, business partners, communities, and shareholders at the same time—'the art of doing business in an interdependent world'. The argument gaining currency is that it makes commercial sense for a company to anticipate and respond to society's emerging demands, on the grounds that sustainable companies are more likely to be profitable companies.[47]

In fact, the case for sustainability is essentially a business case—initiatives are not simply about 'saving the planet' but about cutting waste, reducing costs, and becoming more efficient. In 2006, Google launched a strategy to switch to renewable energy—while this reflects the personal beliefs of the founders of the business, it is also true that Google is a massive user of electricity and renewable energy provides a way to cut costs.[48]

But seriously, does anyone in the *real* world really care about CSR?

[46] Porter, Michael E. and Mark R. Kramer, 'Strategy and Society: The Link between Competitive Advantage and Corporate Social Responsibility', *Harvard Business Review*, December 2006, pp. 78–92.
[47] Savitz, Andrew and Karl Weber, *The Triple Bottom Line: How Today's Best-Run Companies Are Achieving Economic, Social and Environmental Success and How You Can Too*, San Francisco CA: Pfeiffer Wiley, 2006.
[48] Senge, Peter, Bryan Smith, Nina Krushwitz, Joe Laur, and Sara Schley, *The Necessary Revolution: How Individuals and Organizations Are Working Together to Create a Sustainable World*, London: Nicholas Brealey, 2008.

Who Really Cares about CSR?

Well, the way things are working out, it looks like everybody wants a piece of the action, which is one of the reasons why this is such a hot issue for the front-end of the selling organization.

The Green and Ethical Consumer

Whatever business we are in, and at whatever stage of the value chain, demand is ultimately driven by consumers. Shifting consumption patterns are difficult to track—for example, while many consumers claim they would pay a 5 to 10 per cent premium for many ethical products, in practice such brands usually have tiny market shares.[49] However, a recent five-country survey conducted by market research group GfK NOP suggests that consumers in five of the world's leading economies believe that business ethics have worsened in the past five years, and they are turning to 'ethical consumerism' to make companies more accountable.[50] Respondents believe that brands with 'ethical' claims—on environmental policies or treatment of staff or suppliers—would make business more answerable to the public, and that companies should 'promote ethical credentials more strongly'.[51]

Commentators on branding suggest that ethical consumption is one of the most significant branding issues in modern markets, and underlies change in the automotive sector, food, retailing, technology, and health and beauty sectors. Its influence is behind the strong sales growth of hybrid cars, 'cruelty-free' beauty products, and dramatic growth in sales of organic food. The conclusion appears to be that ethical and environmental questions are being posed by growing numbers of consumers, and they are not always overly impressed by companies' responses.[52] The impact of 'ethical consumerism' is large, and of escalating significance.

For example, the Daimler miniature Smart car (the one that looks like a gym shoe on wheels) looked like a massive liability ready for abandonment at one stage. However, the 2008 launch in the United

[49] Grande, Carlo, 'Ethical Consumption Makes Mark on Branding', *Financial Times*, 20 February 2007, p. 24.

[50] Grande (2007), op. cit.

[51] Grande (2007), op.cit.

[52] Edgecliffe-Johnson, Andrew, 'Scepticism Grows Over Claims on Ethics', *Financial Times*, 27 May 2008, p. 3.

States has been a big success—the vehicle has exactly the right green credentials to appeal to buyers for a city car in trendy, left-ish cities like Boston and San Francisco.[53]

However, if you push the question—do consumers really care about ethics and social responsibility?—unsurprisingly the answer is basically that some do and some do not. Research suggests that consumers with high ethical standards make up a distinct segment in many markets, with a willingness to pay higher prices for ethical products, and more inclination to 'punish' producers of unethical products. There is some virtue in testing rather than assuming that consumers care enough about moral issues to pay more.[54]

Business-To-Business Customers

However, the disproportionately loud voice of the 'green consumer' is nowhere more evident than in the reactions of corporate customers to issues of social responsibility. In many sectors, strident demands from business-to-business customers for their suppliers to implement CSR policies and initiatives that are acceptable to the customer organization are rapidly escalating.

For example, the 'vendor compliance' programme at Target Corporation is illustrative. Target Corporation is a successful US retailer with more than 1,500 Target stores and nearly 200 upmarket Super-Target outlets. Target prides itself on its high ethical standards and business principles, emphasizing the protection of human rights and extends these principles and standards to its suppliers. Purchasing officers are required to uphold Target Corporation social responsibility standards wherever they buy in the world, even when these exceed the requirements of local laws—Target engineers do not just inspect suppliers' factories for product quality, but also for labour rights and employment conditions. Target operates a formal 'compliance organization' for its purchasing, to enforce its vendor standards, focusing on vendor education and verification, with the following components: implementation of a compliance audit programme, where audit staff conduct random visits to supplier manufacturing facilities, following which compliance violations are subject to

[53] 'Americans Get Smart', *Sunday Times*, 9 December 2007, Section 3, p. 3.
[54] Trudel, Remi and June Cotte, 'Does Being Ethical Pay?', *Wall Street Journal*, 13 May 2008, p. R2.

administrative probation or severance of the relationship; limitation of subcontractors used by suppliers to those approved by Target; and regular vendor evaluations as well as formal audits.

Similarly, Home Depot, the American DIY chain, insists that all its wood products are sourced from suppliers who can provide verifiable evidence of their sound forest management practices. Home Depot is one of the largest buyers of wood products in the country, and the company wants to be seen as taking a strong position on sustainability.[55]

Companies like Target and Home Depot are no longer unusual in giving attention to the ethical and social responsibility standards demanded of its suppliers throughout the world. The introduction of formal social responsibility dimensions to supplier relationships is becoming the norm rather than the exception with large customers. These social responsibility mandates impact on supplier selection, and on the continuation of relationships with existing suppliers. Organizational customers' evolving social responsibility mandates require effective responses. Certainly, one response may be that a customer's social responsibility demands reduce the attractiveness of that customer to the seller, and the business should be sacrificed. Nonetheless, the spread of vendor evaluation approaches which make CSR demands on suppliers requires continuous and systematic evaluation as the basis for an appropriate response.

Lobby Groups and CSR

There is evidence that companies with poor CSR records may experience serious negative consequences, such as large-scale consumer boycotts, weaker brand image, or reduced sales. Part of this effect may be accounted for by the growth of consumer groups who actively promote awareness of what they believe to be company wrongdoing, and actively promote consumer boycotts.[56] Activist organizations have become much more aggressive and effective in bringing public pressure to bear on companies. They may target the most visible companies, to draw attention to the issue, even if the company in question has little impact on the problem. Nestlé is the world's largest seller of

[55] Senge et al. (2008), op cit.

[56] Snider, Jamie, Ronald Paul Hill, and Diane Martin, 'Corporate Social Responsibility in the 21st Century: A View from the World's Most Successful Firms', *Journal of Business Ethics*, Vol. 48 No. 2 2003, pp. 175–87.

bottled water, and has become a major target in the global dilemma about access to fresh water. In fact, Nestlé's impact on world water usage and availability is trivial—but it is a very convenient target.[57]

In 2008, the activist group People for the Ethical Treatment of Animals (PETA) succeeded in pressuring companies from Timberland to H&M to ban Australian wool because of the way merino sheep are treated. This is somewhat bad news for the Australian wool industry, which supplies 50 per cent of the world's wool for clothing—it is already a casualty of prolonged drought in Australia. However, PETA had little trouble recruiting clothing companies to the ban, as one European retailer said at the time: 'who wants to be on PETA's radar screen?'[58]

Responding to outside pressures, particularly where they are vocal and well organized, in order to defend a company's competitive position may be an appropriate management action. On the other hand, it may not—it may be impossible or undesirable to respond to some pressure groups' demands. In either case, the effects of such responses need to be carefully considered in the context of the entire value chain, and attempts made to control the 'unintended consequences' of such actions.

Suppliers and CSR

The issue of CSR and ethical standards in a company's supply base is the direct reflection of the questions raised above regarding the CSR-related demands made by major customers. Indeed, the ethical and social standards displayed by a seller's own suppliers may form part of a customer's CSR evaluation—as in the limitation of the use of subcontractors in the Target example above. Increasingly, our major customers may require that we adopt a proactive CSR stance towards the entire value chain. While the general trend is clear, strictly managers face choices. If CSR-related demands cannot, or will not, be met by suppliers, then the choice becomes whether or not to continue

[57] Porter, Michael E. and Mark R. Kramer, 'Strategy and Society: The Link between Competitive Advantage and Corporate Social Responsibility', *Harvard Business Review*, December 2006, pp. 78–92.
[58] Capell, Kerry, 'The Wool Industry gets Blooded', *BusinessWeek*, 14/21 July 2008, p. 40.

the relationship, accepting that then alternative suppliers will have to be located and the arrangements made. Conversely, if suppliers are prepared to concede new standards in their behaviour, then there are likely to be implications for the prices they charge, and hence for the company's cost structure, and the prices it must ask of its own customers. This is likely to be a complex calculation. Careful evaluation is required.

Employees, Managers, and CSR

CSR is also seen as impacting on the perceptions of the employees and managers inside the company, and consequently on their motivation and commitment to the company. It is certainly apparent that many of the individuals now entering professional employment and providing the pool of talent from which future corporate leadership will be drawn have important concerns about moral and ethical issues in business. The question is whether CSR initiatives will appeal to those concerns and generate the superior level of employee and manager commitment that should be associated with higher levels of job performance.

Certainly, a research study by McKinsey suggests that as many as 70 per cent of company managers believe there is room for improvement in the way large companies anticipate social pressure and respond to it. Managers see risks for their businesses in some social challenges—such as climate change, data privacy, and healthcare—but opportunities in other challenges—such as the growing demand for more ethical, healthier, and safer products.[59] Further indications of the importance of ethical and social responsibility issues are shown in studies of the perceptions of business school students—who will provide the next generations of managers. Business students appear to believe that companies should work more towards the betterment of society, and want to find socially responsible employment in their careers.[60]

---

[59] Maitland, Alison, 'The Frustrated Will to Act for Public Good', *Financial Times*, 25 January 2006, p. 15.

[60] Knight, Rebecca, 'Business Students Portrayed as Ethically Minded in Study', *Financial Times*, 25 October 2006, p. 9.

Competition and CSR

As we noted earlier, in the UK, 2007 saw an 'environmental arms race' between retailers, each claiming to be greener than the other. Marks & Spencer's announcement that it intended to be carbon neutral by 2012 led to claims from Tesco that it would carbon label all its products, and similar eco-promises from J. Sainsbury. Appositely, one analyst noted 'Whether M&S wants to save the rainforest or save itself from Tesco is the question.' While cynics may suspect there is a degree of posturing and 'holier than thou' grandstanding in these environmental initiatives, there appears an underlying belief that in the current marketplace consumers are discriminating in favour of companies that can demonstrate they are trying to clean up their environmental act. The new retail mantra appears to be: 'Green pays. Green brings in customers.'[61] Mid-2007 saw the supermarkets attacking their own plastic carrier bags and attempting to persuade consumers to forgo this convenience in favour of other packaging—designer re-usable cotton bags marked 'I'm Not A Plastic Bag' at Sainsburys,[62] vouchers for schools for consumers not using bags at Asda, and loyalty card points for reusing plastic bags at Tesco.[63] While responding to competitors' CSR moves may not always be the best approach, the strategic significance of CSR to competitive positioning is growing.

Investors

An ethical investment community is also becoming important. In 2008, Tesco's AGM was plagued by animal rights and environmental issues and protestors. Sometimes things are counter-intuitive, of course. When Google announced its renewable energy strategy in 2006, one leading New York stock analyst downgraded the company, despite clear indications that the initiative would cut costs—his view was that the company was no longer focusing on its real priorities.[64]

---

[61] Davey, Jenny and Ben Laurance, 'Trading Bright Green Ideas', *The Sunday Times*, 21 January 2007, p. 3.5.

[62] Though imitated by some, with bags claiming instead that 'I'm Not a Smug Git' …

[63] Sherwood, Bob, 'Stores Compete to Prove Their Green Credentials Are in the Bag', *Financial Times*, 26 April 2007.

[64] Witzel, Morgen, 'The Business Case for More Sustainability', *Financial Times*, 3 July 2008, p. 16.

Nonetheless, CSR and corporate reputation seem to matter to those making individual and fund investment decisions.

The Danger of Being Too Hot to Handle

The very real business risk tied up in this is that judgements of your ethical standards and your company's commitment to social responsibility are increasingly linked to your attractiveness as a supplier.

Quite simply, your value offering may be undermined because of your company's CSR position. Buyers will either genuinely not want to do business with you because of what you stand for or they will not want to buy from you for fear of sin by association—they do not want to be castigated by their own shareholders or by the media and lobby groups for dealing with you. You have become too hot to handle.

For example, we saw earlier the instance of Microsoft 'firing' suppliers on the basis of their employment policies. In the United States, many large companies, including Microsoft, already insist on good diversity practices from suppliers, and are reducing or terminating the business they do with suppliers who fail to heed requests to diversify their workforces. Indeed, while many US-based multinationals have adopted voluntary corporate responsibility initiatives to self-regulate their overseas social and environmental practices, pressures mount for more active involvement of the US government in mandating such regulation.[65] British-based companies that operate 'supplier diversity policies' include the bankers Morgan Stanley, BAA, and car rental group Avis Budget.[66] Suppliers unable or unwilling to meet the social responsibilities defined by major customers stand the considerable risk of losing those customers.

The Value Chain Shuffle

Interestingly, one response to CSR pressures by companies at the front-end of the value chain is simply to blame companies at earlier stages in

---

[65] Aaronson, Susan Ariel, ' "Minding Our Business": What the United States Government Has Done and Can Do to Ensure that U.S. Multinational Act Responsibly in Foreign Markets', *Journal of Business Ethics*, Vol. 59 2005, pp. 175–98.

[66] Taylor, Andrew, 'Microsoft Drops Supplier Over Diversity Policy', *Financial Times*, 24/25 March 2007, p. 5.

the chain, and pass the costs back to them. For example, interestingly, the green competition between supermarkets has quickly moved to public criticisms of their *suppliers'* excessive product packaging policies, and promises to sanction suppliers who do not reduce packaging (and, of course, carry the additional costs incurred).

Meanwhile, to recover its severely bruised reputation and to attempt to establish its credentials as a socially responsible company, Wal-Mart is pushing for greater diversity in the upper levels of its top law firms,[67] as well as demanding that all suppliers measure the greenhouse gas emission and label products to show how much carbon went into their manufacture.[68] Clearly, sanctions threaten non-conforming suppliers. Recently, Gap withdrew a line of children's clothes from its shelves, following allegations of forced child labour at Indian subcontractors. In common with other clothes retailers, Gap monitors the behaviour of suppliers in its value chain, and in 2007 stopped working with 23 factories.[69]

In a growing number of cases, if you cannot meet a customer's requirements for your company's standards in environmental and employment standards, you have no value and they cannot buy from you. It matters little if the customer's motivation is a genuine concern for social issues, or the desire to look clean, or simply the tactic of passing the buck—the effect is largely the same.

Defend, Attack, or a New Business Model?

However, cynical short-term manoeuvres by some players should not detract from the long-term significance of CSR as a driving force in business, and its significance to the strategic sales initiative. In fact, one important distinction is between defensive and proactive CSR.[70] This distinguishes between responsive and strategic CSR.

---

[67] Birchall, Jonathan, 'Wal-Mart Lays Down the Law', *Financial Times*, 21 February 2007, p. 11.

[68] Harvey, Fiona, 'Winds of Change Beginning to Blow', *Financial Times: Special Report on Sustainable Business*, 12 October 2007, p. 1.

[69] Johnson, Jo and Aline van Duyn, 'Pressure on Clothes Retailers after Gap Child Labour Allegation', *Financial Times*, 29 October 2007, p. 6.

[70] Porter, Michael E. and Mark R Kramer, 'Strategy and Society: The Link between Competitive Advantage and Corporate Social Responsibility', *Harvard Business Review*, December 2006, pp. 78–92.

Responsive CSR involves acting as a good corporate citizen, reflecting the social concerns of stakeholders in the company, and also mitigating the existing or predicted adverse effects of business activities. The domain is generic social impacts and value chain social impacts. The limitation of many citizenship initiatives remains that however beneficial the social effects, such programmes tend to remain incidental to the company's business. The key to mitigating value chain social impacts is best practice, though competitive advantage through such endeavours is likely to be temporary.

Strategic CSR moves beyond good citizenship and value chain impacts to initiatives with large and distinctive effects. The goals are the transformation of value chain activities to benefit society while at the same time reinforcing the company's strategy, and strategic moves that leverage corporate capabilities to improve areas of competitive context. Strategic CSR may involve the introduction of radically different new products—the Toyota Prius hybrid car responds to consumer concerns about car emissions pollution, and provides both competitive advantage for Toyota and environmental benefits. However, the broader goal of strategic CSR is to invest in social aspects of the company's context to strengthen company competitiveness. This is achieved, in part, by adding a social dimension to the company's value proposition and ways of doing business. Only a small number of the social issues that could be addressed have this potential to make a real difference to society and build competitive advantage.

Responsive CSR may include pre-emptive social initiatives. For example, the US cola giants have undertaken to restrict the sales of their products in schools, as a way of avoiding the tough measures proposed by activists concerned with obesity and diabetes in young people.[71] In other situations, the issue may be maintaining parity with competitors in CSR initiatives, just to avoid being screened out by buyers. Indeed, keeping up with the competition in social responsibility initiatives may be the minimum requirement for staying in the market. Falling behind the rest may make you unacceptable to the customer—you have no value to offer.

---

[71] Ward, Andrew, 'Soft Drinks Producers Act to Deflate Calls for Regulation', *Financial Times*, 19 August 2005, p. 5.

However, at its core, strategic CSR is concerned with developing new business models that combine social initiatives with business goals.

CSR as a New Business Model

Social policies may be used more proactively to establish a new form of competitive differentiation in some situations. The positive side of all this is that your company's stance on CSR may add to the value of what you offer customers—even to the level of becoming a selling point. For example, Dell and Hewlett-Packard both actively exploit the energy-saving characteristics of their new computers as part of their value propositions—reflecting big business enthusiasm for environmental initiatives that pay their own way.[72] In this sense, CSR becomes an active part of the value proposition.

For example, in 2005, General Electric—the world's largest company—launched its Ecoimagination initiative. Ecoimagination grew out of GE's long-term investment in cleaner technologies, and places these technologies under a single brand. To qualify for the Ecoimagination brand, products must significantly and measurably improve the customer's environmental and operating performance. The company is rigorous in selecting projects that are both wanted by customers and financially viable. The Ecoimagination vision is driven by the principle that its green initiatives will have a positive impact on GE's competitive position and financial performance. The focus on greener products is part of CEO Jeffrey Immelt's plan to reduce GE's exposure to low-growth industries and reshape its portfolio to more profitable sectors. In 2007, GE reported it had doubled sales of environmentally friendly products to $12 billion over the previous two years, on track to meet its target of £20 billion in green sales by 2010.[73]

Correspondingly, in 2008, Siemens, Europe's largest engineering group, locked horns with GE, claiming that it made nearly double the revenue from environmentally friendly products as its US rival's much-publicized Ecoimagination programme. Siemens claimed sales

[72] Anders, George, 'Dell and H-P Cast Energy Savings as an "Eco-Push" That Pays Its Way', *Wall Street Journal*, 21 November 2007, p. 7.

[73] Harvey, Fiona, 'GE Looks Out for a Cleaner Profit', *Financial Times*, 1 July 2005, p. 13; Guerrera, Francesco, 'GE Doubles Eco-Friendly Sales', *Financial Times*, 24 May 2007, p. 28.

worth $26 billion of environmentally friendly products versus worth $14 billion the made by GE. The company admitted that GE and other rivals had outflanked Siemens in this key marketing advantage. Engineering companies are increasingly seeing greener products as a profit boosting advantage in the market as well as helping the environment. Green products are an increasing competitive emphasis—Siemens leads with 23 per cent of its revenues from environmentally friendly products in 2007, followed by Philips with around 23 per cent of its revenues from this source, and GE with 15 per cent of its engineering business.[74]

In a different market, leading computer supplier Dell, Inc., faces challenges in rebuilding its value proposition, after losing market leadership to Hewlett-Packard. Dell is leveraging its distinctive competitive competences in initiatives with both business and social benefits—using the strengths of its direct business model to generate collective efforts to reduce energy consumption and protect the environment. The initiative centres on improving the efficiency of IT products, reducing the harmful materials used in them, and cooperating with customers to dispose of old products.

Michael Dell's environmental strategy focuses on three areas: creating easy, low-cost ways for businesses to do better in protecting the environment—providing, for example, global recycling and product recovery programs for customers, with participation requiring little effort on their part; taking creative approaches to lessen the environmental impact of products from design to disposal—helping customers to take full advantage of new, energy-saving technology and processes, and advising on upgrades of legacy systems to reduce electricity usage; and looking to partnership with governments to promote environmental stewardship PC. The link between this CSR initiative and the company's business model and value proposition is clear.[75]

Similarly, 2007 saw Microsoft partnering with governments in less developed countries to offer Microsoft Windows and Office software packages for $3 to governments that subsidize the cost of computers for schoolchildren. The potential business benefit for Microsoft

---

[74] Milne, Richard and Fiona Harvey, 'Siemens Tackles GE in Green Push', *Financial Times*, 24 June 2008, p. 25.

[75] This illustration is based on Dell, Michael, 'Everyone Has a Choice', *Financial Times Digital Business—Special Report*, 18 April 2007, p. 1.

is to double the number of PC users worldwide, and reinforce the company's market growth. The social benefit is the greater investment in technology in some of the poorest countries in the world, with the goal of improving living standards and reducing global inequality.[76]

The point is that adding a social dimension to the value proposition adds a new frontier for our thinking about competition. The number of industries and companies whose competitive advantage can involve social value propositions is rapidly growing. Accordingly, it is increasingly important that we consider the resource profile of the company and the ways in which it can leverage and strengthen that profile:

Organizations that make the right choices and build focussed, proactive, and integrated social initiatives in concert with their core strategies will increasingly distance themselves from the pack....Perceiving social responsibility as building shared value rather than as damage control or as a PR campaign will require dramatically different thinking in business. We are convinced, however, that CSR will become increasingly important to competitive success.[77]

CSR Is Customer Value

The most extreme case is where CSR becomes the value proposition. In sectors as diverse as automotives, good, retail technology, and health and beauty, ethical consumerism is at work. Unimpressed by conventional philanthropic commitments, the ethical consumer is focused on environmental impact and the treatment of staff and suppliers.[78] Accordingly, a growing number of companies are thinking 'beyond the green corporation' to a situation where eco-friendly and socially responsible practices drive business performance.[79]

Whether the impact is negative in undermining other aspects of the value proposition, neutral in simply keeping up with the competition, or positive in creating a competitive advantage in the customer's eyes,

[76] 'Footing the Bill: Gates Offers $3 Software to Poor', *Financial Times*, 20 April 2007, p. 1.

[77] Porter and Kramer (2006), op. cit.

[78] Grande, Carlos, 'Ethical Consumption Makes Mark on Branding', *Financial Times*, 20 February 2007, p. 24.

[79] Engardi, Pete, 'Beyond the Green Corporation', *BusinessWeek*, 29 January 2007, pp. 50–64.

the relationship between CSR and customer relationships is complex and increasingly important. What you stand for, and your standards of behaviour, impact on customer value. These qualities may be an important determinant of our ability to differentiate our value offering and position advantageously against the competition. The issue is too big to be ignored in developing strategic relationships with customers.

Some Questions to Ask about Salespeople and CSR

CSR is a big set of issues that is exercising many management minds right now. One challenge is to focus down on to the specifics of what CSR means to customer relationships and the customer choices we make (or customer defections we should anticipate). A starting point in testing the impact of CSR initiatives on buyer–seller relationships might be to try asking a few practical questions of and about how salespeople, sales managers, and account managers who actually meet customers deal with the CSR issue:

- Do salespeople know the company's position on different aspects of CSR— do they know what initiatives are underway?
- Do they buy-in to CSR, or are feelings more antipathetic or even cynical?
- Do they know what competitors are doing in this area and how customers are reacting?
- Are our sales processes aligned with CSR initiatives to leverage this as a competitive advantage in customers' eyes?
- Do CSR initiatives make us more or less attractive to some customers—do we know which, and how this works for them?
- Are there emerging opportunities for building stronger partnerships with major customers based on joint CSR initiatives?
- Are we vulnerable to losing some major customers because our CSR stance does not meet their aspirations for their suppliers—do we know which, and how to respond to this threat?

This will at least provide some guidelines to what value and impact the company's CSR investments are having on selling and relationship-building activities, and what opportunities and threats are developing, rather than just waiting to see what happens when competitors seize the initiative.

Building the Agenda

Traditional approaches to managing sales and account management organizations have not really engaged with the sorts of issues we have discussed in this chapter. If considered at all, 'ethics' was mainly about compliance to codes of conduct and guidelines for appropriate behaviour. Corporate reputation and corporate social responsibility were not really addressed as part of the value proposition that salespeople and account managers took to the customer—more a question of 'PR' and philanthropy on the part of senior management, favouring good causes of their choosing. Nothing much to do with our competitive position in the customer's eyes.

One way or another, things have changed. It is clear that one of the things that we will be judged by will be our integrity and social responsibility stance. This may kill us in some markets, or provide us with a competitive advantage. Issues of integrity and responsibility will inevitably be part of the definition of the relationship between buyers and sellers.

This provides an additional dimension to leadership by the strategic sales organization within the business, which may yet prove to be the most critical dimension. It identifies another opportunity waiting to be grasped by the strategic sales organization and linked closely to the priority for strategic customer management.

10

International: Looking Beyond National Boundaries Because Customers Do

It is perhaps stating the obvious to suggest that the strategic sales organization should be shaped in part by an international perspective on customers and management practices. However, experience suggests that many conventional sales managers do not really agree. They should change their minds. International issues are critical to developing business models and new strategies, to managing the customer portfolio, and to developing the sales organization infrastructure.

In fact, building strong customer relationships is a high priority in most markets wherever they are located, and the strategic sales initiative should play a pivotal role in this activity. At the same time, aggressive globalization and the challenges of gaining a strong competitive edge underline the importance of sales management strategies in gaining competitive advantage in international markets. Increasingly, top managements in many global enterprises are developing their salesforce capabilities, recognizing the importance of the salesforce in core business processes like customer relationship management, supply chain management, and product development management. Multinational firms like Nestlé SA, Novartis, and Caterpillar Inc. have been widely recognized for their successful global sales management systems.[1]

We start by looking at why an international perspective is an imperative for the strategic sales organization, and then focus on how companies can respond to the emergence and rapid growth of global customers who buy on a multinational basis, and the adoption of global account management approaches as an extension of strategic account management. Finally, we look at some of the challenges of global sales management, and particularly the dilemmas about whether to standardize sales management strategy across different countries and cultures, or whether to adapt to local conditions in terms of cultural characteristics, economic wealth, and political stability. The issue is whether international markets are convergent (increasingly the same) or divergent (fundamentally different)—this is not a judgement to be made hastily or incorrectly.

Get Lost—We Don't Do 'International'

Well, yes—actually you do. To all intents and purposes there is no such thing as a domestic market any more. Wherever you are, whatever you do, you are now competing in a global market. The only difference is whether you know it or not. If we aim to play a role at the strategic decision-making level in a company, an international perspective is one of the basic requirements. There are several reasons for this.

The Internet

For a start, it is already clear that the Internet means no one competes only in their domestic market any more. Simply the fact that customers can make product and price comparisons on the Web means you are competing globally. The growth in online auctions and Web-based purchasing consortia reinforce this fact. For example, Agentrics (a merger of the Global Exchange Network and Worldwide Retail

[1] Cravens, David W., Nigel F. Piercy, and George S. Low, 'Globalization of the Sales Organization: Management Control and Its Consequences', *Organizational Dynamics*, Vol. 35 No. 3 2006, pp. 291–303.

Exchange) brings together 50 of the world's largest retailers and over 80,000 suppliers, with a goal of streamlining and automating sourcing globally, and supporting collaboration between retailers and suppliers. Although facing problems of technology integration as well as anti-trust questions, it is estimated that Internet-based procurement systems may cut 30 per cent off costs. In business-to-business marketing, it is telling that even by the early 2000s, major purchasers like Boeing and Motorola were warning that suppliers unable or unwilling to make the transition to Web-based commerce would be locked out of their businesses. Suppliers face competition at a global level even in what would previously have been seen as domestic business.

On top of that, the Internet makes it more viable to digitize both products and channels. Where a traditional product can be converted to digital format, then it can be constructed and delivered to the user directly through the Internet, and conventional distribution may be avoided. Examples include music and software downloads, where the need for a conventional CD to be physically handled by distributors or retailers is reduced or removed. Similar developments include business and consumer information services, insurance and other financial services, e-books, education and training, computer games, television services, and movie rental and purchase. Interestingly, after some years of hesitation, video content creators like Hollywood studios are moving into digital distribution channels, creating services allowing consumers to watch films when and where they want. These moves are stimulated by the goal of new revenue streams and concern that traditional distribution models are declining.[2] Similarly, Sony is cutting US jobs and reviewing its business model to react to the shift of the computer games industry from sales of packaged software in retail stores to networking and online distribution.[3]

However, while product digitization goes hand in hand with the digitization of channel functions, it is not a prerequisite. Consider the airline ticket. While the airline still provides a seat on the aircraft, many of the traditional distribution functions carried out by travel agents or airline retail outlets are replaced by an online reservation number and an online, pre-printed boarding card, and online choice of seats,

[2] Taylor, Paul, 'Coming Soon: Films on File', *Financial Times*, 31 May 2006, p. 12.
[3] Sanchanta, Mariko, 'Sony to Cut US Jobs to Prop Up PS3', *Financial Times*, 8 June 2007, p. 28.

food, and entertainments. Opportunities exist more broadly to digitize certain channel functions for both products and services. The idea of 'lean consumption' underlines the emergence of these opportunities to minimize customer time and effort and to deliver exactly what they want, when and where they want it.[4]

The digitization of products and channel functions is not necessarily associated with the process of disintermediation—replacing distributors with direct manufacturer-owned channels. Rather, companies like iTunes and online insurance brokers are creating new types of online distributors—a process of reintermediation. Indeed, digitization of distribution functions can work closely with conventional channel arrangements—in-store online ordering of out-of-stock products, or collecting online purchases from retail outlets are illustrative developments.

Strategic customer management initiatives have to accommodate forces for globalization and digitization that change the competitive landscape in fundamental ways.

There Is Nowhere Else to Grow

It is also pretty clear that in many mature industries in the developed economies, the mandate for continued corporate growth makes it unavoidable that international markets become a priority. In fact, it is actually quite worrying that under pressure company management seems to have a knee-jerk reaction when challenged on growth prospects—the answer is always the 'emerging markets', the expanding BRIC countries (Brazil, Russia, India, and China).

This is great except for the fact that these are actually some of the toughest markets in the world in which to compete. Success in new and different markets across the world is likely to require new business models and new routes to market. Effective strategic customer management and new sales strategies are likely to be critical issues within this process.

For example, drugmaker AstraZeneca has built a good business in China by hiring local salespeople, many speaking local Chinese

---

[4] Womack, James P. and Daniel T. Jones, 'Lean Consumption', *Harvard Business Review*, March 2005, pp. 59–68.

dialects, to canvass doctors and hospitals to prescribe its products, but it did this by focusing on provincial cities largely ignored by its competitors, who were clustered in the major cities like Beijing. The company has taken its prescription drug sales from $85 million in 2001 to $423 million in 2007, by adapting its sales model to exploit local market characteristics.[5]

New Competitors Are Coming after You

Perhaps even more worrying than the challenges of expanding internationally is the fact that companies from the emerging markets are not simply competing fiercely in their own markets, but also pursuing their own impressive globalization initiatives.

Just think about the following facts. The low-cost car which India was promised has not been produced by any of the global automotive alliances, but by the Indian company Tata—the 'one lakh car' (selling for £1,250) is the Tata Nano. The same company—Tata—now owns Jaguar and Land Rover. The global steel industry has been reinvented by Lakshmi Mittal's ArcelorMittal company, growing out of Indonesia, India, and the former Eastern Europe, which is now the global market leader. Russian steelmakers are rapidly acquiring steel plants in the United States. Although frequently somewhat secretive, the investment vehicles of governments in Asia, the Middle East, and elsewhere are buying companies and brands in the West—the six Gulf States alone control sovereign fund assets of $1.7 trillion. The oil and gas business was once led by ExxonMobil and Chevron of the United States and BP and Royal Dutch Shell in Europe, but now is dominated by Saudi Asramci, Russia's Gazprom, CNPC of China, NIOC of Iran, Venezuela's PDVSA, Brazil's Petrobas, and Petronas of Malaysia, who together own a third of the world's oil and gas production and reserves. At the end of 2007, three of the five largest companies in the world were Chinese (PetroChina, China Mobile, and Industrial & Commercial Bank of China).[6] Astonishingly, in 2008, amid the meltdown of mainstream banks in the credit crunch, Bangladesh's

[5] This illustration is based on Zaminska, Nicholas, 'AstraZeneca Taps China's Hinterlands', *Wall Street Journal*, 13 June 2008, p. B.1.

[6] Dyer, Geoff and Richard McGregor, 'China's Champions', *Financial Times*, 17 March 2008, p. 11.

Grameen Bank made its first loans in New York, bringing its pioneering microfinance techniques (very small loans to high credit risk consumers) to the poor of the United States who do not rate a bank account.[7] Do you see something of a pattern emerging here?

Not only are many sectors now dominated by investment from the emerging markets, the real export from the emerging markets is not capital, it is new ways of doing business, or new business models. Companies which have developed effective ways of doing business in the harsh market conditions they have faced are likely to find Western markets pretty soft targets. Businesses that have survived tough economic conditions have valuable lessons for others.[8]

Think about Mumbai's tiffin boxes, and ask what such radically different approaches could do in other markets.[9] Mumbai's 'dabbawallahs' constitute a 5,000-strong workforce that every day rushes tens of thousands of tiffin boxes (stacked cylindrical tins of food) across the city. The food is prepared in the morning by wives, sisters, and maids, and using a relay system they reach the right person by lunchtime. The empty tins are collected after lunch and returned to the housewives who prepare the food. A coded system of numbers and signs on the tiffin box directs it to the correct office. Every day the dabbawallahs, many of whom are illiterate, deliver more than 170,000 meals with almost no mistakes. The tiffin box system has operated successfully for more than 100 years. The system is highly customer-focused but relies on the dabbawallahs' feet, heads, bicycles, carts, and the luggage compartments of the trains in Mumbai's suburban rail network. This complex system has no computer databases or software, or barcode scanning, or supply chain strategy, but it is both lean and agile. The extension of business models from emerging markets like India has the potential to revolutionize Western markets.

Nonetheless, it is dangerous to make stereotypical assumptions about how these new businesses will operate and how they will compete. For example, Tata is leading India's globalization through

---

[7] Pimlott, Daniel, 'Grameen Bank's Loans to US Poor', *Financial Times*, 16/17 February 2008, p. 8.

[8] Sull, Donald, 'Emerging Markets Give Flight to New Industry Champions', *Financial Times*, 5 August 2005, p. 11.

[9] This illustration is based on Murray, Sarah, 'Food for Thought for the Financiers', *Financial Times*, 19 November 2007, p. 14.

a programme of worldwide acquisition. But the strategy is not to 'Indianize' the companies purchased. Mr Tata explains that moulding an acquired company to look and function more like its parent is a 'more Anglo-Saxon' concept. In the West the expectation is that an acquired business will take on its owners' operating characteristics. He states that Tata does not consider itself capable of micro-managing acquired businesses from India, even to the extent that this approach is sometimes misunderstood as neglect. Mr Tata says his approach is to seek out companies with sound business plans and good corporate ethics, and then to avoid the destructive pressure for short-term profits, in favour of a more patient investment philosophy.

On the other hand, Mittal's acquisition strategy has been ruthless and in some cases brutal. Faced with personnel problems at one acquired plant in the United States, Aditya Mittal's impassive response was 'Feel free to change the management'.[10] When faced with the chance to take over one of his own brother's steel plants in Bulgaria because it was running out of cash, Mr Mittal had no hesitation in swooping.[11] Mittal's strategy has been robust and determined and he has succeeded in reinventing the way the global steel industry works.

But the point we are making is that not all Indian companies behave the same because they are Indian. You should expect diverse business models and management approaches from new types of competitors. The premium on deep knowledge about competition has never been greater.

Global Customers

Then there is the question of global customers—those who buy internationally across numerous geographic locations. They demand a global response from their suppliers. They occupy a special position in the customer portfolio and deserve careful strategic evaluation. Let us turn attention to the challenge of meeting global customer needs.

[10] Reed, Stanley, 'Mittal & Son', *BusinessWeek*, 16 April 2007, pp. 44–52.
[11] O'Connell, Dominic, 'Mittal Swoop on Brother's Steel Plant', *Sunday Times*, 25 May 2008, Section 3 p. 3.

Responding to Global Customer Needs

In many companies, an issue of critical importance to the strategic sales organization will be the continued development of global customers—for example, in retailing and in the IT and automotive sectors. These customers will normally be strategic accounts or major accounts, depending on the relationship they want to have with the supplier (see the customer portfolio, Chapter 2). In either case, they are likely to require a different approach.

For many companies, this is a major challenge because of the growing importance of global customers, who expect to buy on a global basis and to receive favourable treatment across all their worldwide locations. This challenge is illustrated by the growth of global retailing businesses and the development of global account management organizations.

The Growth of Global Customers

In the consumer goods sector, the growth of global retailers has been substantial. In consumer packaged goods, Ahold (the Netherlands), Carrefour (France), and METRO (Germany) each operate in more than 25 countries. Aldi (Germany), Auchan (France), Rewe (Switzerland), Tesco (United Kingdom), and Wal-Mart each operate in 10 or more countries. Similar trends are appearing in industries as diverse as clothing, chemicals, entertainment, financial services, and personal computers. Powerful global customers expect levels of coverage, speed, consistent and high-quality service, and extraordinary attention from their suppliers to reflect their buying power. These expectations require suppliers to provide a single point of contact, uniform terms of trade, and worldwide standardization of products and services.[12]

Retail markets outside the United States show astonishing degrees of buyer concentration. For example, in the food market, notwithstanding the strong position of Wal-Mart and up-market innovations like Whole Foods Market and Trader Joe's, many US retail chains are relatively weak and fragmented and lack the scale to bargain with food companies or to produce their own labels. Many have in effect rented

---

[12] Kumar, Nirmalya, *Marketing as Strategy: Understanding the CEO's Agenda for Driving Growth and Innovation*, Boston, MA: Harvard Business School Press, 2004.

out their shelves to food companies such as Heinz and Kraft.[13] This market structure gives food product manufacturers considerable scope to take a lead role in managing relationships with these customers. By contrast, in Europe, each country market is relatively small, and retail concentration is extremely high. In the United Kingdom, for example, one retailer (Tesco) controls more than 30 per cent of the national grocery market, and the top four firms (Tesco, Asda, Sainsbury, and Morrisons) control 75 per cent of the market.[14] Similar concentration is seen in other European countries with the impact of French retailers like Carrefour. The situation for manufacturers is clearly quite different when powerful retailing companies control such high shares of the market, and different selling relationship choices are necessary.

For example, global customers typically demand more uniform and transparent global prices from suppliers. In 2000, supermarket Tesco acquired a small supermarket chain called Hit in Poland. Hit was obtaining better prices from its suppliers than was Tesco. The lack of a logical worldwide pricing structure allows global customers like Tesco to demand retrospective discounts when they discover what they regard as 'anomalies', at great cost to their suppliers.[15]

Global Account Management

The growth in importance of global customers has led many suppliers to develop specialized organizational units and processes to manage their relationship. Global account management is 'an organizational form and process by which the worldwide activities serving a given multi-national customer are coordinated by one person or team within the supplying company'.[16]

In some companies, Global Account Managers have been developed in parallel to Strategic Account Management functions (see Chapter 2). Procter & Gamble, for example, has established global

[13] Gapper, John, 'America's Time-Warp Supermarkets', *Financial Times*, 11 June 2007, p. 11.
[14] Rigby, Elizabeth, 'Food Retailing Recovery on Special Offer', *Financial Times*, 16 November 2006, p. 21.
[15] Kumar (2004), op cit., p. 119.
[16] Yip, George S. and Madsen, Thomas L., 'Global Account Management: The New Frontier in Relationship Marketing', *International Marketing Review*, Vol. 13 No. 3 1996, pp. 24–42, at p. 25.

customer development teams to present a single face to the global customer. P&G's global customer teams operate in parallel with the company's business units and country organizations, in a form of matrix. The customer teams have specialists in IT, retail merchandising, finance, sales, supply chain, marketing, and marketing research. The teams manage relationships with global retailers and develop joint plans with them, as well as working with business units and country managers to deliver against strategic goals for the customer in each product category and geographic location.

Global account management teams are multi-functional and can only operate effectively by addressing cross-functional coordination and communication around the strategy development for the global customers. Global account managers frequently report to very senior levels of the organization. Effective organizational responses to the global customer are becoming extremely important in a wide range of companies.

For example, global account management strategy at Microsoft provides a good illustration.[17] Global account management (GAM) puts a single executive or team in charge of a single customer and all its global needs. This executive must be able to call on all the company's resources and be able to market all its products to the customer. GAM involves a relationship with the customer that does not just find solutions for operational needs, but builds strategies for the future and develops new business. The main tasks in initiating GAM are selecting the accounts, developing corporate structure that makes GAM a distinct company operation, and recruiting account managers. At Microsoft, account managers, called Global Business Managers, are encouraged to be innovative and have their own budgets. They work across business units, functions, and organizations, and get support in marshalling resources from a headquarters team of 10, and support from a broader group of 150 people worldwide, who contribute in various ways to account planning and operational management.

Microsoft began introducing GAM in 2000, and focuses on multi-million dollar, global corporate customers that depend heavily on

[17] This illustration is based on Senn, Christoph and Axel Thoma, 'Worldly Wise: Attracting and Managing Customers Isn't the Same When Business Goes Global', *Wall Street Journal*, 3 March 2007, p. R.5.

information technology. To be a Microsoft global account, candidates must have enough revenue potential to justify Microsoft allocating significant resources. Account size is only one criterion, the candidate must be willing to collaborate; be ready to share information for developing new products and processes; be willing to establish multilevel relationships with Microsoft; be a leader in their industry (to leverage Microsoft's reputation); possess superior skills and knowledge and be early adopters of new technology; and already have global organizational coordination. Microsoft encourages its senior managers to develop relationships with senior decision-makers in the global account, and be active in ensuring that GAM initiatives get all the resources they require from within Microsoft.

GAM is in many ways similar to strategic account management and suffers from the same vulnerabilities and involves the same choices.[18] However, here there may be less choice involved. If the customer is a global business with buying points across many countries, there may be no option other than to respond on a global account management basis or to lose the business.

Indeed, from a strategic sales perspective, part of the challenge of GAM is translating central decisions into the operations of decentralized sales organizations. One of the issues then becomes the extent to which country-based sales management practices will have to be altered to allow this translation to happen.

Global Market Differences or Global Convergence?

One of the quandaries in sales and marketing strategy is knowing when and how to respond effectively to differences between international markets—what to standardize globally and what to adapt to local market conditions. Adaptation suggests market differences. But what of market convergence and similarities?

---

[18] For an excellent review of global customer issues, see Yip, George S. and Audrey J. M. Bank, *Managing Global Customers: An Integrated Approach*, Oxford: Oxford University Press, 2007.

Global Market Differences

Importantly, market conditions and consequently customer priorities may be significantly different in global markets. For example, some of the most attractive prospects are in emerging markets, where local market conditions are substantially different to those in developed countries. The importance of adapting customer strategy to these local conditions is a critical factor for success.

For example, India with its huge population and a rapidly globalizing economy is a key target market for many companies.[19] Firms like Wal-Mart, Vodaphone, and Citigroup are placing multi-million dollar bets on the country—lured by the 300 million strong middle class. The realities of developing effective customer strategy in India identify many challenges. The infrastructure has received little investment—many roads are crumbling, airports are jammed, power blackouts are common, and water supplies are limited. Improvements are slowed by the sheer scale, by corruption in many public bodies, and by cost.[20] Seventy per cent of India's population lives in the rural countryside. The population is poor, and the infrastructure at its worst in these areas. Successes have been products adapted to these conditions—4 cent sachets of soap, salt, and tea from Hindustan Lever, $20 wind-up radios from Philips, the $900 Hero-Honda Splendour motor cycle—sold in small shops, bus-stop stalls, and roadside cafes.

Foreign companies have many horror stories: Nokia saw thousands of cell phones ruined when a shipment from its factory in Chennai was soaked by rain because there was no room to warehouse the crates at the airport; Suzuki says trucking its cars 900 miles from the Gurgaon factory to the port in Mumbai can take up to 10 days—because of delays on three state borders on the way, and big rigs are banned from congested cities during the day—and once at the port, the autos can wait weeks for the next outbound ship, because there is not enough dock space for cargo carriers to load and unload; When GE sent executives to survey a potential site for a factory to manufacture locomotives in partnership with India Railways, they returned

[19] This illustration is based on Hamm, Steve, 'The Trouble with India', *BusinessWeek*, 19 March 2007, pp. 49–58. Kripalani, Manjeet, 'Rural India, Have a Coke', *BusinessWeek*, 27 May 2002, pp. 30–1.

[20] Hamm, Steve, 'The Trouble with India', *BusinessWeek*, 19 March 2007, pp. 49–58.

discouraged—it took five hours to drive the 50 miles from the airport to the site, and when they got there they found nothing—no roads, no power, no schools, no water, no hospitals, no housing.

It is easy to be misled about the real opportunities faced in selling in overseas markets. For example, it is clear that countries like Russia and India are becoming major buyers of luxury automobiles. Nonetheless, while India's middle class has developed a taste for luxury and the confidence to indulge it, poor roads and the lack of parking in Indian cities often force car owners to have their driver follow behind in a back-up vehicle, to take care of the Porsche when it is not being driven.[21] In fact, more than half of India's passenger car market is in the rural areas. In these areas, Maruti Suzuki, India's largest passenger carmaker, has an interesting sales strategy: when new car customers ask for cars to be delivered at home, it is often because they cannot drive; it is still relatively unusual for women to drive in India; key to Maruti's strategy in a market where first-time buyers account for 35 per cent of sales is teaching people to drive—Maruti sponsors neighbourhood driving schools, some with female instructors to encourage women learners. Because buying a car is a major family decision, dealerships accommodate buyers in large groups, and arrange Hindu blessings of vehicles to bring good luck. Niche markets are important—for example to reach teachers in rural areas, Maruti sent salespeople to 30,000 schools and sold 10,000 cars. Maruti had 55 per cent of the Indian passenger car market in 2007 (and is planning to export 100,000 small cars a year to Europe).[22]

When it is different in overseas markets, it may be very different. When local competitors are strong, they may be very strong. You need to know these things before you invest, not afterwards. This places some priority on extending and enhancing the market sensing capabilities of sales organizations (see Chapter 3).

Accordingly, assumptions about local market conditions should be challenged and questioned in many cases. Those local conditions shape and define what customers will need and require from suppliers, and those needs may be very different. However, there are

---

[21] Leahy, Joe, 'Road of New Rich Littered with Potholes', *Financial Times*, 1 August 2007, p. 24.
[22] Yee, Amy and John Reed, 'How Maruti Clocks Up Custom', *Financial Times*, 4 September 2007, p. 14.

also important issues to consider about how well sales management and account management practices and policies cross national
boundaries—or more how well they cross cultural and economic
divides.

... Versus Global Convergence

However, while much marketing and sales thinking emphasizes differences between international markets, when we come to consider
strategic sales rather than operational sales issues, that thinking may
have exaggerated the importance of international market differences.[23]

One important issue in understanding global trends in sales management (rather than simply selling) is whether real differences exist
between different cultures and countries. In particular, this raises a
crucial question—how important are country differences when we
make multi-country salesforce decisions on things like the level of
management behaviour-based control and incentive compensation
(Chapter 6).

Thomas Friedman's best-selling book—*The World Is Flat*[24]—offers
the compelling proposal that globalization is removing barriers
between countries—including the impact of physical, technological,
cultural, and political differences. Friedman's argument is that while
these changes are happening at different rates, many management
processes around the world are becoming more similar. He defines
the process as a triple convergence, where there are new competitive
players, competing on a new playing field, who are developing new
processes and practices for horizontal collaboration. He underlines
10 'flatteners' that have played a key role in these changes—such as
international management education and the Internet.

However, the global convergence of business capabilities and performance is also examined by Suzanne Berger in *How We Compete*.[25]
The results of a five-year study of 500 international firms conducted
by the MIT Industrial Performance Center suggest the need for some

---

[23] This section is adapted from Cravens, Piercy, and Low (2006), op. cit.

[24] Friedman, Thomas, *The World Is Flat: The Globalized World in the Twenty-First
Century*, Harmondsworth: Penguin, 2007.

[25] Berger, Suzanne, *How We Compete: What Companies around the World Are Doing to
Make It in Today's Global Economy*, New York: Doubleday Business, 2005.

International   293

caution in interpreting the extent of 'flatness' when comparing advanced industrial economies with the rest of the world. While economic growth and changes in China and India are impressive, much of the rest of the world, although changing, is not 'flat' (including Africa, Latin America, and large areas of the Middle East and Asia). Berger points to challenges in transformation and observes that much of the world is still 'round'. The MIT research has a heavy emphasis on technology, but is a nice counterpoint to *The World Is Flat*.

For example, in the global sales management field, recently SAP AG implemented a global incentive programme in 50 countries where it operates, replacing locally based programmes. The benefit is taking advantage of economies of scale and fostering a global culture. Importantly, SAP and other firms are learning that similarities across countries are making the old approaches of regional and local management control less effective in today's global business environment.

The Key Issues with Global Customers then Become...

The convergence of sales management practices across countries in a flattening world may be a high priority in meeting the demands of global accounts in particular. This may replace the individual country-based practices developed in an earlier era of 'think globally, act locally' to reflect country and market differences.

For example, Hewlett-Packard recognizes the need to meet the challenges of globalizing the sales organization. In response to increasing evidence of convergence in global market characteristics and practices, H-P's management is examining the adequacy of its multinational customer relationship strategies. The company has launched major initiatives to globalize the firm's corporate sales strategy. Country-focused sales organizations are being realigned to serve global customers.[26]

The dilemmas facing senior sales executives are complex in managing global sales strategies. Global account management involves deciding how to identify and serve international accounts. But should one global salesforce be used or should account responsibilities be delegated to country salesforces? How should salespeople be allocated between direct and non-direct salesforces around the world? How

[26] Cravens, Piercy, and Low (2006), op cit.

important are country differences in multi-country salesforce decisions like sales management control and incentive compensation? These dilemmas underline the strategic issues in managing across national boundaries to which we now turn.

Managing Strategic Sales across National Boundaries

In fact, knowledge about global sales management practices outside the United States and Western Europe is limited.

However, even within Europe, cultural differences may be important to sales management initiatives. One interesting study compares salespeople within Europe on the basis of their Latin or Anglo Germanic cultural groups—groups whose origins lie in distant political and religious history. This research found that the cultural groupings explained differences in salespeoples' selling strategies and most interestingly that cultural differences indicated different responses to 'coaching' (through behaviour-based control systems)—Latin salespeople seemed to respond better to behaviour-based control than did Anglo and Germanic salespeople. The researchers suggest that managers responsible for salesforce restructuring within Europe are likely to face some obstacles reflecting cultural and national differences.[27]

But if we think on a broader front about emerging markets evidence is even more scarce. There are few published studies on sales management in developing countries to guide management decisions. However, our research sheds some light on some of the relevant issues.[28] The findings discussed below are based on information provided by over 1,000 field sales managers responsible for the direct supervision

[27] Rouziès, Dominique and Anne Maquin, 'An Exploratory Investigation of the Impact of Culture on Sales Force Management Control Systems in Europe', *Journal of Personal Selling & Sales Management*, Vol. 23 No. 1 2002/3, pp. 61–72.

[28] This section is based on Cravens, Piercy, and Low (2006), op cit.; Piercy, Nigel F., George S. Low, and David W. Cravens, 'Examining the Effectiveness of Sales Management Control Practices in Developing Countries', *Journal of World Business*, Vol. 39 2004, pp. 255–67; Baldauf, Artur, David W. Cravens, and Nigel F. Piercy, 'Examining the Consequences of Sales Management Control Strategies in European Field Sales Organizations', *International Marketing Review*, Vol. 18 No. 5 2001, pp. 474–508.

of salespeople in business-to-business selling situations. The countries included Austria, Greece, the Gulf States (Bahrain and Saudi Arabia), India, Israel, Malaysia, Nigeria, and the UK.

Global Sales Management

Our perspective is based on trying to answer two general questions: (*a*) to what extent has a global convergence of strategic sales management processes occurred and (*b*) what management insights can we gain by examining global sales management control processes and their consequences, in a range of countries including those from the developed and developing countries?

More specifically, we are interested in how developed countries compare to developing countries regarding their sales management practices and particularly how the effects of sales management behaviour-based control and compensation-based control vary between and across the countries studied.

The Research Findings

The major relationships studied and findings are shown in Table 10.1, and we highlight the evidence of convergence and divergence between the countries shown in the results. In fact, the findings overall show compelling evidence of convergence in sales management practices. However, that convergence is far from complete. The sales management world appears to be flattening but is not yet completely flat.

We were particularly interested in whether the effectiveness of sales management control and other practices would reflect differences in culture, income, and political stability in the countries examined.

Culture

The countries in the study vary considerably in their cultural characteristics. Hofstede's famous work on culture identifies four dimensions considered relevant to management practices: power distance, uncertainty avoidance, individualism, and masculinity.[29] For comparing sales management differences across the countries in the study,

---

[29] http://www.geert.hofstede.com

Table 10.1 Synthesis of eight-country sales manager research findings[a]

	Evidence of convergence?	Evidence of divergence?
The impact of sales manager behaviour control strategy on the following:		
1. Salesperson success characteristics	Yes. Stronger relationship for Israel and Nigeria, weaker for the UK	Sales manager behaviour control strategy has stronger effects in countries with low political stability and a higher uncertainty avoidance culture
2. Salesperson behaviour performance	Yes. Much stronger relationship for Israel and Nigeria. Not significant for Malaysia	Sales manager behaviour control strategy has stronger effects in countries with low political stability and a higher uncertainty avoidance culture. Behaviour control may be less effective in countries with a high power distance culture
3. Salesperson outcome performance	Several differences. The relationship is much stronger for Israel and Nigeria, but not significant for the Gulf States and India	Sales manager behaviour control strategy has stronger effects in countries with low political stability and a higher uncertainty avoidance culture. Behaviour control may be less effective in countries with a high power distance culture
4. Sales unit effectiveness	Some differences. India and the Gulf States not significant, but Nigeria very strong	Sales manager behaviour control strategy has stronger effects in countries with low political stability and a higher uncertainty avoidance culture. Behaviour control may be less effective in countries with a high power distance culture
The impact of incentive pay on the following:		
1. Salesperson performance	No impact, except Israel and the Gulf States	Incentive pay may be more effective in higher uncertainty avoidance cultures because it clarifies the 'rules'
2. Sales unit effectiveness	Mixed impact	Incentive pay may be more effective in higher uncertainty avoidance cultures and in low political stability countries

[a] Adapted from Cravens, Piercy, and Low (2006).

we used the power distance and uncertainty avoidance dimensions of culture as potentially the most insightful.

The power distance dimension of culture refers to the degree of equality or inequality between people in a country's society. Low power distance may facilitate more collaborative, less formal relationships between the sales manager and the salesperson, than would be the case with the greater social divide represented by high power distance. We found some indications that sales manager behaviour control activities may be less effective in high power distance countries— salespeople may prefer clear directives to 'coaching' and social interaction with the manager.

Uncertainty avoidance focuses on the level of tolerance for uncertainty and ambiguity within a society. Low uncertainty avoidance indicates less concern about ambiguity and more tolerance for risk. We found some indications that in high uncertainty avoidance cultures (e.g. Israel, Nigeria), sales manager behaviour control shows a strong relationship with salesperson performance. This suggests that introducing clear 'rules' and working closely with salespeople may be particularly effective. Conversely, there are signs that the collaborative nature of behaviour-based control may face more difficulties in high power distance cultures (e.g. India, Malaysia) where salespeople may expect a greater level of social distance to be maintained between supervisor and employee.

Income and Political Stability

Economic wealth seems to explain relatively little in interpreting the results, with the exception of Nigeria, the poorest country in the study. Here there is evidence that behaviour-based control has a particularly strong impact on sales unit effectiveness, because it reduces uncertainty and economic risk for the salesperson. Political stability may also explain some of the relationships in the results. The lower income/low political stability countries also show a stronger impact of behaviour control on sales unit effectiveness (Nigeria), as well as a high impact of compensation control on sales unit effectiveness (Israel and India).

Nonetheless, crude stereotyping should be avoided. It is worth remembering that in low-income countries even relatively humble sales jobs are one of the routes for the poor to buy into middle-class dreams. Many taking jobs as salespeople will be among the most able and ambitious—this is, for example, part of the economic drama unfolding in India.[30]

What Do the Research Findings Tell Us about Global Sales Management?

The findings in Table 10.1 show a high degree of convergence between the countries, particularly in terms of the positive impact of sales manager behaviour control strategy, and interestingly the limited impact of incentive compensation (except for Israel and the Gulf States).

The relationships between sales manager behaviour control, salesperson performance, and sales unit effectiveness clearly support Friedman's *The World Is Flat* premise. The strongest evidence of convergence is for the relationships between behaviour control, salesperson success characteristics, and salesperson behaviour performance. The top line finding suggests that we may introduce these sales infrastructure approaches in global sales operations with some confidence that they will be effective (although the research only looks at eight countries).

Incentive pay has no apparent impact on performance in most of the countries. In certain of the developing countries managers reported a relatively high percentage of incentive pay for salespeople compared to the developed countries. This finding may indicate the need to consider the effects of high incentive rates in these developing countries. The traditional assumption that high financial incentives are more effective in emerging markets may be dubious. Incentive pay has, at best, a mixed impact on sales unit effectiveness. Overall, the evidence concerning incentive pay is that it has no effect in most countries.

However, while the evidence of convergence is compelling, there remain country differences linked to factors like national culture characteristics, economic wealth, and political stability. It would be unwise to ignore these differences in thinking about global sales management. However, importantly, these culture- and economic/political-related factors only appear to impact when there are very large differences

---

[30] Bellman, Eric, 'In Mumbai, Humble Sales Jobs Help Poor Buy into Middle-Class Dreams', *Wall Street Journal*, 19 November 2007, pp. 14–15.

to the rest of the world. In our research countries, for example, India and Nigeria are among the poorest countries in the world with some of the lowest scores for political stability; Malaysia does not simply have a high level of power distance, it is the highest in the Hofstede research of countries across the world; Greece does not just have a high uncertainty avoidance culture but the highest in the world. The evidence is that divergence in the effectiveness of sales management practices is linked to *extreme* differences in cultural, economic, and political characteristics.

The question still remains whether adopting the same sales management strategy across a range of overseas countries will be effective. If there are local differences in the response of salespeople to differing control approaches, they may easily outweigh the attractions of a standardized global approach to sales management. The danger remains that insensitive application of conventional sales management strategy across countries and cultures still carries the risk of damaging the business and missing opportunities in some of the highest prospect international markets. The warning signal is when the countries in question show very large differences in cultural, economic, and political stability factors.

Building the Agenda

The need for an international perspective on strategic customer management is almost a no brainer. How can you be strategic in a company without being international? We laid out the case for adopting an international perspective in the strategic sales organization. We then looked at the impact of global customers and the development of global account management approaches. Finally, we looked at some of the challenges in global sales management.

Examining the international aspects of strategic customer management provides the final part of the imperatives for the strategic sales organization that we defined in Chapter 1 (Figure 1.3). In that sense, the agenda has now been built!

Of course, life is rarely that straightforward. Agendas are never exhaustive and rarely fully completed—things move on, the priorities change. Nonetheless, we believe that we have constructed a framework, based on leading-edge practices and incorporating up-to-date research findings, that provides an operational tool for managers to address some of the most important questions faced by their companies in managing relationships with the marketplace.

Now would be the appropriate time to go back to the 'Diagnosing the Changing Salesforce Role' diagnostic that we introduced in Chapter 1 as a planning mechanism (Appendix 1.1). Having worked through the issues we have uncovered and tested them against the position in your company, you should be able to identify the high priority gaps and new opportunities most relevant to the company. From this analysis, an action plan should be developed and taken forward in the ways best suited to getting things done and changed in your organization. We believe that the strategic customer management perspective and the strategic sales organization based on that perspective will be among the most significant company changes developing over the next few years. The stakes are high, but so are the risks of persisting with the *status quo*. It is likely that important careers will be developed out of the strategic sales change process.

Epilogue

Management books like this one work best if they stimulate productive conversations about important issues between people in organizations who can address those issues. In our case, those conversations may be between sales executives, marketing people, organization development specialists, strategic account management, and above all in importance—senior management in the organization. The issue is how the front-end of the organization should be shaped and managed to deliver value in new and rapidly changing customer and market conditions.

Sometimes conversations like these are better if there is structure and a shared mechanism for assessing the issues to debate. To this end, we include a diagnostic as an Appendix to this chapter—*How Strategic Is Your Sales Organization?* The diagnostic contains ten questions about each dimension of our strategic sales organization model (Figure 1.3) and asks you to assess the key points around each of them. They are all issues considered in the relevant chapters of the book. For those of a quantitative disposition, this gives a score out of a 100 for each dimension.

These things work better as a group exercise where we pool insights, rather than an individual effort. Importantly, there are no implications that you should aim to score maximum points on each dimension. Broadly, scores above 60 suggest that on this dimension you are looking at a strategic sales organization, while score below 40 suggest you definitely are not. Scores in the mid-range are more difficult to evaluate, and the issue becomes the direction in which you are moving. The most interesting outcome is actually the profile: in what areas are you already operating as a strategic sales organization and where is more work needed for this to be true. What would be the added-value for the company, if you were to move in this direction?

The goal of this diagnosis is to take a view on what you have got at the moment. This opens the way to the really important conversation about what you need and how a more strategic sales organization can add value to the company in the challenges it faces.

Appendix 10.1: How Strategic Is Your Sales Organization?

The diagnostic asks you to evaluate your sales organization in terms of its strategic characteristics. Consider each of the statements and decide how true or untrue it is as a description of your sales organization.

This will produce two things: a score out of 100 for each dimension of the strategic sales organization (scores over 60 generally indicate strategic status, scores under 40 indicate a non-strategic status, and mid-range scores indicate areas to watch); and a profile of the strategic characteristics of the sales organization in question. Consider what conclusions this analysis allows you to draw and record these on the form.

The results provide an indicator for the present strategic status of the sales organization but open the way to considering how strategic the sales organization needs to be to meet customer and market challenges, and the areas where attention should be focused to achieve this.

INVOLVEMENT	How are we doing?									
How true are the following statements?	Completely untrue									Completely true
1. Sales organization executives have a clear model of the company's business strategy in its main markets.	1	2	3	4	5	6	7	8	9	10
2. The customer portfolio is regularly and systematically modelled for each main market.	1	2	3	4	5	6	7	8	9	10
3. The customer portfolio is a central part of developing business strategy.	1	2	3	4	5	6	7	8	9	10
4. The company recognizes the investment priorities in the customer portfolio.	1	2	3	4	5	6	7	8	9	10
5. The company recognizes the relationship requirement differences in the customer portfolio.	1	2	3	4	5	6	7	8	9	10
6. Business strategy includes appraisal of the dominance of large customers and defines criteria for deciding when to reduce dependence.	1	2	3	4	5	6	7	8	9	10
7. Sales organization executives have a clear role in making decisions about strategic customers.	1	2	3	4	5	6	7	8	9	10
8. Business strategy recognizes both the attractions of strategic customers and the risks and plans for contingencies.	1	2	3	4	5	6	7	8	9	10
9. The company is realistic about the type of relationship required by strategic customers.	1	2	3	4	5	6	7	8	9	10
10. The selection of strategic customers is systematic and reflects the priorities of business strategy regarding volume and business risk.	1	2	3	4	5	6	7	8	9	10

INVOLVEMENT—TOTAL SCORE OUT OF 100	
CONCLUSIONS	

INTELLIGENCE	How are we doing?									
How true are the following statements?	Completely untrue									Completely true
1. The company has a high 'market IQ'.	1	2	3	4	5	6	7	8	9	10
2. The sales organization plays a major role in market sensing and communicating market changes to management.	1	2	3	4	5	6	7	8	9	10
3. Market intelligence from the sales organization plays a large role in shaping how management understands changing market boundaries and definitions.	1	2	3	4	5	6	7	8	9	10
4. The sales organization maps market structure to provide decision-makers with insights into how the market operates and where the opportunities are to be found.	1	2	3	4	5	6	7	8	9	10
5. Sales executives play a key role in gathering intelligence and information to show decision-makers priorities for investment and the need for defence strategies in the market.	1	2	3	4	5	6	7	8	9	10
6. The sales organization provides decision-makers with a clear view of how different customers understand the company's strengths and weaknesses and the real external opportunities and threats.	1	2	3	4	5	6	7	8	9	10
7. Sales executives have a clear and up-to-date understanding of major customers' end-user markets and the customer's strategy in those markets.	1	2	3	4	5	6	7	8	9	10
8. Sales executives play a role in providing major customers with end-user market information to show the customer new sources of competitive advantage.	1	2	3	4	5	6	7	8	9	10
9. With major customers selling is about providing advice and strategy-focused support not sales transactions.	1	2	3	4	5	6	7	8	9	10
10. The sales organization is a driver of new ideas and value-innovation in the business.	1	2	3	4	5	6	7	8	9	10

INTELLIGENCE—TOTAL SCORE OUT OF 100	
CONCLUSIONS	

INTEGRATION	How are we doing?									
How true are the following statements?	Completely untrue									Completely true
1. Sales executives have a clear model of the critical processes that define, create, and deliver value from the company to the market.	1	2	3	4	5	6	7	8	9	10
2. This model is communicated and understood by decision-makers in the company.	1	2	3	4	5	6	7	8	9	10
3. We are generally very successful in avoiding the customer problems associated with poor integration between departments, functions, and external suppliers.	1	2	3	4	5	6	7	8	9	10
4. The sales organization has a clear priority for integrating and coordinating everything in the company and its supply organization that contributes to identifying, meeting, and delivering customer value requirements.	1	2	3	4	5	6	7	8	9	10
5. Relationships between the sales organization and other departments are characterized by cooperation and partnership not conflict.	1	2	3	4	5	6	7	8	9	10
6. Sales executives are active participants in important integration mechanisms like cross-functional teams, process teams, and superior internal communications.	1	2	3	4	5	6	7	8	9	10
7. Sales executives work closely with the company's purchasing department to link sourcing and purchasing strategies to customer value.	1	2	3	4	5	6	7	8	9	10
8. Sales executives work closely with other company executives managing joint ventures and collaborations to link their partnership strategies to customer value.	1	2	3	4	5	6	7	8	9	10
9. The sales organization and the marketing organization have a clear and productive relationship.	1	2	3	4	5	6	7	8	9	10
10. Sales executives devote time and resources to managing internal interfaces between departments and units to enhance the delivery of customer value.	1	2	3	4	5	6	7	8	9	10

INTEGRATION—TOTAL SCORE OUT OF 100	
CONCLUSIONS	

INTERNAL MARKETING	How are we doing?									
How true are the following statements?	Completely untrue									Completely true
1. Sales executives focus on the internal market inside the company to achieve implementation of their strategies.	1	2	3	4	5	6	7	8	9	10
2. Sales executives systematically and realistically evaluate the barriers inside the company to the successful implementation of their strategies.	1	2	3	4	5	6	7	8	9	10
3. Screening for implementation problems at the earliest stage of planning change is part of how the sales organization operates.	1	2	3	4	5	6	7	8	9	10
4. Sales executives develop implementation strategies to get things to happen in the company as part of their work with customers.	1	2	3	4	5	6	7	8	9	10
5. Sales executives' implementation strategies are realistic and appropriately resourced.	1	2	3	4	5	6	7	8	9	10
6. The sales organization plays a key role in developing internal marketing programmes to support customer strategies.	1	2	3	4	5	6	7	8	9	10
7. The goals of internal marketing are well understood in the sales organization.	1	2	3	4	5	6	7	8	9	10
8. Internal marketing to support customer strategies is structured and appropriately resourced.	1	2	3	4	5	6	7	8	9	10
9. The sales organization plays a key role in monitoring the links between internal and external customer satisfaction and quality judgements.	1	2	3	4	5	6	7	8	9	10
10. Sales executives play an influential role in developing company policies to enhance customer satisfaction through appropriate employment and reward systems.	1	2	3	4	5	6	7	8	9	10

INTERNAL MARKETING—TOTAL SCORE OUT OF 100	
CONCLUSIONS	

INFRASTRUCTURE	How are we doing?									
How true are the following statements?	Completely untrue									Completely true
1. The company recognizes and supports realignment of sales organization structures and processes with the needs of business strategy.	1	2	3	4	5	6	7	8	9	10
2. The sales organization actively considers the needs of people entering the sales profession and how those needs are changing.	1	2	3	4	5	6	7	8	9	10
3. Sales executives have a clear view, which is regularly tested and updated, on the critical drivers of salesperson performance with different customer assignments.	1	2	3	4	5	6	7	8	9	10
4. Sales executives distinguish between salesperson outcome and behaviour performance and the competencies associated with each.	1	2	3	4	5	6	7	8	9	10
5. Sales manager control strategy focuses on salesperson behaviour performance in building long-term customer relationships and outcome performance in managing transactional relationships.	1	2	3	4	5	6	7	8	9	10
6. The time available to sales managers to coach and facilitate as opposed to selling to their own accounts is carefully monitored to get the best results.	1	2	3	4	5	6	7	8	9	10
7. Sales managers receive regular and focused training and development in their managerial roles and how these roles are changing.	1	2	3	4	5	6	7	8	9	10
8. Sales executives have a clear and tested view of the role of compensation control for sales people and managers in different selling situations.	1	2	3	4	5	6	7	8	9	10
9. In team-based selling situations, teams are carefully selected and their performance monitored as teams.	1	2	3	4	5	6	7	8	9	10
10. Processes of change in the management of the sales organization are carefully linked to the implementation of business strategy.	1	2	3	4	5	6	7	8	9	10

INFRASTRUCTURE—TOTAL SCORE OUT OF 100	
CONCLUSIONS	

INSPIRATION	**How are we doing?**									
How true are the following statements?	Completely untrue									Completely true
1. The sales control strategy recognizes the leadership role of front-line sales managers and supports them in this role.	1	2	3	4	5	6	7	8	9	10
2. Our salespeople are chosen and developed to display leadership characteristics in their dealings with customers and colleagues.	1	2	3	4	5	6	7	8	9	10
3. The sales organization recognizes and values line manager skills in getting things done and rewards these characteristics.	1	2	3	4	5	6	7	8	9	10
4. The leadership style of sales executives in the sales organization is closely matched to the needs of the sales organization and how they are developing.	1	2	3	4	5	6	7	8	9	10
5. Sales executives are selected, trained, and developed in appropriate leadership skills and behaviours.	1	2	3	4	5	6	7	8	9	10
6. The sales organization has a clear view of the needs for transformational leadership in appropriate circumstances and supports this.	1	2	3	4	5	6	7	8	9	10
7. The sales organization has a clear view of the needs for transactional leadership in appropriate circumstances and supports this.	1	2	3	4	5	6	7	8	9	10
8. Sales executives play a full and appropriate role in the leadership role across the company.	1	2	3	4	5	6	7	8	9	10
9. Sales executives play a full and appropriate leadership role in external relationships with suppliers and partners.	1	2	3	4	5	6	7	8	9	10
10. Sales executives play a role in appropriate external professional bodies, and are recognized as leaders in their field.	1	2	3	4	5	6	7	8	9	10

INSPIRATION—TOTAL SCORE OUT OF 100	
CONCLUSIONS	

INFLUENCE	How are we doing?									
How true are the following statements?	Completely untrue									Completely true
1. Senior sales executives are recognized across the business as key players in deciding the future.	1	2	3	4	5	6	7	8	9	10
2. Senior sales executives play a full role in the social and everyday life of the company.	1	2	3	4	5	6	7	8	9	10
3. Sales executives know who is powerful in the business and how patterns of dependence and interdependence are important to achieving their goals.	1	2	3	4	5	6	7	8	9	10
4. Senior sales executives exert influence in the business because of their understanding of problems and ability to get employees and colleagues on their side, not just because of organizational rank.	1	2	3	4	5	6	7	8	9	10
5. In approaching their tasks, sales executives are skilled in winning support and allies within the company.	1	2	3	4	5	6	7	8	9	10
6. Sales executives have a clear idea about the sources of support and opposition to sales initiatives within the company and address these issues effectively.	1	2	3	4	5	6	7	8	9	10
7. Sales executives understand their sources of influence within the business and how they can be used.	1	2	3	4	5	6	7	8	9	10
8. Sales executives are skilled in changing the thinking of people in the business by not just changing what people think but how they feel about important issues.	1	2	3	4	5	6	7	8	9	10
9. In addressing organizational change, sales executives include strategies of influence in their plans.	1	2	3	4	5	6	7	8	9	10
10. Sales executives devote time and effort to winning the 'hearts and minds' of employees and managers across the company to support customer strategies.	1	2	3	4	5	6	7	8	9	10

INFLUENCE—TOTAL SCORE OUT OF 100	
CONCLUSIONS	

INTEGRITY	How are we doing?									
How true are the following statements?	Completely untrue									Completely true
1. Sales executives understand the organization's corporate reputation and actively exploit the impact of corporate reputation on customer relationships.	1	2	3	4	5	6	7	8	9	10
2. Senior sales executives constantly monitor the emergence of ethical dilemmas that impact on customer relationships.	1	2	3	4	5	6	7	8	9	10
3. Salespeople are aware of the need to be seen to behave in an ethical way and have clear management guidance in this area.	1	2	3	4	5	6	7	8	9	10
4. People in the sales organization have a simple and clear framework for evaluating the ethical dimensions they may encounter in customer relationships.	1	2	3	4	5	6	7	8	9	10
5. Salespeople and sales managers are fully aware and informed on the company's corporate responsibility initiatives.	1	2	3	4	5	6	7	8	9	10
6. Salespeople and sales managers are supportive of the company's corporate responsibility issues and understand the link to customer value.	1	2	3	4	5	6	7	8	9	10
7. Salespeople and sales managers have a good view of what customer opportunities are dependent on the company's corporate social responsibility initiatives.	1	2	3	4	5	6	7	8	9	10
8. Salespeople and sales managers have a good view of what customer vulnerabilities are linked to the company's corporate social responsibility policies.	1	2	3	4	5	6	7	8	9	10
9. The sales organization provides a foundation for a strategic corporate responsibility platform with customers.	1	2	3	4	5	6	7	8	9	10
10. Sales processes are aligned with corporate social responsibility initiatives to leverage them as an advantage in the customer's eyes.	1	2	3	4	5	6	7	8	9	10

INTEGRITY—TOTAL SCORE OUT OF 100	
CONCLUSIONS	

INTERNATIONAL	How are we doing?									
How true are the following statements?	Completely untrue									Completely true
1. The sales organization underlines to management the impact of international competition and global customers.	1	2	3	4	5	6	7	8	9	10
2. Sales executives play a major role in the selection of overseas markets and international sales strategies.	1	2	3	4	5	6	7	8	9	10
3. The sales organization provides the company with knowledge about new types of competition and new competitors impacting on domestic and global markets.	1	2	3	4	5	6	7	8	9	10
4. Sales executives are influential in shaping the company's response to new types of competition.	1	2	3	4	5	6	7	8	9	10
5. Senior sales executives play a major role in the selection of global customers.	1	2	3	4	5	6	7	8	9	10
6. Senior sales executives play a major role in developing global account strategies.	1	2	3	4	5	6	7	8	9	10
7. Sales executives are well-informed and up-to-date about differences between overseas markets and the domestic market.	1	2	3	4	5	6	7	8	9	10
8. Senior sales executives are closely involved in managing global sales efforts.	1	2	3	4	5	6	7	8	9	10
9. Careful choices have been made on managing global sales that reflect market differences and similarities (e.g. culture, economic wealth, political stability).	1	2	3	4	5	6	7	8	9	10
10. The sales organization is recognized in the company as providing an international perspective on business strategy.	1	2	3	4	5	6	7	8	9	10

INTERNATIONAL—TOTAL SCORE OUT OF 100	
CONCLUSIONS	

Index

academy companies 211
accountability 213
accounts departments: consequences
  of un-integration from sales 122
activists 222
added-value sales strategies 50
Agentrics 282–3
Airbus 60–1, 224
Alliance Boots 56
allocating skills 214
Anderson, Erin 182
Apache Geronimo project 81
Apple 73, 74, 235
  iPhone 113–14, 235
  iPod 73, 74, 98, 235
  iTunes 98, 235, 284
ArcelorMittal 285
Argyris, Chris 215
Asda 56, 57, 250–1, 272, 289
  and Kellogg 58
Association of Medical Research
  Charities 249
assurance 169
AstraZeneca 284–5
automotive components sector 63–5, 67

BA: Gate Gourmet and 78–9
BAE 248
BAE Systems 252
Bank of Scotland 258
banking industry 285–6
Belbin, R. Meredith 201–2
Berger, Suzanne 294–5
Best Buy, USA 197, 222
Bloombergs 258
Boeing 123, 224, 283
  and Dell Inc. 53, 112
Bonoma, Thomas V. 214
bonus schemes 173, 195, 198, 199
Booz Allen Hamilton 173
Bower, Joseph 150
brand development 119
bribery 248, 254–6
BRIC countries (Brazil, Russia, India,
  China) 284

Bridgestone 255
British Telecom: and Marconi 74–5
Brown, Richard 225
Business Management Performance Forum 91
business process organizations 128–9
business relationships 53–9
  changes in 73–4
  difficult customers 54–9
  walking away from unprofitable 53–4
business risk 83, *83*, 86, 93
business strategy identification 39–44,
  40
business-to-business customers: and
  CSR 268–9
business-to-business marketing 10–11, 16,
  283
buyer–seller relationships 51–2, *52*, 70,
  110–12, 248
  and CSR 263–79
  dominant customer strategy 65–7, *66*
bystanders 222

Cable & Wireless 60
Cadbury 18–19
Capon, Noel 128
car industry 285, 286–7
carbon footprints 57
cash-flow customers 86
Caterpillar Inc. 281–2
Cato the Younger 231
CBD (Customer Business Development)
  organizations 20
Cespedes, Frank 136
change, process of 237, 244–5
Chrysler 64–5
Cialdini, Robert 241, 242–3
CIGNA health insurance group 167
Cisco 27
cloud computing 98–9
Cognosis 225
collaboration 213, 227–8
  success factors 228
Colvin, Geoff 235
commission schemes 195, 198
commoditization 13, 15–17